This is dedicated to my mother, Jennifer, for giving me that blank red hardbound notebook, and for the rest.

Contents

Acknowledgements

I am very grateful to James Russo, who assisted with some of the research in this book, and to Niranjan Casinader, for his helpful advice on a little matter of geography. Thanks also to Rosalyn Black, who helped me to work through some of these ideas, Celia Hannon for the conversations, and finally to my wife, Emma Rujevic, for her editorial feedback, love and support.

About the Author

Lucas Walsh is Associate Professor and Associate Dean (Berwick) in the Faculty of Education at Monash University. Walsh has worked in corporate, government and not-for-profit sectors and has held four research fellowships. He was previously Director of Research and Evaluation at the Foundation for Young Australians and managed the International Baccalaureate's Online Curriculum Centre in the United Kingdom.

Introduction

The global labour force is changing. During the last 30 years, working life has become profoundly different from previous generations. Nowhere is this more evident than in the worlds inhabited by young people. Getting work is becoming more competitive, and once gained, working life is often more fluid. Marginalisation from work is pronounced. Globally, as many as 290 million 15- to 24-year-olds were not participating in the labour market in 2013 – 'almost a quarter of the world's youth, and a group almost as large as the population of America' (*The Economist* 2013d). It has been estimated that almost 74 million young people were looking for work, in 2014 an increase of nearly 3.5 million since 2007 (ILO 2015; 2013). While advanced economies are dogged by persistent unemployment, a proliferation of temporary jobs and growing youth disillusionment, poor-quality, informal, subsistence jobs have increasingly become the norm in developing countries (ILO 2013). Throughout countries within the Organisation for Economic Co-operation and Development (OECD), young people must rely on casual work, have less control of planning their lives either financially or socially, change their job status more regularly, and pursue further study without a guarantee that it will lead to satisfying and secure forms of work. The Global Financial Crisis (GFC) of 2007–08 accelerated these conditions.

The GFC is a focal point of this book. Its effects highlight how precarious the working lives of young people can be during an economic downturn. As the OECD pointed out at the time:

> Young people . . . suffered a disproportionate share of job losses during the global economic crisis. In the third quarter of 2010, the OECD-average youth unemployment rate represented 18.5 [per cent] of the

labour force aged 15/16–24, with over three million more youth having joined the ranks of the unemployed compared with the corresponding quarter of 2007. But unemployment does not capture the full hardship for youth, as many of those who have left education do not even appear in labour market statistics. (OECD 2010, p. 1)

Soon after the GFC, youth unemployment soared throughout Europe. In Greece, youth unemployment exceeded 53 per cent, while in Spain, the figures surpassed 55 per cent. Some reports suggested that there was a flight of young people from Spain across Europe seeking opportunities to work (Johnson 2012). In 2012, nearly 30,000 young people from Spain relocated to Germany in search of work. Substantially more Greeks, Polish and Romanians also moved to Germany (*The Economist* 2013a). By mid-2013, youth unemployment in Greece rose as high as 58.8 per cent, while Spain's rate peaked at 55.7 per cent (Eurostat 2015, January 30). The potential damage to the social and economic fabric of these countries is significant, and was quickly manifest in widespread protests and unrest (such as those generated by the Occupy movement) (news.com.au 2011).

Echoing the international experience, young Australians' post-school futures are increasingly characterised by uncertainty, insecurity and fluidity in relation to working life (ACTU 2012). Getting a job is a major concern for many young Australians. Along with housing, it was one of the two key election issues for young voters in the lead-up to the 2013 federal election (NFAW 2013). This is further reflected in the National Survey of Young Australians published by Mission Australia, which in 2011 showed a large rise in the proportion of young people valuing getting a job, from 16 per cent in 2010 to 22.7 per cent (Mission Australia 2011). Another youth survey published the following year, which focused on young people aged 15–19, suggested that '[u]nless we provide them with the job-specific, work-ready skills and the kind of qualifications employers are looking for, our youth face an uphill battle to secure employment' (Mission Australia 2012).

Their participation in the labour force has been considerably affected by both long-term and more recent changes following the GFC. Time and time again, the evidence suggests that the most vulnerable young people include teenage males who are not engaged in education (particularly those who leave school early), those residing in remote and regional areas, Indigenous young people, and young people from disadvantaged backgrounds (Walsh 2010). Precarious work is also identified particularly with young women (Wilson 2013).

The fluidity and precarity of the workforce experienced by young people have six main features. Firstly, the number of full-time[1] job opportunities for teenagers has been steadily declining since the 1980s (Robinson & Lamb 2009; Robinson et al. 2010). Secondly, the rate of casualisation across the Australian workforce in general increased from 18.9 per cent in 1988 to around 25 per cent in 2012 (Stacey 2013). Within this, there has been an increase in the uptake of casual and part-time work[2] by young people aged 15–24. One-fifth of all casual workers are aged 15–19. From 2001 to 2011, the prevalence of casual work increased significantly for this age group and to some extent for 20- to 24-year-olds for the period, but far less for older age groups (ACTU 2012). While some young people prefer casual and part-time work because of the benefits that flexibility offers, the overarching context of labour market change has challenged the ability of young people to plan their lives and maintain close social relationships (Woodman 2012a). Many want to work more but are unable to do so. Underemployment, defined by the Australian Bureau of Statistics (ABS) as part-time workers who are available to do more work, rose significantly following the GFC, a trend that has not abated since (Stanwick et al. 2013). While employment conditions generally improve after the age of 25 (Stanwick et al. 2013), it would appear that for many, the options for young people to secure full-time work are increasingly out of reach. Thirdly, globalisation is creating challenges for young people seeking work in Australia. As Birrell and Healy (2013a) suggest, young working holidaymakers from overseas are intensifying competition for jobs with young local workers. Particularly vulnerable are those 'without post-school education, who are seeking less skilled, entry-level jobs'. Fourthly, a growing share of local workers aged 55 and over is staying in the workforce (Birrell & Healy 2013b). Between May 2003 and May 2013, the share of those aged 60–64 in the workforce increased from 39 per cent to 54 per cent. This increasing competition for work particularly affects young people who are qualified but lack experience. Fifthly, a trend arises from a perceived global mismatch between skills and jobs. Recent surveys of business confirm a widely held perception that young people are underprepared for working life and lack foundational skills in literacy and numeracy, as well as soft skills such as communication and problem-solving (CCIQ 2011; Mission Australia 2013). Finally, there is a disproportionately high level of youth unemployment. Figures from 2014 suggest that youth unemployment represents just under 40 per cent of all unemployment in Australia. More than one in three unemployed[3] Australians is aged between 15 and 24 (Brotherhood of St Laurence 2014, p. 4).

These trends have not gone unnoticed in education policy: 'There is concern that the gap between education and the work readiness of young people is widening. Early and intense educational intervention is needed to help young people develop the work readiness, career development and work knowledge' (ACARA 2013b, p. 4). Young people's employment and response to the increasing fluidity of working life is a major concern of policymakers, educators and business. These concerns, and the problems underpinning assumptions made about young people that shape responses to these concerns, are critically discussed throughout this book. These immense changes require a re-examination of young people's preparedness for employment in the 21st century and, at a deeper level, what it means to be 'young'.

Drawing from economic and labour force trends, politics and policy, technology, demographic change, recent thinking in education, sociology and research conducted directly with young people themselves, this book builds on recent research into young people's transitions to take a fresh look at how educators, parents, businesses, policymakers and young people need to think about transitions in the 21st century. The discussion, which looks in detail at both long-term labour force trends and more recent factors, such as the GFC, provides a current and striking picture of the contemporary worlds of work faced by young people – worlds that are becoming very different from previous generations.

Understanding the challenges facing 'generation next' in their transitions to work presents wider questions about how teaching, schools and schooling can be improved to enable young people to navigate 'a sea of uncertainty' (Wyn 2009, p. iii) facing them beyond the school gates. In exploring the changing nature of young people's transitions from school to work, this book asks whether schools and the teaching profession are adequately designed to prepare young people for the contemporary workforce. It connects key challenges facing the teaching profession and schooling to the rapidly changing conditions and nature of young people's transitions from school to work and life in general. It provides an overview and critical analysis of this relationship by exploring key research data over the last decade – particularly since the GFC.

This book offers some approaches to thinking about how policymakers, educators and other actors seeking to improve educational outcomes might respond to these challenges. It develops the concept of 'adversity capital' to understand how young people might be better prepared to navigate working life. The concept of adversity capital has been used in other areas of youth studies, but the following discussion redevelops the concept in the contested and changing area of young people's transitions. In doing so, this book questions whether approaches promoted by business, the OECD and some educators are in fact desirable and in the best interests of young people (or the contemporary labour market in general).

While international trends, policy and practice set the wider context of discussion, Australia serves as a unique case study that has significance to educators and policymakers throughout the world. Despite having undergone an unprecedented period of prosperity, Australia's young people are nevertheless increasingly exposed to conditions of workforce fluidity and precarity that bear similarity to broader conditions that are transforming young lives throughout the world. Australia is also a case study of neoliberal policy whose trajectory bears certain characteristics of austerity measures adopted in Europe but without the same underlying economic problems experienced in other countries. These conditions arise from both local and global factors, and demand an urgent rethinking of how educators and policymakers are preparing young people for changing worlds of work.

The structure of this book

The discussion is divided into two parts. Part One includes three chapters that explore the key trends underpinning and transforming young people's transitions from school to work in relation to economic, demographic, technological and other global trends. It describes a labour force that, in some ways, is fast becoming unrecognisable from previous generations in which conventional notions of careers, security and even 'adulthood' are increasingly problematic. It also looks at how some recent attempts by governments to respond to issues such as young people's employment have failed to understand these changes in young people's transitions.

The discussion starts in Chapter One with the GFC and works its way out to these broader factors and drivers of change. The GFC had a profound impact on young people's transitions from school to working life – even in countries that fared relatively well such as Australia (Robinson et al. 2010). Compared to many other countries, Australia's young population was to some extent shielded from the worst of the GFC. In 2010, for example, a higher percentage of young people both in education and not in education were employed compared to the OECD average. Specifically, just under 47 per cent of 15- to 19-year-olds and 74.2 per cent of 20- to 24-year-olds in Australia had some employment as compared to the OECD average of 19.1 per cent for 15- to 19-year-olds and 20.7 per cent for 20- to 24-year-olds. Unemployment rates were also lower. In 2011, just over 11 per cent of 15- to 24-year-olds in Australia were unemployed compared to the OECD weighted average of 16.2 per cent (Stanwick et al. 2013, p. 19).

But beneath these trends are persistent forms of marginalisation, insecurity and precarity. For example, record numbers of young people looking for full-time work must make do with casual work or marginalisation from the workforce. Core groups of young people, such as those from low socio-economic status (SES) and Indigenous backgrounds, experience disproportionately high levels of insecurity and marginalisation from work and study. After decades of uninterrupted economic growth, it needs to be asked: does prosperity need to be accompanied by insecurity, and if so, are we best preparing young people for the pathways ahead?

Chapter One sets the economic context by examining these trends in detail. It sets the context for the central argument of this book – that young people's worlds of work are changing and that there is a need to rethink schooling to keep pace with these changes. These changes are not purely economic, but are interconnected with broader social, cultural and political factors that necessitate a refocus of how and where learning by teachers and students takes place, and how 'success' is defined within these contexts. Success means more than young people's grades or employability. It relates to how and whether young people experience belonging and navigate precarity and the world in general.

Other macro trends, such as an ageing population, the profound impact of information and communication technology (ICT) and other dimensions of globalisation, are transforming the participation of young people in work and life. These trends are discussed in Chapter Two.

Surveying a range of disconnections between educational institutions and governments and business, Chapter Three investigates a perception both in Australia and internationally that there is a global mismatch between skills and jobs. A number of surveys of business in Australia, for example, suggest a perception amongst employers that young people are underprepared for working life – ranging from underdeveloped foundational skills in numeracy to soft skills such as communication and problem-solving. Disconnections in recently proposed neoliberal government policy responses are also critically analysed, and located in relation to wider policy discourses in Australia, the United States and Europe.

These discourses are themselves problematic, and the concept of 'adversity capital' is proposed and critically discussed in Chapter Four as a means of analysing, understanding and meeting these challenges.

The development of soft skills, in particular, reflects a wider need to prepare young people for worlds of insecure work in Australia and internationally. They form part of adversity capital, which enables young people to be more adaptive, flexible and resilient. The need to develop adversity capital is located within a broader social ecological context. This chapter commences Part Two of this book, which explores possible responses from the perspectives of young people and their communities; teachers and the teaching profession; and schools and other actors that could contribute more to schooling, such as business, the third sector, parents, young people and governments.

Chapters Five and Six, accordingly, look at the implications of the changing nature of young people's transitions for teachers and schooling. Specifically, the discussion critically analyses the capacity of teachers and schooling to respond to the changing labour force and broader challenges facing young people. Key challenges facing the teaching profession are explored, from the initial education of teachers through to the development of school leadership and how schooling in general is understood. The roles and nature of schools are also discussed from an ecological perspective that takes into consideration the array of actors that are and could be working with schools to prepare young people for contemporary working life.

To provide an international and comparative perspective, research, case studies and illustrations are included from North America, Europe, Asia, Scandinavia and countries within the OECD. Brief examples and implications are also drawn from vocational education and training and higher education to provide a wider contextual view of education pathways.

Through these two parts, the book aims to provide a macro perspective of two fundamental questions facing all educators and policymakers. Firstly, how aligned is schooling to young people's expectations and experiences of fluid worlds of work and global change? Secondly, is an industrial model of education capable of preparing young people for an increasingly post-industrial society?

A brief note about data

This book draws on a wide range of data. One major source is the annual report *How Young People Are Faring*, which was produced by the Foundation for Young Australians in collaboration with researchers from the University of Melbourne, led by Professor Stephen Lamb (2008–12), and the National Centre for Vocational Research (Stanwick et al. 2013). This report is explicitly selective, presenting data on important educational markers from national and international surveys and collections. Data used in the reports were derived from a range of sources, including annual ABS surveys of education and work, labour force surveys, longitudinal surveys of youth, census data, other national sources, and data from international comparisons.

Data are also drawn from sources such as the International Labour Organization (ILO), Eurostat and the United Nations. These data sources are also selectively used to highlight key trends according to the measures used by these organisations and countries, with some limited bases for comparison. Nuanced differences between these measures make detailed comparisons difficult. For example, while ABS definitions of labour force status reflect ILO guidelines, there are some variations.

Given the reliance on ABS data for the Australian context, it is useful to state their key definitions upfront. The definitions of employment and unemployment adopted by the ABS are as follows. The labour force survey includes 'usual residents' and civilians aged 15 or over. It is thought that age 15 is the lowest practical limit at which it is feasible and cost-effective to measure the participation of young people in economic activity with acceptable accuracy. If a person is employed for an hour or more in work (e.g. paid work or unpaid work in a family business/farm) in the 'short' reference period, that person is classified as employed. Likewise, if a person is absent from a regular job for a short period or is on paid leave, she/he is also classified as employed. Individuals who identify themselves as being engaged in various forms of self-employment, or who own businesses that they do not work in, are also classified as employed. A person is classified as unemployed if she/he has not undertaken some work in the reference period (i.e. not an hour or more of work), has taken active steps to find work and is currently available for work. If the individual does not meet either of the requirements for employment or unemployment, she/he is classified as economically inactive (and not in the labour force) (ABS 2013a). As the ABS notes, what should constitute the short reference period is contentious. Some propose one day, whilst others propose one week. In Australia, the one-week reference period is used because most people are in full-time employment, and it is thought that this reference point will result in lower variability and therefore be a more statistically reliable measure of unemployment.

Other international definitions of unemployment are used throughout this book. In a similar manner to the ABS, the UN Millennial Development Goals adopt the ILO definitions of employment, which one would expect given that the former is a project nested within the UN and the latter is an agency of the UN (2015). Given these overlaps, the above discussion about what the ABS constitutes as employment, unemployment and not in the labour force is relevant and would essentially be replicated here. However, the ILO defines any individual engaged in some work related to economic activity (i.e. employee, employer, family business worker) as employed. It states that 'for operational purposes the notion of "some work" may be interpreted as work for at least one hour' (ILO 1982, paragraph 9b2). The ILO has more recently released standards in relation to the underutilisation of labour, which have also been adopted within Australia and other countries with sophisticated labour market surveys in operation. As implied in the discussion of ABS methods and definitions above, the ILO leaves open the question of whether the reference period for employment activity should refer to a single day or a week.

Statistics reported in the Millennial Development Goals report are the OECD's 'standardised unemployment rates', which are adjusted international rates of unemployment to fit with ILO concepts. These standardised rates are calculated from annual average estimates (or the period considered most representative over the year), thereby avoiding the variances that would occur if different reference periods were used. It is stated that these unemployment rates, based on official national information, should provide the best basis currently available for making reasonable international comparisons and assumptions.

It is noted that there are differences in how particular countries determine age groupings, which have implications for international comparisons in unemployment statistics. In general, where a minimum school-leaving age exists, the lower age limit of youth will usually correspond to that age. This means that the lower age limit often varies between 14 and 16 years (and for some countries is even lower than 14; e.g. in Haiti, it is 10 years), according to the institutional arrangements in the respective country. Six countries use 29 as the upper age limit: Colombia (1989–90), Costa Rica (1980–86), Honduras (1991–98), New Caledonia (1996), Panama (1983) and Suriname (1987). There are also differences in the operational definition of adults. In general, adults are defined as all individuals above the age of 25, but some countries apply an upper age limit. The upper age limit would obviously affect only the ratio of youth-to-adult unemployment rates, and the effect is likely to be very small (United Nations 2015).

International comparisons of unemployment rates across countries are delimited by the use of different data sources for unemployment figures in different jurisdictions. The most reliable data are considered to be available from labour force surveys. Census of Population and Housing data might be accurate, but less timely. Administrative data are considered the least reliable due to the potential for double counting and lags between when individuals find work and when they are removed from administrative lists.

Eurostat figures, which are used in this book, base their unemployment estimates on the European Union Labour Force Survey, which Eurostat coordinates. The definitions of labour force status are also based on the ILO guidelines. One notable difference to the ABS data is the fact that the labour force is restricted to those aged between 15 and 74, although this is unlikely to significantly impact either employment or unemployment rate comparisons.

Eurostat data differ in other ways. For example, the category of underutilisation in the Eurostat data includes the following groups of people: the unemployed, underemployed part-time workers, persons available to work but not seeking, and persons not available to work but seeking employment. At first glance, this differs from the ABS underutilisation rate, which only includes the first two groups. However, the ABS 'extended labour force underutilisation rate' is comparable to the Eurostat data. In addition to the unemployed and underemployed, this rate also includes 'people who are actively looking for work and who could start within four weeks, but are not available to start in the reference week' and 'discouraged job seekers' (ABS 2013c).

Finally, in Chapter One, comparisons are made of levels of unemployment and underutilisation between European countries such as Spain and Greece, in which data are analysed in terms of young people rather than only those in the labour market to include some types of underutilised labour who are outside the labour market (e.g. persons available to work but not seeking, persons seeking work but not immediately available). Comparisons between such countries change dramatically when young people's unemployment is considered as a percentage of the relevant overall population, rather than as a percentage of those young people participating in the labour market. Consequently, some of the data have been constructed through combining unemployment data/underutilisation data with population estimates data from Eurostat sources.

Defining young people

As part of the development of the Millennial Development Goals, the UN developed a list of indicators to measure progress towards the various stated goals (United Nations 2015). In this context, the UN defines youth unemployment as the proportion of people aged 15–24 who are unemployed. Following on from the discussion above, this definition is also widely used by the ABS.

Nevertheless, international definitions of what constitutes 'young' vary considerably. Even within major data sources within Australia, such as the ABS, discrepancies emerge. For example, in the employment publications, young people are classified as those individuals between 15 and 24 years of age (ABS 2010), in part because it is considered infeasible to collect data from people younger than 15 (ABS 2003). However, there are enough exceptions to conclude that the ABS uses the construct of young people rather fluidly. For example, in relation to the *Mental Health of Young People* publication, the focus of the survey was on people between 16 and 24 years of age (ABS 2007b). Another article in the *Australian Social Trends* publication discussing the demographic characteristics of the Australian population in different geographic areas refers to young people as being between 20 and 34 years of age (ABS 2008). This criterion is similar – although not identical – to that used to define the construct of a 'young adult' in another *Australian Social Trend* article focused on housing, which adopted 18–34 years of age (ABS 2006). By contrast, the Australian Institute of Health and Welfare (AIHW) adopts a different definition of young people from ABS publications. The AIHW defines young people as those aged 12–24 and acknowledges that this categorisation overlaps with that of children (individuals aged 0–14) (AIHW 2011).

This book adopts a fairly fluid definition of young people. For some comparisons, the age bracket of 15–24 is used; but we will also be looking at people in schooling under the age of 15 and up to 30 years of age. As we shall see, the very notion of what it is to be young is contested and shaped by political, social and economic change. In the context of transitions from 'childhood' to 'adulthood', distinctions between young people and adulthood are problematic and changing (Wyn 2009). Experiences of 'being young' are characterised by greater fluidity than other age groups (United Nations 2014). Demographic changes, 'the standardisation of the young lifestyle' and other definitional changes have reshaped what constitutes being 'young' in contemporary society (Bernardini 2014, pp. 42–43). While much of the data used in this book focus on those aged 15–24, the discussion also reflects on those in school, as well as those impacted by recent policy approaches that effectively extend the definition of youth out to the age of 30, amounting to an infantilisation of young people. Somewhat paradoxically, young people are at the same time compelled to experience the demands of 'adulthood' earlier in life, such as those who juggle work and school, while still being labelled as 'young'. Research is therefore included from a wider demographic that includes young people through to the age of 30 to provide a breadth of examples from which international comparisons can be made.

Use of the term 'soft skills'

The term 'soft skills' will be used throughout this book as a widely accepted description of certain literacies, 'generic and basic skills' such as social intelligence, communication and emotional resilience (Roberts 2009; Roberts & Wignall 2010). But this term undervalues the power and significance of these skills in preparing young people for working life. Accordingly, a better way of describing them is needed but not presented in this book.

A final note about context

This book reflects on current and very recent policy and its potential impact on young people. These include several proposals by the Australian federal government that have yet to be legislated or implemented. The purpose of including these is to illustrate a larger policy *attitude* or narrative that provides insight into how young people are understood and treated as the objects of social and economic policy. Some major initiatives, such as the Australian Curriculum, continue to be under review and are subject to change. Similarly, policy proposals are critically analysed, though many have yet to take effect and will possibly never be implemented. Consequently, some examples included in this book will probably be superseded between authorship and publication.

Part I

Navigating Seas of Uncertainty: The Impact of the GFC and Beyond on Young People

1
Young People, Precarity and a Workforce in Transition

The last several years have been an uncertain time for countries throughout the world. Economic and political orthodoxies have been challenged, within wider calls for austerity. New ways of living and working are emerging, with some groups experiencing these very differently to others. Recent economic instability has had a profound impact on young people. This was particularly pronounced following the GFC in 2007–08. In countries such as Greece and Spain, youth unemployment exceeded 50 per cent within the four years following the downturn. Young people in Australia, despite its comparative economic prosperity, also felt the impact of the GFC. The Organisation for Economic Co-operation and Development (OECD) observed in its report, *Jobs for Youth: Australia*, that 'past experience suggests that in Australia, like in most other OECD countries, any deterioration in labour market conditions is disproportionally felt by the youth' (2009, p. 1). Socio-economic and geographic factors magnify the impact of economic instability on certain young people, affecting, in turn, their participation in education and employment, which are explored in more detail in Chapter Two.

Accompanying these trends are long-term structural changes to the workforce, which in combination set the economic context of this book. Young people face declining opportunities for full-time work, increasing part-time and casual work, underemployment, underutilisation and unemployment. This chapter explores the impact of recent economic instability and, in particular, traces the impact of the GFC year by year alongside longer-term structural changes, on young people in Australia, as well as in parts of Europe.

The aftermath of the GFC: 2008 to present

In the years following the GFC, the working lives of many young people became unstable. They became more insecure, and growing numbers of young people not in study experienced unemployment. To illustrate the severity of the impact of the GFC, we can see the steady intensification of insecure working conditions and precarity in the years following the downturn.

Prior to the GFC, unemployment for those aged 15–24 was at the lowest recorded level since the 1970s (OECD 2009). This low level of unemployment reflected greater numbers of young people choosing to study before entering the workforce, as well as growth in part-time rather than full-time work (Lamb & Mason 2008). But as in many other countries, the impact of the GFC was immediately felt in Australia and rippled across the years that followed.

Data collected during the last several years by Professor Stephen Lamb and his team of researchers at the Centre for Research on Education Systems at the University of Melbourne (2009–12) make for sobering reading. Between 2008 and 2009, the proportion of teenagers not learning or earning full-time jumped from 13.4 per cent to 16.4 per cent – the highest level since the recession of the early 1990s. During this period, the rate of unemployment among teenagers rose by over 6 per cent, one of the largest annual increases for this group in 20 years. In 2009, a quarter of 20- to 24-year-olds were not engaged in full-time work or full-time education (Robinson & Lamb 2009, p. vii). This increase from 2008 also reversed the downward trend from the previous decade. Young men were more likely to be unemployed, while young women were more likely to be in part-time work or not in the labour force.[1] Fewer teenagers began apprenticeships in 2009, the level of commencements having stalled following the GFC (Robinson et al. 2010).

Between the first quarter of 2008 and 2009, the number of Australian teenagers in full-time work fell significantly from 249,000 to 208,000 (Colebatch 2009). One estimate suggests that all but 400 of the 30,600 jobs lost between January and July 2009 were lost by teenagers (Martin 2009). This decrease was neither matched by the number of full-time students nor matched by an increase in full-time employment.

Counterbalancing these fairly dramatic figures were greater numbers of young people choosing to study before entering the workforce, with 83 per cent of 20- to 24-year-olds completing Year 12 at school or attaining a post-school vocational education and training (VET) qualification at Certificate III or higher in 2008 (Robinson & Lamb 2009, p. 25) – a steady rise but still short of the 90 per cent attainment targets set by the federal government for 2015 (COAG 2009), particularly in regions such as the Northern Territory. Between 2001 and 2009, Year 12 attainment of people aged 20–24 increased from 70 per cent to 75 per cent. But for most disadvantaged, the rate of increase was marginal, fluctuating between 50 and 60 per cent (ABS Survey of Education and Training, cited in Bentley & Cazaly 2015, p. 16).

Labour force data from 2009 showed just over 29 per cent of 20- to 24-year-olds were in full-time education (Robinson & Lamb 2009, p. 19). Data from the last decade have shown that school completers[2] are more likely to gain further qualifications (65 per cent by age 23), while early school leavers[3] are less likely to obtain any further qualifications (57 per cent by age 23). This gap in qualification levels between school completers and early school leavers widens in the post-school years (Robinson & Lamb 2009, p. viii). For school leavers, the transition to the labour market via certain pathways other than higher education slowed or stagnated. For example, estimates for 2008 indicate that the percentage of teenagers undertaking traineeships and apprentice-ships flatlined after a decade of growth (Robinson & Lamb 2009, p. 12; Robinson et al. 2010).

And for those seeking full-time work post-school, opportunities fell steeply following the economic downturn. A significant amount of part-time work was undertaken on an involuntary basis; that is, young people indicated a preference for full-time employment, but increasingly had to accept part-time work. Many students engaged in full-time post-school study took on more hours of part-time work. (We will explore the implications of this below.)

The data have consistently shown that further or post-school qualifi-cations are increasingly important in helping young people to make the transition to the labour market after leaving school. Census data from 2006 indicated that about six in ten Australians attained a post-school qualification by age 24. Just under a third had a university degree or higher, with 31 per cent attaining a VET qualification. Young women were much more likely than males to have a university qualification (33 per cent compared with 23 per cent of young men) (Robinson & Lamb 2009, p. viii). As the minimum level of qualifications required for work continued to rise, post-schooling providers of training, university and further education faced the challenge of meeting growing demand. Australia lacked and continues to lack solid long-term alternative path-ways for those young people not taking the conventional pathway from school to higher education, particularly given the immediate impact of the economic downturn on apprenticeships and training opportunities – which, as indicated above, contracted significantly.

Amongst the most vulnerable in making the transition from school to work or further training and study were those from low socio-economic backgrounds and living in regional and remote areas. Census data from 2006 showed that a young person living in the wealthiest areas was three times more likely to attain a university degree or higher by the age of 24 than those living in the poorest areas. The 24-year-olds living in metropolitan areas had more than double the rate of attainment of university and higher-level VET qualifications as rural areas, in which vocational certificates are particularly valuable. For just under one-third of this group, this was their highest post-school qualification (Robinson & Lamb 2009, p. 31).

Globally, the rate of young people's unemployment had reached an all-time high of 75.8 million people aged 15–24 out of work (UN 2012a). A year on, the unemployment rate of young people hovered at 12.6 per cent, compared to an adult unemployment rate of 4.8 per cent (UN 2012a). In the UK, this rate rose from 13.5 per cent in December 2007 to 19.5 per cent in June 2009, before it plateaued at around the 20 per cent level for the next several years (Eurostat 2015, 30 January). Rates in parts of Europe were even higher.

In Australia, levels of teenage disengagement from work and study remained as high in 2010 as in the previous few years. Teenage males continued to be particularly affected by the economic downturn. They had greater difficulty finding full-time work. Unemployment rates in general continued to be much higher for teenagers than for adults. Despite modest improvements, the percentage of school leavers not fully engaged in education or work was at its highest level in two decades. The unemployment rate of teenagers not in full-time education approached 18 per cent. Full-time job opportunities for teenagers continued to decrease, offset by a small increase in participation in full-time education. Levels of participation by 20- to 24-year-olds in earning and learning improved; however, nearly a quarter of this age group were still not engaged in full-time education or full-time work (Robinson et al. 2010).

By the first quarter of 2011, the unemployment rate for people aged 15–24 in OECD countries was 17.4 per cent compared with 7 per cent for adults (aged 25 and over) (UNRIC 2012b). A record number of young people in Europe were unemployed. Young women particularly struggled to find work. The rate of unemployment for this age group continued climbing to 22.1 per cent in the 27 European Union countries and 21.3 per cent in the euro area – up from 21 per cent and 20.6 per cent, respectively, in the previous year (Eurostat, Unemployment Statistics, cited in UNRIC 2012a). Around 5.5 million young people were out of work (European Commission 2014, p. 1). Amongst the highest levels registered were in Greece, Ireland and Spain, where youth unemployment rates had almost doubled. The GFC effectively wiped out any positive gains in employment during the beginning of the new millennium (ILO 2012). As the UNRIC (2012a) noted:

> With the exception of Austria, Germany and Switzerland, none of the advanced economies saw a return of unemployment rates for younger people to pre-crisis levels in 2011. This will have substantial long-term consequences, lowering the career path expectations of young entrants into the labour market and diminishing the incentives for the coming generation to take up long and expensive studies.

While the rate of young Australians not engaged in education, employment or training (NEET) was less than the OECD average in 2011,[4] the rate is still striking given how well Australia fared economically compared to many of its counterparts in the OECD.

Unemployment continued to be consistently higher for teenagers. One in four long-term unemployed were aged 15–24. Since 2008, the percentage of young Australians without a job for a year or longer had almost doubled. More young people who were not in some form of study or training had part-time jobs. Among those in the labour force, three times as many teenagers (15–19) and more than twice as many young adults (20–24) had part-time jobs compared to the mid-1980s. An average of nearly one in five teenagers changed their labour force status every month in 2011, compared with one in ten older workers. Young people changed employers more regularly (Robinson et al. 2011, p. 11).

In 2012, 81 million young people globally were unemployed (and notably 152 million of those who had jobs resided in households that earned less than the equivalent of 1 euro (or around AU$1.50) a day (UNRIC 2012a). In Greece, youth unemployment hit 53 per cent, and in Spain, 55 per cent. Some reports suggested that there was soon a flight of young people from Spain seeking opportunities to work in countries such as Germany (*The Economist* 2013a), although Spain had experienced similarly high levels of youth unemployment in the past. Fluctuations like this were not new. In June 1986, when Spain began publishing youth unemployment data, it was 43.8 per cent. It then declined consistently over the first five years of the series, falling to 28.8 per cent in March 1991. Over the next three years, the Spanish youth unemployment rate increased rather dramatically to approximately 1986 levels, at 43.1 per cent in March 1994. It then declined steadily for a seven-year period, falling to 20.9 per cent in September 2001. Over the next seven years, cyclical fluctuations were less dramatic, with the rate reaching a historic low of 17.2 per cent in March 2007, just prior to the GFC. Youth unemployment then spiked dramatically, increasing more than threefold in just over five years to be at 55.4 per cent in December 2012 (Eurostat 2015, 30 January). The potential mid- to long-term damage to the social and economic fabric of these countries soon became apparent. Widespread protest and civil unrest erupted throughout Europe in the wake of the GFC (news.com.au 2011).

In Australia, the rate of unemployment was far lower but still significant. On the upside, more young people were participating in education. School retention to Year 12 rates (the final year of schooling in Australia) reached an all-time high (79 per cent). Furthermore, university-level attainment among 24- to 35-year-olds increased from 24 per cent to 35 per cent between 2001 and 2011 (Robinson & Lamb 2012, p. 7). And as suggested above, as a corollary of declining full-time jobs, rates of part-time employment increased significantly – in the case of teenagers, it had tripled over the previous 30 years. In 2012, a quarter of 18- to 19-year-olds was not in full-time study or work despite government targets aiming to get more young people qualified or into a job (COAG 2012b). Many were seeking full-time work but could not get it. Unemployment for teenagers (15–19) was about three times the overall rate of unemployment in Australia (Robinson & Lamb 2012).

By 2013, the number of young people out of work in OECD countries was nearly a third higher than in 2007 (*The Economist* 2013c). OECD data suggest that around 26 million young people in advanced economies were NEET. World Bank data indicate that over ten times as many young people in developing economies were estimated to be 'inactive' (*The Economist* 2013b). This amounts to almost 290 million young people neither working nor studying, which, as *The Economist* pointed out, was 'almost a quarter of the planet's youth' (*The Economist* 2013b). The figures in Europe were particularly severe. Prior to the GFC, the youth unemployment rate in Greece had experienced a reasonably steady decline from 1999 (the second year in which data are available) to 2008, during which it fell from 31.7 per cent to 21.1 per cent. It then increased dramatically over the course of the next five years, reaching a peak of 58.8 per cent in June 2013 (Eurostat 2015, 30 January).

In Australia, the effects of the GFC continued to be offset to some extent by participation and attainment in education. Both education participation and attainment rates amongst young people continued to increase. For example, four out of five students (82 per cent) who commenced secondary school in 2013 stayed in school to Year 12, a significant increase from 75 per cent in 2008 (FYA 2014). But young people also experienced higher unemployment rates than older age groups. Around 250,000 young people were leaving school and entering the workforce each year (Birrell & Healy 2013a). The underemployment rate for 15- to 24-year-olds had increased from 11.3 per cent in 2008 to 14.9 per cent in 2013 (ABS 2014). High rates of casualisation and involuntary part-time work reflected a labour force that had become more precarious, insecure and fluid. High rates of underemployment and unemployment persisted despite the fact that Australia overall had emerged from the GFC relatively unscathed.

By early 2014, 40 per cent of Australia's unemployed were young people (Brotherhood of St Laurence 2014). The overall unemployment rate for 15- to 24-year-olds reached as high as 12.2 per cent (more than double the general unemployment rate), with much higher rates in certain regions, such as rural and regional communities (Pro Bono 2014). But these pockets of unemployment were not confined to regional and remote areas. As Kelly and Mares (2013, p. 4) suggest, labour markets were 'shallow in significant parts of Australia's biggest cities'. Ken Henry, former Secretary of Treasury (2001–11), found that in the decade leading up to the GFC, youth unemployment had been trending downwards – from over 380,000 in 1992 to less than 160,000 in August 2008. By 2014, the number of unemployed people aged 15–24 increased to around 260,000 (Henry 2014a).

In Europe, unemployment had skyrocketed, although in areas such as Spain, the level had begun to plateau. By 2014, the rate of youth unemployment in Spain was 53.2 per cent, higher than Greece, and highest of the 28 countries in the EU (Eurostat 2015, 30 January). In Greece, despite a recent decline, over half of young people in the Greek labour force were unemployed (Eurostat 2015, 30 January). Following a significant decline during 2014, the youth unemployment rate in the UK was at 16.4 per cent as of September of that year (Eurostat 2015, 30 January). While this rate almost returned to pre-GFC levels, the Spanish and Greece rates remain close to historic highs. Young people in the Spanish and Greek labour force are now three times more likely to be unemployed than their counterparts in the UK. Specifically, approximately one in two Spanish and Greek young people participating in the labour market remain unemployed, compared with around one in six British young people (Eurostat 2015, 30 January).

The Australian experience has broad similarities with Europe in that the main causes of unemployment and disengagement of young people include early school leaving without qualifications, lack of relevant skills and lack of work experience, precarious employment followed by spells of unemployment, limited training opportunities, and a paucity of effective labour market programmes (European Commission 2011). Throughout these years, young people across these economies faced declining opportunities for full-time work; increasing part-time and casual work; underemployment, underutilisation and involuntary part-time work; and youth unemployment. Let us unpack each of these in more detail.

Declining full-time work

In the longer term, participation in the labour force globally has been decreasing. In the decade following 1998, participation of young people in the labour market decreased from 54.7 to 50.8 per cent (ILO 2010, p. 3). Despite uninterrupted economic growth for the 17 years leading up to the GFC, there were no significant gains in full-time job opportunities for young Australians in general over this period (Lamb & Mason 2008). Since 1986, the age at which young people enter full-time work has increased for both males and females (Stanwick et al. 2013).

These longer trends highlight a significant change in the labour force for teenagers. Data over the last few decades clearly indicate declining numbers of teenagers in full-time jobs. This trend was exacerbated by the GFC. Since 2008, the number of teenagers in full-time jobs fell from just under 270,000 to about 200,000 in 2012 (Lamb & Robinson 2012, p. 12). As suggested above, a large proportion of this drop can be accounted for by the growth in the numbers staying in school. Nevertheless, opportunities for those who are not in education to find stable full-time work have become scarcer since the GFC. This decline in full-time work has implications for those teenagers not in study or training. Life for those seeking secure jobs has become significantly more precarious.

Despite downward trends in full-time employment, the percentage of teenagers seeking work has maintained a fairly stable rate. Data published in 2012 suggested that more than one in five teenagers not engaged in education indicated they were trying to find full-time work (Robinson & Lamb 2012, p. 11). By 2013, the proportion of young people aged 15–24 seeking full-time work had increased to its highest level in 15 years (27.3 per cent) (Australian Workforce Productivity Agency 2014, p. 13). By mid-2013, over one in five teenagers who were not engaged in education were trying to get full-time employment (Stanwick et al. 2013).

For those going on to study, a better, but still problematic, picture emerges. The Life Patterns Project, a study by researchers from the University of Melbourne, provides some valuable, if statistically limited,[5] insights into transitions from education to work for young Australians, and the generational change that has occurred during the last three decades. The study compares and contrasts students who left school in 1991 (Cohort One) with students who left school in 2006 (Cohort Two). It has found that 85 per cent of individuals from both cohorts had undertaken some form of post-secondary study, with 77 per cent of individuals from Cohort Two having completed a tertiary qualification. Both cohorts had a similar belief in the efficacy of post-secondary study. Almost half of participants from both cohorts (Cohort One, 47 per cent; Cohort Two, 44 per cent) believed that there was a very strong link between undertaking post-school study or training and getting a better job. Both cohorts frequently pursued, or were pursuing, a second tertiary qualification: 58 per cent of Cohort One (as of 2002; at age 28–29) and 40 per cent of Cohort Two (in 2013; at age 24–25) (Cuervo et al. 2013).

In 2013, almost one-third of Cohort Two study participants (aged 24–25) were yet to secure employment in their field of study. Moreover, almost a quarter of participants were looking for work outside their area of study as they were unable to find suitable work within their field. A similar proportion (just under one-quarter) felt that they needed another degree to get a suitable job in their field of study. The number of participants in Cohort Two reporting that there were very few jobs in their field of study increased substantially between 2012 and 2013, from approximately three in ten participants to four in ten participants (Cuervo et al. 2013). Participants in Cohort One were somewhat more likely to believe that they were in a job that was in their 'career area' than participants from Cohort Two. Approximately 53 per cent of Cohort One held this belief compared with approximately 45 per cent of Cohort Two at age 24 (Cuervo et al. 2013).

The authors of the study suggest that Cohort Two is both more pessimistic and realistic about the notion of having job security in the future. At the age of 23, 40 per cent of Cohort One participants believed that it was very likely that they will be in well-paid, secure employment in five years' time compared with less than 30 per cent of Cohort Two. Cohort Two participants were also less likely to believe that they would be married, have children or be in a position of authority (Cuervo et al. 2013).

Increasing part-time and casual work

Positive gains in the employment of young people have mainly been made in part-time work, reflecting greater uncertainty in the working lives of many young people. Working life in general is increasingly competitive and 'fluid'. ABS data from 2012 suggest that around 40 per cent of the workforce is 'non-permanent' (ABS 2012). The rate of casualisation across the Australian workforce increased from 18.9 per cent in 1988 to around 25 per cent in 2012. As the Independent Inquiry into Insecure Work pointed out in 2013, casual work is particularly concentrated among young people with 20 per cent of all casual workers being aged 15–19 (ACTU 2012). Since 2001, the occurrence of casual work increased considerably for this age group and to some extent for people aged 20–24, but far less so for older age groups (ACTU 2012).

For growing numbers of young people, the transition from school to work will involve one or more part-time jobs. In 2010, just under 58 per cent of men and 74 per cent of women in their late teens were in part-time employment, while 44.3 per cent and 26 per cent of young men and women, respectively, aged 18–19 were in full-time work (Pocock et al. 2010). Among those in the labour force, three times as many teenagers and more than twice as many young adults had part-time jobs in 2011 compared to the mid-1980s (Robinson et al. 2011, p. 6). The proportion of teenagers in part-time work, who were not in education, increased from 8.7 per cent in 1986 to 30 per cent in 2012. The proportion of 20- to 24-year-olds more than doubled during the same period – from 8.3 per cent to just over 19 per cent. This reflects the long-term pattern of replacement of full-time employment with more part-time jobs within the teen and young adult labour markets (Robinson & Lamb 2012, p. 48).

These trends are evident elsewhere in the world. In Europe, for example, the percentage of workers employed on a part-time basis has increased over the past three decades for both younger workers and other workers. In countries such as Spain, Greece and the UK, the manner of these increases has been highly variable. For example, the fluidity in working life experienced by young people is particularly pronounced in Greece. There has been relatively little change in the percentage of workers 25 years of age and over who are employed part-time. Despite a slight increase in the part-time employment rate between 2008 and 2013 (5.2 per cent to 8 per cent), more than nine in ten workers in this age group remain employed full-time. Between 1983 and 2004, the part-time employment rate of 15–24-years-olds in employment was comparable to, albeit somewhat higher, than that of older workers. However, since around 2005, the part-time employment rate of young people in Greece increased more rapidly than the equivalent rate for older workers, peaking at 21.1 per cent in 2013 (Eurostat 2015, 2 February).

In Spain, a similar story emerges, albeit one in which the discrepancies between younger and older workers are more pronounced. In 1991, less than 1 out of every 20 workers aged 25 and over was employed part-time. By 2013, this rate had risen to around 3 out of 20 workers. By contrast, where just over 1 in 20 workers aged 15–24 was employed part-time in 1991, this had increased to 8 in 20 workers by 2013. Moreover, the part-time employment rate since the GFC has almost doubled for young people. Coupled with the almost threefold increase in the youth unemployment rate during this period, only a small minority of young people in Spain are employed on a full-time basis compared with the situation pre-2007 (Eurostat 2015, 2 February).

The situation is slightly different in the UK. Traditionally, part-time work was more common amongst all workers, particularly amongst workers aged 25 and over. Although workers in this age group are slightly more likely to be employed part-time in 2013 than 30 years ago, most of the growth in part-time employment in the UK has been amongst younger workers. Specifically, in 1983, the part-time employment rate for older workers was approximately twice that of younger workers (21.2 per cent vs 10.6 per cent). However, by 2013, the situation had reversed (25.2 per cent vs 40.2 per cent). This reflects a 19 per cent increase in the part-time employment rate for older workers across these three decades, whilst the equivalent increase for younger worker was almost fourfold (Eurostat 2015, 2 February).

Another notable trend is the proliferation of temporary work amongst young people. As of 2013, in each of these three countries, young people who are employees remain approximately three times more likely to be on a temporary employment arrangement than older people (Greece 26.4 per cent vs 9.4 per cent; Spain 64.7 per cent vs 21 per cent; UK 14.7 per cent vs 4.9 per cent) (Eurostat 2015, 2 February). Furthermore, differences between these countries are significant. Greek employees of all ages are almost twice as likely to be temporary employees as their UK counterparts, and Spanish employees are more than twice as likely to be temporary employees as their Greek counterparts (Eurostat 2015, 2 February). Advanced economies in general are heavily reliant on temporary contracts – over a third of young people according to one estimate, 'which make[s] it hard to gain skills' (*The Economist* 2013b).

There are many reasons for increases in part-time and temporary work in these countries, particularly amongst young people. Some of these reasons are arguably relatively benign, and may even be viewed positively from an employee perspective. For example, the changing gender composition of the workforce (in which women are more likely to work part-time) and the fact that young people are more likely to pursue further education indicate that some young people may have a preference for seeking part-time work. Part-time and casual work is not without benefits. Children and young people in work gain a variety of skills and valuable experience. Some take jobs for extra pocket money. Others do so to help pay for school materials and to augment family income. However, other reasons might be seen as more problematic from an employee point of view, such as increased competition, enabling employers to develop a more flexible workforce within increasingly deregulated labour markets.

Aside from a lack of security, part-time work can be detrimental in other ways – particularly to young people who work while studying. To give a brief example: in 2013, the Australian-based McDonald's chain of restaurants received criticism for illegally employing a 14-year-old girl to work an overnight shift for nearly 15 hours. A fine of AU$15,000 was served in the Perth Industrial Magistrates' Court on McDonald's for unlawfully employing a child aged younger than 15 years to work at its Rockingham outlet. This case brings to light three concerning trends in youth employment that have been recognised in recent years that challenge the many benefits of having a job.

The first problem is a legal one. It was reported that the 14-year-old female worked five separate shifts that were completed after 10 p.m. in breach of the Children and Community Service Act. An explicit purpose of the Act is to protect children and young people from exploitation in employment. As Western Australia's then commerce minister Michael Mischin pointed out, her shift was nearly 15 hours in duration, including working during the prohibited hours of 10 p.m. to 6 a.m. (AAP 2014). Some young people enter the workforce without sufficient understanding of their rights in the workplace. Concerns not only relate to hours of employment but to a lack of understanding of occupational health and safety regulations that serve to protect children, young people, the business and their customers. Children and young people face pressures to respond to the demands of their workplace in which some find that failing to fill a shift one week will find them excluded from opportunities to work in the shift of their choice in the next.

A second concern relates to the impact on young people who work while studying. In one shift, the female worker apparently commenced work at 3.21 p.m. on a Saturday afternoon and did not conclude her shift until after 6 a.m. the following day. Then, Minister Mischin also observed, 'A further shift was not completed until after midnight on a night preceding an ordinary school day' (AAP 2014). The 2009 House of Representatives *Inquiry into Combining School and Work: Supporting Successful Youth Transitions* found that many children and young people face the challenge of juggling school and work (HOR 2009; House of Representatives 2009). Figures from 2009 indicate that around 22 per cent of students aged 15–19 worked between 11 and 15 hours each week. Approximately 9 per cent worked 16 hours or more (ABS, cited in HOR 2009, p. 16). Just over 48 per cent were employed in the retail sector, while just fewer than 30 per cent worked in fast food and hospitality (HOR 2009, p. 15). For those working while studying, balancing study commitments with work is a challenge for many young people. This applies not only to post-school study and training but also to those still at school. The Inquiry found that working too many hours could undermine educational and general wellbeing. One survey of students found that they could manage up to 12–15 hours of work a week without impacting on their schooling (HOR 2009, p. 17). Of course, this differs depending on the type of job, type of study and individual learning needs. But research by Maslen (2009) suggests over half of senior secondary students in Australia are juggling the demands of school and part-time work, and for many balancing the various demands of school, recreation and work can be significant. The House of Representatives Inquiry highlighted that too much work can become an impediment, with adverse effects on students' performance at school. The work experience gained is valuable and is sometimes seen as a stepping stone to a permanent job (HOR 2009). But statistically, teenagers working part-time jobs are only marginally more likely to transition to full-time employment than those who are unemployed (Robinson et al. 2011). In the long term, participation in part-time work has also been shown to have negative effects on women in particular, such as a 'wage scarring' and lack of career progression (Chalmers & Hill 2007; Chalmers 2013). We shall return to these issues later in the book.

Unemployment

From a global perspective, the UN has repeatedly observed the severe impact of the GFC on young people – particularly in the area of unemployment (UNRIC 2012a, 2012b). They are amongst the first to lose jobs, and economic downturns can deeply impact on their transitions from school to work. 'During economic downturns', the 2012 UN *World Youth Report* notes, 'young people are often the "last in" and the "first out" – the last to be hired, and the first to be dismissed. This issue has particularly severe implications for the school to work transition, the period when young people enter the labour market to look for their first job' (UN 2012a). While youth unemployment rates vary significantly throughout the world, they tend to be higher than those of adults (UNRIC 2012a). And unemployment rates can vary greatly within countries. In Australia, for example, more young people experience unemployment in regional and remote areas (Brotherhood of St Laurence 2014).

Following the GFC, between 2008 and 2011, the percentage of young Australians without a job for a year or more nearly doubled (Robinson et al. 2011). The unemployment rate for all teenagers in the labour force, at 16.6 per cent, was three times higher than for all adults in Australia (Robinson & Lamb 2012, p. 7). By 2013, it was reportedly as high as 40 per cent in some disadvantaged suburbs (McDougall 2013). According to a 2014 report released by the Brotherhood of St Laurence, an average of 12.4 per cent of young people aged 15–24 were out of work in the year to January 2013 (Brotherhood of St Laurence 2014).

As we found above, young people most at risk of marginalisation from earning and learning live in rural and remote areas (Lamb & Mason 2008; Robinson & Lamb 2009). In regions such as northern Adelaide, west and north-west Tasmania and far north Queensland, for example, unemployment reached as high as 20 per cent in 2014 (Brotherhood of St Laurence 2014).

Importantly, the unemployment rate has not returned to levels prior to the GFC. Increases in unemployment have persisted since 2008 (Stanwick et al. 2013). It continues to hover at around two to three times the national average and is much more of an issue for 15- to 19-year-olds than for those aged 20–24.

Underemployment, underutilisation and involuntary part-time work

Youth underemployment, a measure of those willing and able to work but who cannot get it, has increased. It is in part linked to the long-term changes to the labour force described above, as well as more recent instability in the wake of the GFC. Many women aged 18–19, for example, would prefer to work more but are unable to do so (Pocock et al. 2010).

A significant proportion of young people in general are seeking full-time work but cannot get it (Lamb & Robinson 2012). In 2011, a third of the 814,700 part-time workers who would prefer to work more hours were aged 15–24 (ABS 2011a). Teenagers face particular challenges. As we found earlier, more than one in five teenagers not engaged in education indicated they were trying to find full-time work (ABS 2011a). While just under half of those aged 15–19 preferred to work less than 30 hours per week, around 28 per cent of underemployed part-time workers in this age group had insufficient work for a year or more. By 2012, the underemployment rate for 15- to 24-year-olds was nearly double that of the whole population (12.6 per cent compared to 6.9 per cent) (Stanwick et al. 2013, p. 16). As mentioned above, by June 2013, the number of young people seeking full-time work had reached its highest level in 15 years.

The concentration of young people in part-time work in Australia, which includes a significant proportion in involuntary part-time work, is significantly high compared to OECD countries. The OECD defines involuntary part-time work as comprising those who usually work full-time but who are working part-time because of economic slack (i.e. unused proportion of economic capacity), those working part-time but have fewer hours in their jobs because of economic slack and those working part-time because full-time work cannot be found. According to this data, the share of involuntary part-timers aged 15–24 in the labour force was just over 13 per cent in 2011. The percentage of involuntary part-time workers has at times been higher in Australia during the last decade compared to some other OECD countries for which comparable data are available. The share of involuntary part-timers aged 15–24 as a percentage of part-time employment was just under 35 per cent in 2011, compared to, say, 4.8 per cent in Norway (OECD 2013b).

While these figures serve as a starting point for understanding the challenges of underemployment, they are by no means perfect indicators. (The measure of 'involuntary part-time work' is itself contested.) They do not necessarily capture the acute challenges facing certain young people in the Australian labour force. While the proportion of part-time workers who are underemployed generally decreases as they get older, the experience of insecurity or dissatisfaction with working life during these formative years is not without negative consequences. For example, school leavers who want full-time work, but have to take part-time jobs instead, can remain vulnerable to marginalisation from secure work for years.

Another measure, the rate of labour force underutilisation – which includes the unemployed plus the underemployed as a proportion of the labour force – indicates that for 15- to 24-year-olds, the rate reported in 2013 was 23.7 per cent, compared to 11.9 per cent for the entire labour force. (Within this figure, the unemployment rate for teenagers was 17.7 per cent, while it was 8 per cent for 20- to 24-year-olds [Stanwick et al. 2013, p. 6].) Labour force underutilisation rose following the GFC – a trend that has not reversed since 2008. It has been higher for females than for males – 14.4 per cent compared to 11 per cent in 2012 (Stanwick et al. 2013, p. 16).

Measures of underutilisation reveal more troubling trends beyond unemployment. Eurostat data include those who are unemployed, underemployed part-time workers, persons available to work but not seeking it and persons not available to work but seeking employment. While the levels of youth unemployment experienced in the UK were lower than Spain and Greece, the situation for young people in the UK is far more troubling if you include other measures of labour underutilisation and focus on looking at unemployed as a percentage of the total population (rather than as a percentage of the labour market). By contrast, the reverse is true for Greece. Including additional measures of labour underutilisation does not appear to significantly alter the picture of the labour market in Greece. This is because most (77 per cent as of September 2014) young people who can be classified as underutilised were in fact unemployed. Despite one in two young people in Greece's labour market being classified as unemployed, fewer than one in seven young people in the overall population were unemployed and fewer than one in five classified as underutilised. This suggests that a high proportion of young people in Greece are engaged in other non-labour market-related activities (Eurostat 2015, 30 January).

Spain's outlook is alarming irrespective of the measure used (Eurostat 2015, 30 January). In addition to the high levels of unemployment described above, a further one in ten young people in Spain fit into one of the other categories of labour underutilisation. In particular, a relatively high percentage of young people in Spain (5.4 per cent in September 2014) were available to work, but not seeking employment (Eurostat 2015, 15 January, 30 January). It may well be that young people are discouraged by both the prospect of seeking employment in the current labour market or participating in further study.

Including the broader measures of labour underutilisation significantly alters the picture that emerges when analysing the labour market situation in the UK. In contrast to Greece, where more than three-quarters of those underutilised young people could be classified as unemployed, unemployed young people make up less than half of the underutilised in the UK. The situation in the UK is particularly notable for the relatively high proportion of young people currently employed part-time and wanting to work more hours (6.6 per cent of all young people, as of September 2014) (Eurostat 2015, 15 January, 30 January). A particularly vulnerable group here are those on zero-hours contracts, in which employers do not have to provide any minimum working hours. It was reported that from 2013 to 2015, the number of people employed on zero-hours contracts in their main job had risen from 586,000 to 697,000, with a large proportion being students in full-time education or working part-time, and being aged either under 25 or 65 and over. The increase has been attributed 'to increasing recognition of the contracts by staff when asked by researchers about their employment terms', but the figures are no less striking. Around 30 per cent of people on these contracts want to work more hours. Major employers of young people, such as Burger King, Domino's Pizza, McDonald's and hotel and catering businesses, offer zero-hours contracts. According to the UK Office for National Statistics (ONS), more than 50 per cent of businesses in hotel and catering sectors used no-guaranteed-hours contracts in August 2014 to varying extents (Inman 2015).

In the UK, for the most part, the GFC does not appear to have impacted significantly on the labour underutilisation rate of middle-aged people (25–54 years of age), which has fluctuated between 9 and 11 per cent since 2008. This can be contrasted with the underutilisation rate of young people, which has fluctuated more substantially and was clearly trending upwards until the end of 2013, when it reached a high of 26.1 per cent (Eurostat 2015, 15 January, 30 January).

However, perhaps what is most striking is the large gap between the labour underutilisation rates of young people and middle-aged people across all time periods in the UK. By this metric, young people in the UK are certainly relatively disadvantaged compared with middle-aged people in this region, and currently face a higher labour underutilisation rate than their counterparts in Greece (22 per cent of all young people underutilised in the UK compared to 18.4 per cent in Greece, as of September 2014). This trend certainly is not immediately apparent when analysing youth unemployment data, and reflects both that labour force participation of young people in the UK is higher than in Greece and that the UK has a far higher proportion of individuals in other labour underutilisation categories, particularly underemployed part-time workers (Eurostat 2015, 15 January, 30 January).

Conclusion

Economic downturns have long-term impacts on young people's participation in work. Many who become disengaged during these periods struggled to get back into work. This applies in advanced economies such as Australia as well as in developing countries, such as Argentina, Brazil and Indonesia. Following Indonesia's financial crisis in 1997, young people forced out of work were less likely to be in work ten years on 'and if they were, to have only informal jobs' (*The Economist* 2013b).

Following the GFC, the significant increase in young people's disengagement from work in 2008–09 heightened concerns for the effect of this across young people's lives (Robinson & Lamb 2009). The link between young people's engagement in work and study and their satisfaction with various aspects of their life is well established. Survey data from 2007 showed that 58 per cent of Australian young people engaged in full-time work or study reported being very happy with their life, whereas 48 per cent of those who were in neither full-time work nor education gave that response. Those young adults engaged in full-time work were much happier about their career prospects, the work they do, their future and their standard of living than those who were unemployed, not in the labour force or in part-time work (Robinson & Lamb 2009, p. 52). Young people such as apprentices, who have a degree of financial security and a career pathway, are happier about their life in general (Dockery 2010).

By contrast, those marginalised can experience depression and isolation. Disengagement from work has implications across other domains of life, from personal life satisfaction to one's health and relationships with friends, family and community. It can be debilitating, isolating, and incur social, economic and personal costs – for those who are disengaged, for the communities in which they live, and for the broader economy and society. The evidence suggests that part-time work or withdrawal from the labour force can have a negative impact on young people's levels of satisfaction with non-economic aspects of their lives, such as their use of spare time, independence and social life (Hillman & McMillan 2005, p. 22).

Increasing rates of secondary school completion has been the great hope of successive governments seeking to improve young people's transitions. Engagement in school-based learning significantly affects young people's ability to successfully negotiate educational transitions, particularly in post-school education. But by international comparisons, Australia's rate of secondary school completion has lagged behind several OECD countries (Robinson et al. 2010).

Of these key educational transitions, most concerning is the disengagement of those young people in the 16- to 24-year-old age bracket. Once these young people have become disengaged from work and study, it is much harder for some to get back in. Disengagement at this age has a detrimental effect on young people's outlook, options and futures. The long-term impact of global downturns on youth employment is likely to be felt for decades. When looking at those NEET, Australia only ranked 17 out of 32 countries for 15/16- to 24-year-olds. Again, this is striking given how well Australia has fared overall in comparison to other countries following the GFC (Stanwick et al. 2013). And given that Australia is fundamentally enmeshed in the global market, there is little to suggest that it is immune from the global trends discussed in the introduction of this book.

Those who go on to study and training post-school tend to fare better in life across a range of indicators (LSAY data, cited in Robinson et al. 2010). In the Life Patterns Project, 80 per cent of participants in Cohort One who had completed a post-secondary qualification reported being in full-time work at age 24/25, compared with 65 per cent of participants in Cohort Two. The trend was similar for participants who reported that they were 'still studying' (50 per cent vs 37 per cent), although, conversely, was in the opposite direction for participants who had not discontinued or not pursued post-secondary studies (59 per cent vs 66 per cent) (Cuervo et al. 2013).

As workers get older, not only are they more likely to be employed on a permanent basis, but are less likely to work irregular hours. However, most young people are still working irregular hours when they are 25 years old. For example, around 60 per cent work weekends, and around three-quarters work irregular hours of some description. Working non-standard shifts particularly affects individuals who are employed in a job not related to their desired career, and those employed part-time and/or on a sessional/casual basis (Cuervo et al. 2013).

Employment opportunities in general are shifting from traditional bases such as manufacturing to industries such as education and tourism. And the fluidity of working life means that across the life cycle, employment may not be tied to one job or sector. By some estimates, the typical secondary school student will have as many as 13 different jobs in four different industries across their lifetime (Kahn et al. 2011). While most young Australians will go on to get 'good jobs' (Stanwick et al. 2013, p. 7), this book is primarily concerned with those who find themselves unemployed post-school, as well as those struggling to get secure work. The data above suggest that a growing and significant proportion of young people find themselves adrift at sea, caught in broader tides over which they have little control and for which they are ill-prepared when they leave the school gates.

Given recent downward turns in the economy, coupled with longer changes in the labour force, we need to ask whether enough is being done by educators to prepare young people for working life. Working life in general has become more fluid and insecure. And young people from certain backgrounds and places face deep and often structural barriers. SES, ethnicity and educational attainment matter. We return to these issues throughout this book.

Despite the confronting trends outlined in this chapter, compared to many other countries, Australia fared well in light of the economic turbulence experienced throughout the world following the GFC. But the key trends outlined during this discussion challenge a number of assumptions about how young Australians are faring in their transitions from school to work, further study and training. These challenges strike at the very heart of how we understand the very nature of successful 'transitions' and perhaps even the very notion of what constitutes 'maturity' and 'career' in this era of fluid and less secure work. But given that Australia's economy has fared far better than Greece, Spain or the UK, does prosperity need to be accompanied by insecurity?

The evidence suggests that while many young people enjoy the flexibility of casual work, it is difficult for them to plan for the future. For example, securing a mortgage to purchase a house and starting a family are more challenging without a secure, stable income. Many young people in casual work must consequently defer big life decisions. Young people, like most people in general, seek security, connection and a sense of where they are going in life. But economic change is effectively warping the experience of transition from school to work, and has major sociological implications. These pathways are characterised by different markers of transition to the ones with which many of us are familiar. These markers include when (and if) young people start families, purchase homes and get full-time stable work. The data clearly suggest that these events associated with 'maturity' are happening later in life. But this is not necessarily by choice. The current housing market, for example, deters many new entrants. Raising a family is another decision that appears to be deferred. In 2011, young women were slightly less likely to give birth than in 2001, following a broader trend in which many women are giving birth at older ages (Stanwick et al. 2013).

Many young people have part-time jobs but want to work more or be in more satisfying work. They want a sense of where they are going, a decent level of income to live on and seek security.

Some lack a basic knowledge of how to seek work. They are disadvantaged by a lack of work experience as well as networks to navigate the job market (ILO 2010 in Mann 2012). There is evidence to suggest that young people want more hands-on learning and practical experience, 'especially people who may have been excluded from the academic focus of traditional education programs' (Davies et al. 2011, p. 36; see also Bryce & Withers 2003; House of Commons 2009). They want to connect their learning to life. Is schooling fulfilling this need? There is a deeper issue of how well conventional approaches to opening up these opportunities – ranging from careers advice to young people to the ongoing professional development of those teaching them – are aligned with changing environments of learning and labour. To illustrate this point: in a society in which the majority of young people expect information and communications technologies (ICTs) to be infused across life from home to school, work and social life, can the same be said of their teachers and employers? For example, too many teachers continue to struggle to work easily with digital media and 'keep up' with their transformational impact and usage by young people.

At a time when there is great emphasis on defining educational success according to certain measures (e.g. using data from the National Assessment Program – Literacy and Numeracy [NAPLAN]), there is a fundamental question as to the degree to which educators are fostering the relevant skills, competencies and literacies for contemporary working life beyond 'the basics' of numeracy and literacy. These range from problem solving and communication skills, to cultural competencies that will be so important to Australia's engagement with the region in the Asian century. The need for these skills has been acknowledged as important, but much of the work on this during last 15 years has been focused on adults, rather than young people. Literacy and numeracy remain crucial. As important but undervalued are oracy and the learning of languages other than English. The Australia in the Asian Century White Paper (Australian Government 2012) rightly suggested that far more needs to be done in the latter area in particular – a point that has been made for over a decade now by organisations such as Asia Education Foundation.

These skills are important because the pathways that young people tread are changing. They are foundational in pathways to secure work, pathways out of disadvantage, and pathways to their region and the world.

A related challenge lies in developing skills to match economic need. Predicting what the labour force will look like is extremely difficult. (Just look at how technology has transformed industry and working life.)

When I facilitated a series of seminars engaging big employers of young people in Australia in 2012 and 2013, I asked participants to name what the nature of industry and workforce-readiness will look like in a generation. Some people in business (like many of us) struggled to do so, while in the same breath suggesting that young people are ill-prepared for worlds of work.

One final question to end this discussion is related to the degree to which our conventional pathways from school to life beyond rely on conventional, industrial models of education to develop young people for an emerging post-industrial society. How do these models define 'success' and are they equipping young people with the knowledge, skills, and dispositions to learn, engage and adapt to the challenges of the 21st century? These questions are at the heart of this book.

2
The Big Four: Structural Marginalisation, Globalisation, Demographic Change and Technology

Introduction

The challenges facing young people in worlds of work outlined in the previous discussion are complexly interwoven with other domestic trends, such as embedded forms of marginalisation, as well as broader effects of globalisation. While Australia did not feel the effects of the economic downturn of 2007–08 as profoundly as many other countries, the ripple effects of the GFC serve as a stark reminder that these challenges continue to be enmeshed in the global. For example, young people are facing competition for work with temporary migrant workers as well as growing numbers of older people who are staying in the workforce longer. Young working holidaymakers from overseas, in particular, may be saturating the domestic labour market, occupying jobs typically taken by young people. As a result, it is argued that many young people seeking work have been driven to undertake low-level training as a kind of refuge from unemployment (Birrell & Healy 2013b). Overlaying this shifting labour market is the need for higher qualifications to get work, a trend that is emerging internationally.

Broader challenges and opportunities await young people seeking to work in a region that is experiencing unprecedented growth and in which Asian countries are exerting new kinds of geopolitical influence. In light of these, this chapter also outlines the key issues in how Australia engages the Asian region and the ways that schooling is failing to prepare young people for international engagement and the challenges of living in 'the Asian Century'.

Technology is another driver of change. These effects have implications beyond work; they are reshaping the way that people are engaging with the world.

In Chapter One, it was noted that particular groups were at risk of marginalisation, such as those living in regional and remote communities. The first part of this chapter will provide a deeper examination of who is most at risk of marginalisation from work, focusing on domestic trends within Australia. The discussion then outlines some key macrolevel drivers of change, such as demographic shifts, the ubiquity of ICTs and cultural diversity.

The work of Arjun Appadurai provides a useful lens through which to view these drivers within the context of globalisation. He describes five 'scapes' of modern global cultures, which provide a conceptual framework for understanding these drivers of change. These drivers are important for understanding the wider context and a key question asked in this book: in a highly competitive global labour market, what is the future of working life and how adequately are our schools preparing young people? In building a case for change, these drivers set the context for the discussion to follow.

Who is most at risk of marginalisation?

Within Australia, persistent trends continue to show that particular categories of young people experience marginalisation from earning and learning. As we saw in the previous chapter, a significant proportion of young people who are not in work, education and training are from disadvantaged backgrounds, particularly those from low SES families, Indigenous young people, those living in regional and rural areas, those who struggle to do well at school and who attain low levels of education, as well as young people with a disability or health problem.

Socio-economic and geographic factors

The impact of socio-economic and associated geographic factors on educational and employment outcomes is significant and widely understood (Keating 2009; Lamb & Mason 2008). SES and parental background, for example, impact on educational attainment. Early school leaving occurs more frequently among young people whose parents left school early (Robinson et al. 2010). Socio-economic and geographic factors intersect. Young people living outside metropolitan areas are, for example, less likely to remain in school to Year 12, and they have fewer pathways post-school (Walsh 2010). Data published in 2009 suggest that young people living in the wealthiest areas of Australia were three times more likely to gain a university degree by the age of 24 than those in the poorest areas. Those from the wealthiest families obtain a university degree or higher at more than double the rate of those from disadvantaged families (Robinson & Lamb 2009). Data have also shown that people from lower socio-economic backgrounds are significantly more likely to lower their educational and occupational expectations (Sikora & Saha 2011, p. 10). Young people living in disadvantaged communities have less connection with people who are employed, university educated or living outside the area (Pope 2006). They often have limited access to the networks and connections that can provide the opportunities for social and economic wellbeing (Tennant et al. 2005). They have less exposure to people working in skilled and professional contexts and are less likely to form a positive association between school and work than their more affluent peers (Todhunter 2009).

Consequently, where young people live has a significant impact on their education and employment opportunities. Educational inequities often manifest along geographic lines, with significant distinctions existing between urban, rural and remote young people across Australia (Lamb & Mason 2008; Robinson & Lamb 2009). For example, according to ABS Census data of Housing and Population from 2006, young adults living in the city areas of Australia had more than double the rate of attainment of university qualifications than those living in very remote areas (32.3 per cent compared to 14.5 per cent) (Robinson & Lamb 2009, p. 31). The farther young people live from city locations, the higher the percentage without any post-school qualifications. The proportion of teenagers not in full-time education or employment is also uppermost in those states and territories that have rural and remote populations, including the Northern Territory, Queensland and Western Australia, and 52.4 per cent of young people in remote locations had no post-school qualifications compared to 38.7 per cent of city dwellers (Robinson & Lamb 2009, p. 31).

Indigenous young people

Educational inequity is particularly concentrated amongst Indigenous young people, for whom marginalisation is also related to socio-economic context and magnified by geographic location, with remote and rural Indigenous young people significantly more disengaged than urban young people.[1] For young Indigenous people living in these areas, policy efforts to raise secondary school attainment have not translated into significant post-schooling opportunities, and their rate of disengagement from work and study is pronounced. The highest numbers of young Indigenous Australians live in states featuring more regional and remote communities, with the Northern Territory having the highest proportion in relation to the rest of the population (Hughes & Hughes 2010). These trends predate the GFC (Long & North 2009; Productivity Commission 2009). For example, in 1996, the unemployment rates of young Indigenous adults were around twice as high as those of non-Indigenous Australians, but 10 years later they were nearly three times higher (Long & North 2009, p. 52). Young Indigenous Australians were less likely to have a full-time job. In the decade 1996–2006, rates of participation in full-time work did not change for Indigenous teenagers and increased slightly for young adults (Long & North 2009). Apparent retention rates of Indigenous students from the first to final years of secondary schooling remain well below those of other young people, although this gap has decreased over the last 20 years. While 30.7 per cent of Indigenous young people stayed on to Year 12 in 1995, 45.4 per cent stayed on in 2009 (Robinson et al. 2010, p. 44). The proportion of people aged 20–24 who completed Year 12 or above improved from 45 per cent in 2008 to 59 per cent in 2012–13 (Productivity Commission 2014). The proportion of Aboriginal and Torres Strait Islander 17- to 24-year-olds participating in post-school education, training or employment grew from 32 per cent in 2002 to 40 per cent in 2012–13, but was still low compared to non-Indigenous rate of 75 per cent in 2011–12 (Productivity Commission 2014). Gains have therefore been favourable, but modest when compared to the overall population (DPMC 2015). Despite substantial efforts driven by education policy and various programmes dedicated to increasing Indigenous participation in schools, the statistics on Indigenous student retention and attainment of school and post-school qualifications remain far below those for the rest of the population.

Interrelated incidences of low levels of educational attainment, unemployment, poverty, poor health, high levels of incarceration, racism and a long-term legacy of dispossession perpetuate inequities in education and employment. The cumulative impact of these circumstances has a significant impact on the wellbeing and post-school futures of young Indigenous people.

The impact of globalisation

Overlaying these localised and often structural forms of marginalisation are wider and often more fluid global trends and phenomena. Young people's lives are enmeshed in complex flows of people, ideas, products and ideologies – with tensions arising in the intersections and interactions between these flows. 'Globalisation', Appadurai suggests, 'has shrunk distances between elites, shifted key relations between producers and consumers, broken many links between labor [sic] and family life, obscured the lines between temporary locales and imaginary national attachments' (1996, pp. 9–10). Appadurai's notions of ethnoscapes, technoscapes, finanscapes, mediascapes and ideoscapes provide a useful way of framing how we think about the impact of globalisation on young people in the context of their engagement with and disengagement from worlds of work.

These conceptual scapes refer to five dimensions of cultural flows and form the bases of 'imagined worlds'. They are fluid and irregular, and 'characterise international capital as deeply as they do international clothing styles. These terms with the common suffix – scape also indicate that these are not objectively given relations that look the same from every angle of vision but, rather, they are deeply perspectival constructs, inflected by the historical, linguistic and political situatedness of different sorts of actors: nation-states, multinationals, diasporic communities, as well as subnational groupings and movements (whether religious, political, or economic), and even intimate face-to-face groups, such as villages neighborhoods and families' (Appadurai 1996, p. 33). Appadurai suggests that these scapes 'set the basis for a tentative formulation about the conditions under which current global flows occur: they occur in and through growing disjunctures among ethnoscapes, technoscapes, financescapes, mediascapes and ideascapes' (p. 37). There have always been disjunctures in these flows; however, the 'sheer speed, scale, and volume of these flows are now so great that the disjunctures have become central to the politics of global culture' (p. 37). These disjunctures have important implications for how we understand young people's navigation of worlds of work, which is discussed in the following sections.

Global flows of work

The first scape that we outline in relation to young people is the ethnoscape, which refers to the 'persons who constitute the shifting world in which we live' (Appadurai 1996, p. 33). It encompasses groups in movement, such as immigrants, refugees and temporary guest workers. Although the movement of people has always existed, the scope and scale of both the realities of having to move and the fantasies of wanting to move have grown alongside more affordable travel and international ICT. Geographic movement, and the possibility of geographic movement, permeates the lives of more people as they move much further today than previously. Appadurai (1996) cites examples of Sri Lankan refugees finding themselves living anywhere from South India to Switzerland, while the Hmong have migrated from London to Philadelphia.

In Australia, long-term migrations of people have shaped the fabric of its society, from the migration of the first Australians to the mass migration of peoples from all over the world during the 20th century. These flows are visible in the make-up of young people in Australia, which is defined by its cultural diversity. Demographer Graeme Hugo (2012a) highlights that 'there are 62 birthplace groups with more than 10,000 members in Australia, making it one of the most ethnically diverse in the world'. And it is becoming more diverse. By 2011, the percentage of Australians born in Australia, New Zealand or the UK–Ireland had decreased from 97.9 per cent in 1947 to 81.7 per cent. Just over a quarter (26 per cent) of Australia's population was born overseas. One in five young Australians is born overseas and speaks a language other than English (mainly Asian) at home (Muir et al. 2009). One in five had at least one parent born overseas. Asia looms large in Australia's cultural make-up. Over 10 per cent of the population identified themselves as Asian – double the percentage from a decade earlier (Beech 2013). Half of the top ten languages spoken at home include Mandarin, Cantonese, Vietnamese, Hindi and Tagalog (ABS 2011b).

Educational attainment differs across these groups. One report by the National Centre for Vocational Education Research (NCVER) points out that the achievement of Year 12 qualifications and higher education qualifications for 20- to 24-year-olds from non-English-speaking backgrounds is higher than for Australians as a whole. Participation in higher education for 20- to 24-year-olds whose language spoken at home is not English is also far higher than for those whose language at home is English (Stanwick et al. 2013, p. 13).

Recent policy measures have intensified flows within the ethnoscape, which have implications for young people seeking work. The Rudd–Gillard government's permanent-entry migration programme, set at a then record high level of 214,000 in 2012–13, led to large influx of temporary migrants to work in Australia. Young working holidaymakers from overseas are intensifying competition for jobs with young local workers (Birrell & Healy 2013b). As of March 2013, there were 1.1 million temporary visa holders (not counting New Zealanders) in Australia. Most held work rights. The number of visas issued in these temporary visa subclasses is largely uncapped. In the year to May that same year, there was a rise of 168,000 recently arrived overseas born migrants aged over 15 years old in Australia – 108,200 of whom were employed. This is almost as large as the increase in Australia's total employment during that period (126,000 people). In 2012–13, the number of Working Holiday Maker (WHM) visas issued was roughly equivalent to the number of young people who leave school and enter the workforce each year (around 250,000). All these WHMs were aged 30 or less and included significant numbers fleeing foreign job markets in which finding a job was difficult (e.g. from Taiwan and Ireland). Many were seeking work in Australia rather than a holiday supplemented by work (Birrell & Healy 2013b).

As a consequence, argue Birrell and Healy (2013a), many young Australians competing for those jobs were 'seeking refuge in low-level training courses because of lack of employment opportunities'. They contend, 'It is young local workers who are the main losers in the competition for employment. This is especially the case for those without post-school education, who are seeking less skilled, entry-level jobs . . . Young people also have to compete for less skilled entry level work with an increasing number of job hungry temporary migrants looking for the same work' (Birrell & Healy 2013a).

Competition for good quality jobs has also intensified. Following on from our discussion in Chapter One, a combination of an increase in the number of university graduates, combined with greater mobility of qualified workers across countries, is intensifying competition for skilled work, which appears to be driving 'credential inflation'. It is argued that the value of academic credentials has consequently decreased over time (Ortlieb 2015). In a more competitive labour market, employers can demand higher qualifications (Foster et al. 2007; Modestino 2010). This in turn drives out of the labour market those without post-school qualifications, such as graduate degrees.

Credential inflation is evident in the US, where studies show that the 'college premium', that is, the income power of college graduates, is largely enjoyed by those with postgraduate and professional degrees, rather than those with undergraduate qualifications. The generational divide is perhaps most clearly visible in analyses of the relative earning power of different groups in the population. On the one hand, incomes derived from graduate degrees have not kept pace with growth in the incomes derived from postgraduate qualifications, while on the other hand, we see the growth of billionaires – the 'one per cent' identified by the Occupy Movement – since the 1980s (Côté 2013). For example, in the US, the annual earnings of males aged 20–29 not enrolled in educational institutions in the three decades leading up to 2009 declined by 15 per cent, in contrast to a 31 per cent increase for those with master's degrees, while those with a bachelor's degree only experienced a 5 per cent increase (Côté 2013, p. 8; Sum & McLaughlin 2011).

These inflationary pressures may be striking at the core promise of national education systems in countries such as the US, UK and Australia. This promise, or 'opportunity bargain', is that gaining higher qualifications will lead to desirable work (Brown et al. 2011). In the US, it is argued that the mobility of young people from middle-class backgrounds is being challenged and constrained by the entry of professionals from emerging economies such as India. One of the perverse outcomes of this competition is illustrated by Brown et al. (2011, p. 5), who note the use of the Dutch auction in countries such as Germany, which sees those with brightest CVs competing for jobs by offering to accept the lowest paying wage.

Demographic change

Wider demographic change is salient here. On 31 October 2011, the UN marked the occasion of the world's population passing seven billion. Global demographic changes suggest broader local and international challenges to young people in the future. The make-up of world's population is changing. Globally, there were more than six children aged 15 or less for every person aged 65 or older in 1950. In 2070, it is estimated the latter will outnumber the former, and there will be only three working-age people to every two people aged 65 and over (Cohen, cited in Hugo 2012b). Half the population of the world now lives in countries where those of childbearing age are having fewer than two children on average. The fertility rate of half of the world is below replacement level. However, certain parts of the world are experiencing rapid growth in population. This is particularly the case in poorer regions. Data published by the United Nations Department of Economic and Social Affairs, Population Division (2014) show particularly high rates of fertility[2] in parts of Africa. By contrast, in Europe, East Asia and the Americas, it is suggested that there has been 'an over-correction'. Contrast Niger, where the fertility rate is 7.16, to Singapore, whose rate is at 0.78, and 'whose citizens appear intent on extinction' (Seccombe 2013). UN data indicate that this shift occurred around the time that the world population reached seven billion (Seccombe 2013).

Within Australia, key challenges arise in addressing the needs of an ageing population that is also experiencing tensions arising from unprecedented diversity. The median age of Australians is expected to increase from 36.8 years in 2007 to 45.2 years in 2056 (ABS 2013b). The number of young people as a proportion of the population is shrinking and the proportion of people over 65 years is expected to increase from

13 per cent to 25 per cent by 2056. Migration notwithstanding, the number of young Australians as a proportion of the population has been declining as the population has been ageing (ABS 2013b). On one level, this trend may seem alarming; however, in absolute terms, there will be almost 50 per cent more people aged 12–25 by the year 2050 than there is today. This increase amounts to a growth from 4.3 million to 6.3 million (ABS 2013b; FYA 2014). The ageing of the population nevertheless may have significant implications for the nature of the workforce and redistribution of income across the economy.

An ageing of the population might suggest that demand for labour might increase; however, in some countries, this has not flowed on to jobs for young people. Japan's youth unemployment levels, for example, have never quite recovered from the financial crisis of the early 1990s despite its ageing population (*The Economist* 2013b). Older age groups in fact absorbed some of the available work (Genda 2005). In Australia, the proportion of those working in their later years of life is increasing. Birrell and Healy (2013b) highlight that between May 2003 and May 2013, the share of those aged 60–64 in the workforce increased from 39 per cent to 54 per cent. This increasing competition for work particularly affects young people who are qualified but lack experience. The growth in older citizens requires innovative approaches to sustainability given changes in the age of the working population. There are two implications. Firstly, the axis of welfare distribution and healthcare may shift towards supporting those in retirement. With proportionately fewer people working, this may create significant challenges to government health and welfare expenditures. Secondly, the capacity of young people to get work may be challenged by the growing share of local workers aged 55 and over who are staying in the workforce. The ratio of the working-age population to individuals aged 65 and over will halve during the first 40 years of this century. Citing an Australian Government (2010) report, the Foundation for Young Australians note that, in 2002, there were five working people for every person over the age of 65 in Australia. By 2042, this ratio will have fallen to 2.5:1 (FYA 2014).

Income inequality is also increasing. Inequality, as measured by the percentage of income received by the highest income earners, is trending upwards. Since around the year 2000, income inequality has been at its highest level since the 1940s (Piketty, in Cassidy 2014; FYA 2014). Income inequality is a growing feature of advanced economies. In Britain, Howker and Malik suggest the emergence of an 'age apartheid' in Britain (Howker & Malik 2010) arising from 'a dangerous degree of demographic discrimination – a situation in which a large group of the old prosper unfairly at the expense of the young' (Lewis 2012). This discrimination arises from a decline in the benefits enjoyed by the post-world-war generation, such as affordable housing, secure employment, free tertiary education and a more generous welfare safety net. The result is a generation that on some key indicators is worse off than their parents.

Less severe generational tensions have been noted in Australia in areas such as housing affordability (Huntley 2006). Housing affordability and availability is the number one issue of personal concern to young people aged 17–24 (as compared to national or global concern) for which they would like to see politicians take action (AYAC 2013; FYA 2014). This echoes findings by the Australia Institute (2013), in which rent availability and affordability (mentioned by 47 per cent of survey respondents) ranked only behind jobs (57 per cent) as the issue of personal concern most likely to influence the vote of people aged 17–24 at the 2013 federal election. (It failed to feature in the policy of the major political parties in that election.)

Mechanisms within the tax system, such as negative gearing, have fostered enormous growth investment in housing, producing 'a generational lock-up of the housing market' that inhibits entry by young people seeking to purchase a home (Lewis 2012). While it is argued that older home owners faced their own challenges in securing home ownership, such as during a period of interest rates (up to 18 per cent) in the 1980s (O'Neill, cited in Lewis 2012), a 2013 report by the International Monetary Fund (IMF) found that Australia had the third highest house price-to-income ratio in the world. Similarly, in countries such as Belgium, Canada, Norway and Sweden, Australia's house prices have risen to historically high rates (IMF 2013).

One final trend worth noting is immigration, which has also grown at historic levels and has been a major driver behind population growth. Aside from Luxembourg and Israel, Australia has the fastest population growth in the OECD. Since the year 2000, the population has grown by 25 per cent, or around 400,000 each year, which as the Australia Institute points out, is equivalent to the entire population of Sydney that year. More immigrants have arrived in Australia since then than during the intense period of migration between 1950 and 1980 (Krockenberger 2015).

But despite its cultural diversity, Australia is characterised by tensions evident in the widespread experience of racism. The evidence consistently points to high levels of racism that are acutely experienced by young people in schools (Casinader & Walsh 2014; Mansouri et al. 2009; Priest et al. 2014). It suggests that schools, teachers and students are not adequately equipped to deal with racism (Mansouri et al. 2009; Mansouri & Jenkins 2010). It reflects a wider schism in the way that young Australians deal with cultural difference at home and abroad, and it suggests a need to better develop cultural competencies to navigate diversity. These competencies will be explored further in Chapter Four.

Immigration is not only shaping the fabrics of the Australian economy and society but also its relationship to the region. With the ageing of the population and young adults making up a smaller proportion overall than previously, the future workforce arguably has to come from somewhere unless either fertility rates change significantly[3] and in a sustained way, or through migration. If that workforce is to come from Australia's regional neighbours, then how Australia engages with the region in the so-called 'Asian Century' becomes all the more important.

Young people in the Asian century

The impact of cultural flows within the ethnoscape is perhaps no more striking than when we look at Australia's place within the Asian region. In 2014, the *Washington Post* published a striking info-graphic highlighting the fact that about 3.6 billion of the world's 7.1 billion people reside in South and East Asia. More people live within the circle of territories spanning approximately 6,000 km across from the eastern border of Pakistan to the Northern Mariana Islands, and encompassing Mongolia to the North and East Timor to the south, than outside of it (Dewey 2013). This circle encompasses an area about four times the size of Australia, and it has 157 times its population. Within this figure, by 2030 two-thirds of the world's middle class will reside in Asia, compared with just over one-quarter of the world's middle class in 2009 (Kharas 2010). In economic terms, over 70 per cent of Australia's total export earnings in 2013 came from Asian markets – its exports, and consequently broader engines of employment, are now linked to this growing middle class's demand for goods and services, such as education, food, healthcare and tourism. This has intensified Australia's links with the region (AusTrade 2014).

These highly diverse and dense populations live just north of Australia, and yet Australia's engagement with the region has been patchy. This is particularly evident in relation to Australia's policies in both higher education and schooling. With the decolonisation of the developing world and the growth of world trade during the middle of last century, Australian higher education providers saw opportunities for cultural and economic gain through exchanges. The Colombo Plan for Co-operative

Development in South and South-East Asia (1951), for example, boosted government sponsorship of overseas student study in Australia. In the 1960s, the mobility of students was mainly one way from the developing world to the West. In the following decades, international education policy also encouraged Australians studying abroad. Another way of promoting goodwill was through the provision of aid to assist social and economic development, but, by the 1980s, international education shifted its focus towards developing international markets in education as part of a policy shift from 'aid to trade' (e.g. through the recruitment of full-fee-paying overseas students). By the late 20th century, there was a swing back towards aid, which largely remained until the arrival of the Abbott government in 2013, which entered office in 2013 with some controversial policy proposals related to Australia's international engagement, including massive cuts to international aid and highly punitive approaches to the processing of refugees.

Alongside this, Prime Minister Abbott announced in June 2013 that his government would revitalise Australia's educational engagement with the region, in which 'within two years . . . there will be a new Colombo Plan that doesn't just bring the best and the brightest from our region to Australia but that takes Australia's best and brightest to our region' (Abbott 2013). He recognised that Australia's engagement with regional economies is vital to future prosperity. Australia conducts more trade with Asia than the rest of the world combined. Asia's real GDP is expected to more than double from US$26 trillion in 2011 to US$67 trillion by 2030. This amounts to more than the projected GDP of the Americas and Europe combined (Asialink 2012, p. 6). As White (2012) observes:

> Now the industrial revolution is finally reaching the rest of the world, and the effects are being felt quickly. The global balance of wealth and power is swinging back towards Asia . . . within a few years China will again be the world's richest country. A decade or two later India will . . . become the second richest, pushing the US into third place . . . Indonesia could well be in fourth. This is what the Asian Century is all about, and why it is so significant.'

He rightly notes, 'For the first time in our history, our Asian neighbours will not just be richer than us, but richer than our Western allies (White 2012).

In the same speech, Abbott (2013) added that 'we should better appreciate not just how much Australia can give our neighbours but how much they can give us, in cultural insights as well as in trade benefits.

But that's hard when there are, for instance, 17,000 Indonesians studying here but only some 200 Australians studying there. So a modern version of the Colombo Plan, operating as a two way rather than as a one way street, and funded from existing resources, should reinforce our own and overseas future leaders' understanding of all the things we have in common.'

Australian education policy both directly and inadvertently provides insight into Australia's relationship to the region. Australian schooling, for example, has struggled to meet one basic requirement for regional engagement: language. Deficiencies in preparing young people for the Asian Century are starkly evident in the data around language instruction in schools. A 2010 Asia Education Foundation report found that 18.6 per cent of the total Australian student cohort (K-12) were studying Japanese, Korean, Indonesian or Chinese – representing a decrease from 24 per cent in 2000 (Asia Education Foundation 2010, p. 4). In 2011, only 300 students who were not from a Chinese background were studying Chinese at Year 12. Teaching of Japanese declined 20 per cent since 2005, and Korean was taught in very few schools. Indonesian was losing 10,000 students a year. Kathe Kirby (2011) warns that if this pattern continues, there will be no students studying Indonesian at Year 12 by 2020.

As she suggests, the challenges of raising student participation in Asian languages are well documented throughout the 67 reports into languages education since the 1970s. Where 'most students in other developed countries exit schooling with two or more languages in order to leverage the opportunities of their interconnected world', Australian graduates are lacking the same language competencies (Kirby 2011). This reflects a wider deficit in the response of schools to internationalisation. Despite recognition of the importance of internationalisation in education during the 1990s, 'the process of integrating an international or intercultural dimension into the teaching, research, and service functions of the institution' (Knight 1994, p. 9) has been slow.

Wider policy responses to the challenges of engaging the Asian Century have been tepid (White 2012). The previous Labor Government, for example, promoted a largely 'business as usual' approach in its response to the *Australia in the Asian Century* White Paper (Australian Government 2012). As White concludes, 'It turns out that Gillard's Asian Century White Paper is not really about the Asian Century after all. Asia's ascent to wealth and power instead serves simply as a narrative backdrop to spin a reassuring story about a country with a bright future and a government that knows what it is doing. The White Paper presents an unremittingly optimistic view of Asia's future and Australia's place in it: Asia will keep growing, and Australia will keep growing too, and we won't need to change a thing' (White 2012).

A largely commercial view of Australia's relationship to the region has left young people underprepared for the challenges of globalisation. This deficit is also reflected in Australian business practices. In a survey of 380 businesses by the Australian Industry Group and Asialink, less than 50 per cent had any senior executives or board members with language ability or Asian experience (Asialink 2012; McGregor 2013).

Technology

Turning now to Appadurai's technoscape, young people are increasingly enmeshed in the fluid 'global configuration' of technology (1996, p. 34). When presenting this notion in the latter 1990s, Appadurai was rightly responding to the rapid speed of flows of culture and people enabled by mechanical and informational technology around the world, uninhibited by traditional boundaries such as the nation-state. Key actors, such as multinational enterprises, ranging from global banking institutions to Facebook, have played a major role in facilitating this technological movement.

In Australia, the Internet took some time to penetrate society. While a minority of Australians had access in 2001, by 2006, this was reversed, with 63 per cent of Australians online (ABS 2007a). By 2013, according to World Bank figures, the number of Internet users was estimated to be around 83 per 100 people (World Bank 2014). As of December 2013, just under nine in ten teenage Australians had a mobile phone; 69 per cent of these users had a smartphone, and 56 per cent used their mobile phone to go online, with nearly three-quarters going online more than once a day (ACMA 2014).

Related concepts here are Appadurai's mediascapes and ideoscapes, which are interrelated within a 'landscapes of images' (1996, p. 35). The term mediascape has two aspects. The first relates to 'the distribution of the electronic capabilities to produce and disseminate information' (p. 35), by which Appadurai is referring to 'traditional' institutions such as newspapers, magazines, television stations and film-production studios. In the Web 2.0 era, this could now be further extended to incorporate the explosive use of social media, and the blurring of the lines between production of media and consumption of media, opinion and news, celebrity and journalist, layperson and celebrity, and so on. The second aspect relates to 'the images of the world created by these media' (p. 35). Appadurai argues the most important aspect of mediascapes is that they generate 'large and complex repertoires of images, narratives, and ethnoscapes to viewers throughout the world' (p. 35). Mediascapes tend to account for reality through the use of images and the generation of a narrative, with its associated plots and characters, which enables the lives of others to be imagined. This imagining links to the desire to transform ones' life, for example, through material acquisition or geographical movement. The narrative power of ICT is infused throughout Australian education policy, and other education systems throughout the world. The promise of education as a basis for both physical and virtual mobility lies at the heart of educational policy. It is articulated in Australian policy, such as The Melbourne Declaration on Educational Goals for Young Australians (MCEETYA 2008). But as we shall see later on in this book, that promise is becoming increasingly tenuous for many young people. Images of mobility and global citizenship clash with precarity and the rootedness of structural forms of marginalisation.

Nevertheless, the rise of social media has heightened perceptions of global interconnectivity and a diminished sense of 'the tyranny of distance'. Facebook had 11.5 million Australian users in 2013, which amounted to more than half of the population, although this figure includes multiple accounts and inactive users, with the number of users steadily declining (news.com.au 2013) as young users move to other platforms and apps. An illustration of how the world has become interconnected comes from a study by the Università degli Studi di Milano and Facebook, which analysed connectivity of 721 million users worldwide. The 2011 study found just 4.74 degrees or 'hops' of separation between users (Backstrom 2011).

Young Australians now take as given that ICT will be accessible throughout daily life (Walsh et al. 2011). They are almost eight years old when they first use the Internet. Just over three-quarters of Australians aged 9–16 go online daily (Green et al. 2011). On average, young people aged 12–17 use the Internet 6.3 days a week at an average rate of 2.9 hours a day. Ninety-one per cent of school-aged young people describe it as a 'somewhat', 'very' or 'extremely' important aspect of their lives (ACMA 2009, pp. 7–8). While it is used for watching video clips (85 per cent), playing games (78 per cent), emailing (67 per cent) and social networking (63 per cent), the Internet was most widely used for schoolwork (86 per cent) (Green et al. 2011). A 2009 report indicates that 90 per cent of people aged 12–17 regularly used social networking services (ACMA 2009, p. 8). A survey of 753 high school students in Western Australia aged 12–16 found that 23 per cent of teenagers were online for four or more hours on a weekday (and not for school work). Over 85 per cent of students had a social networking site account, with 56 per cent using it six to seven days a week. Moreover, 66 per cent had 200 or more 'friends' on their social networking services (Dooley & Scott 2013).

With this growth in online engagement is a blurring of boundaries. The nominal division between 'real' and 'online' has become somewhat arbitrary, as the boundary has dissolved with the ubiquitous use of technology. Several years ago, I was at a forum on cyber-bullying in which a young speaker informed the room that an easy way to discourage a young person from engaging in discussions about the dangers of using ICT is to put the word 'cyber' before the noun under discussion (as in 'cyber-bullying' or 'cyberspace'). The evidence suggests that on- and offline worlds intersect and shape each other. For example, 24 per cent of 16- to 17-year-old Internet users have met someone face to face they first met online (ACMA 2013, p. 72).

Digital technology is also blurring the boundaries between public and private life, and reshaping how young people engage with the world. These shifts reflect wider changes in what constitutes public and private. ICT has blurred boundaries between work and home. (Just think of a time when you read working-related email out of working hours.)

Technology has also enabled the delivery of lower-cost education – particularly in areas such as vocational education through simulations and online access to skills development in areas such as programming. The permeating of technology is also flowing through business practices. One recent report suggests that '[n]ew technology is unleashing a storm of "disruptive innovation" which is forcing firms to rethink their operations from the ground up' (*The Economist* 2013b). On the flip side, it is also making jobs redundant across a range of sectors.

It is also important to note that ICT is not entirely ubiquitous, with structural barriers persisting in access and the capacity to use them effectively. Many educators experience barriers and access to adequate training. While some practitioners are using technology in confident and inventive ways, many others are using it in limited or tokenistic ways that underutilise its potential. Perhaps most importantly, broad assumptions and generalisations about young people's technological access and ease of use are highly problematic. There is a strong pattern of unequal access to ICT amongst learners, which risks exacerbating existing patterns of disadvantage (Walsh et al. 2011).

A key barrier is a lack of digital literacy in teachers and learners. Students expect ICT to play an integral role in their learning and yet levels of literacy are uneven amongst some educators (Walsh et al. 2011). By another Australian measure, the *National Assessment Program – Information and Communication Technology Literacy*, 62 per cent of Year 6 students and 65 per cent of Year 10 students 'met or exceeded the relevant Proficient Standard' (ACARA 2011). Samples of Year 6 and Year 10 students from across Australia are tested every three years 'on their ability to use ICT to appropriately access, manage, integrate and evaluate information, develop new understandings and communicate with others in order to participate effectively in society' (ACARA 2011). These results suggest that more work needs to be done to lift the proficiency in at least one in three students. There is a significant gap between young people's digital literacy and competency (and that of their teachers and trainers, which we will discuss further in Chapter Five). Based on extensive research with young people, boyd suggests that the problem goes deeper than technological literacy but to basic literacy in general (boyd 2014).

Nevertheless, technological literacy will be increasingly significant in the future workforce, with young people the inheritors and potentially major drivers of its future development. But a 2014 report found that 'while teenagers are active participants online . . . they are not the main drivers of growth and development of the digital economy. Compared to adult Australians teenagers – not-surprisingly – generally have lower incomes and fewer opportunities to fully benefit from online transactional activities, content and services. However, despite these limitations, the activities that teenagers do undertake online are preparing them to fully engage in the digital economy later in life' (ACMA 2014).

Technology will continue to play a major role in shaping the future labour force by replacing human labour through the automation of a wide variety of work and attendant reorientations of the labour market (*The Economist* 2014). With the end of the mining boom and the decline of manufacturing in Australia, it is widely accepted that the labour market will become increasingly oriented to service industries aligned to emergent 'new knowledge economies', such as tourism and education. (We shall return to these economies later in the book.)

Political change

Another related scape developed by Appadurai, the ideoscape, relates to 'ideologies of states and the counterideologies of movements explicitly oriented to capture state power, or a piece of it' (1996, p. 36), as well as the perception of the people influenced by them. Appadurai links this with Enlightenment ideas such as freedom, welfare, rights, sovereignty, representation and democracy. He argues that the Euro-American 'master narrative', which held together these ideas, is no longer as internally coherent, and, that instead, these terms have been reimagined by various nation-states as their political cultures have evolved. Ideoscapes are characterised by 'the differential diaspora' of keywords such as freedom and welfare. Appadurai suggests that the political narratives that govern communication between elites and followers in different parts of the world involve problems of both a semantic and pragmatic nature: semantic to the extent that words (and their lexical equivalents) require careful translation from context to context in their global movements, and pragmatic to the extent that the use of these words by political actors and their audiences may be subject to different sets of contextual conventions that mediate their translation into public politics. Such conventions are not only matters of the nature of political rhetoric: for example, what does the ageing Chinese leadership mean when it refers to the dangers of hooliganism? What does the South Korean leadership mean when it speaks of discipline as the key to industrial growth? (1996, p. 36)

In Western Liberal Democracies, these narratives have increasingly valorised neoliberal notions of choice and flexibility and an idea that economic growth is valuable for its own sake. They enframe policy agendas and rely heavily on economistic views of social wellbeing. But as we shall see below and in the following chapter, these words can mean very different things depending on the context. Welfare, choice and flexibility are problematic in the lives of many young people experiencing precarity. With these shifting and complex boundaries and narratives comes a need to understand better and develop the knowledge, tools and competencies in young people to navigate these worlds, which we shall also explore further in Chapter Four.

Financescapes

The international education policy agendas outlined above illustrate strong connections between cultural engagement and trade, reflecting tensions and intersections between the ethnoscape and financescape. The financescape encompasses the 'disposition of global capital', which is becoming far more complex as a consequence of almost instantaneous transfers in a web of interrelated financial markets (Appadurai 1996, p. 34). Popular economics writer Michael Lewis (2014) highlights the dizzying speed with which financial markets now operate: a trade order sent from Chicago to New York takes around one-tenth of the time it takes to blink. They have also intensified the fluidity of international markets and, with this fluidity, the possibility of rapid economic downturns such as the GFC.

Intensified and unstable flows of capital are linked to workforce precarity, as the flow-on effects of the GFC have shown. Amongst other things, the crisis in global finance brought about a displacement from, and mass migrations in search of, work internationally. The knock-on effects at the local level are complex and sometimes contradictory. The interplay of scapes has significant implications for young people in this regard. Appadurai writes that the 'global relationship among ethnoscapes, technoscapes, and financescapes is deeply disjunctive and profoundly unpredictable because each of these landscapes is subject to its own constraints and incentives (some political, some informational, and some technoenvironmental), at the same time as each acts as a constraint and a parameter for movements in others' (1996, p. 35). Policy–political approaches to foreign languages instruction and international education outlined above also have tensions and may arguably be seen to run counter to each other.

The disjunctive and unpredictable intersection of these flows is evident in certain tensions between the global flows of workers and national labour force policies (the ideoscape). For example, we have already seen that young people most vulnerable to marginalisation from earning or learning live in remote and regional areas (Robinson et al. 2011). Recent policy proposals have proposed that young people should move to areas of employment (Cox 2014), that is, away from rural areas. As we shall also see in the next chapter, such proposals could contradict existing policy attempting to increase regional employment, such as The National Stronger Regions Fund. Similarly, other policy proposals have suggested that young people could relocate to regional areas to undertake seasonal work such as fruit-picking. However, global flows of temporary migrants described above are crowding out opportunities for young Australians to work in rural areas. Political incentives (be they in the form of opportunities to get work or punitive measures such as Work for the Dole schemes) run counter to certain flows within the ethnoscape, reflecting the disjunctive nature of its relationship to other scapes and flows within them. We shall investigate this further in the next chapter.

Conclusion

Globalisation is shaping the experience of working life in different ways. As we saw in the introduction to this book, while advanced economies such as Australia are characterised by persistent unemployment, casualisation and growing discouragement of young people, developing countries feature low-quality, informal and subsistence work (ILO 2013). These disparities are consistent with Appadurai's suggestion: 'We cannot simplify matters by imagining that the global is to space what the modern is to time. For many societies, modernity is an elsewhere, just as the global is a temporal wave that must be encountered in their present'

(1996, p. 9). But waves of globalisation mean increasing intersections of less-advanced economies with advanced ones, namely in the form of cheap labour. Using fertility data from the CIA World Factbook, US economist David Merkel suggests that the world population will peak around 2030 at 8.5 billion (Seccombe 2013). If this is true, it suggests that a reshuffling of domestic populations seeking foreign labour may be inevitable, which in turn will further impact the future labour forces of domestic economies.

Technoscapes are complexly interwoven with ethnoscapes and financescapes. Appadurai suggests that technoscapes do not necessarily reflect traditional economic assumptions, such as economies of scale or market rationality but rather reflect more complex relationships, such as those involving flows of money and both highly skilled and unskilled labour. Factors such as the speed of finance mentioned and virtual and physical migrations of labour, such as WHMs, create complex global flows that have different logics and tensions but which also contribute to a broader economic fluidity and volatility. And yet structural forms of marginalisation also persist beneath, within and because of these flows.

Beyond the profound structural changes influenced by globalisation and demographic change, there is a need to equip young people as working life is shaped by the different scapes outlined above. Skills and competencies, such as digital literacy and cultural competency, are important for navigating these fluid and sometimes hostile terrains. In the Asian Century, cultural competencies assume greater significance, not only in navigating Australia's geopolitical and economic relationship to the region and world but also in navigating cultural diversity that pervades local life. Other dispositions are required for developing resilience to deal with changing labour force conditions, as well as broader challenges in negotiating daily life. The macro-drivers outlined in this chapter call for a reinvigorated discussion of the soft skills that are necessary for young people to engage in working life. We explore these in detail in Chapter Four.

A final point made here is that young people should not be treated as a homogeneous group. They are diverse in need, background, ethnicity and a range of other ways that are salient to considerations about how to prepare them for working life. But these macro-drivers also suggest that they have some things in common when viewed from wider economic, political, social and cultural contexts. These considerations are significant and provide the setting for the following discussion about adversity capital, the teaching profession and relevance of schools in Part Two of this book.

3
Neoliberal Policy and Precarity

Introduction

The discussion so far has explored some key data related to young people's transitions, highlighting the particular force that the GFC had on young people. In Chapter Two, it located some of these trends with broader, global changes that have impacted on how young people's study, work and life in general. This chapter returns to the ideoscape. Globalisation in many of the countries discussed has been coupled with neoliberalism. Neoliberalism has enframed policy responses to young people's transitions and has been particularly visible in recent federal government policy proposals in Australia.

The discussion starts by examining some of the more extreme consequences of global workforce insecurity and the resultant experiences of precarity by many young people. We then critically examine some of these recent policy proposals and aspirations by the Liberal–National Coalition government (2013–present) and highlight certain disconnections and disjunctures from both the material reality and perspectives of young people navigating insecure work. It critically analyses the extent to which these proposals align to the lived experiences of young people and expectations of other stakeholders, such as business. The evidence suggests that a misalignment is taking place. The following analysis will unpack and examine this in more detail.

Preparing for precarity

The global and Australian trends outlined throughout this book so far highlight an increasingly fluid workforce that is, for many young people, insecure and precarious. The wider context of employment is important.

Employment growth in Australia has failed to keep pace with population growth since the 1970s, which, as economist William Mitchell argues, 'is why the unemployment rate is now more than 340 per cent higher than it was in 1971' (Mitchell 2015). This trend continues. Between the start of 2013 and early 2015, employment overall grew by 2.1 per cent, in comparison to a 3.7 per cent growth in the population.

Beneath this data, it is important to understand what sociologist Andy Furlong (2007, p. 102) refers to as 'the grey area between employment and unemployment' in relation to the quality and nature of the working conditions of young people. In the context of Western Europe, precariousness is characterised by extremely low wages; the absence of employment protection; high employment insecurity; and low levels of employee control over hours, wages and conditions (Rodgers 1989, p. 3).

Many young people throughout the world experience precarity, a 'precarious existence' (Chomsky 2011). Writing in the European context, Kalleberg observes that precarity is linked to feelings by labourers of powerlessness and devaluation 'as they faced living and working without stability or a safety net' (2009, p. 15). Those experiencing precarity lack 'a sense of belonging to a self-sustaining community grounded in a profession or craft' with 'a "shadow of the future" hovering over their deliberations and dealings with others, who may be here today and gone tomorrow, in a series of passing relationships' (Standing 2012, p. 590). Berlant describes the erosion of 'the good life' during the latter 20th century, including ideas of 'upward mobility, job security, political and social equality, and lively durable intimacy. The set of dissolving assurances also includes meritocracy, the sense that liberal-capitalist society will reliably provide opportunities for individuals to carve out relations of reciprocity that seem fair and that foster life as a project of adding up to something' (2011, p. 3).

Precarity is not a new phenomenon. While the post-war years leading up to 1975 were characterised by relative stability and the availability of 'good jobs', it is argued that this period was in fact an exception. Precarious work has been around as long as work (Campbell 2013; Kalleberg 2009; Quinlan 2012). The period described in this chapter bares similarity to the late 19th century/early 20th century period of capitalism (Cuervo et al. 2013). More recently in Australia, key policy such as changes to industrial relations, which 'altered the conditions under which employees would undertake their work', 'has fostered and reinforced the precariousness of labour market generally' (White & Wyn 2008, p. 175).

What is significant about the period described in this book is a generational rift that runs through the current era of precarious work that disproportionately affects young people. This rift, as we shall see, takes many forms. In France, for example, a paradox has been observed in which a generation is emerging that is 'middle-class in terms of education, and underclass in terms of socio-economic position' (Chauvel 2010, p. 75). As we saw earlier in the book, Genda (2005) notes that in Japan the potential negative effects to the employment of middle-aged and older workers were somewhat shielded by cuts to young people's employment during the 1990s recession. In Australia, a more complex picture emerges, as we shall see below (Cuervo et al. 2013).

Many young people throughout the contemporary world are involuntarily becoming part of 'the precariat'. Standing (2011) uses the term 'precariat' to describe the emerging class of people, including young people, who are increasingly vulnerable to these recent and longer-term changes in the labour force. Many suffer 'from the programs of deunionization, flexibilization and deregulation that are part of the assault on labor throughout the world' (Chomsky 2011). Standing describes the precariat as 'a distinctive socio-economic group, so that by definition a person is in it or not in it. This is useful in terms of images and analyses, and it allows us to use what Max Weber called an "ideal type". In this spirit, the precariat could be described as a neologism that combines an adjective "precarious" and a related noun "proletariat"' (Standing 2011, p. 7).

There are debates over whether these groups of individuals experiencing precarity can be constituted as a class, per se (see Breman 2013; Skoczylas & Mrozowicki 2012). The basis of this grouping is questionable given the diversity of people experiencing precarity internationally. While it is premature to refer to this group as a 'class', Standing's powerful narrative serves to highlight the extent to which growing numbers of people experience precarity throughout the world. Of particular concern are those in work are living 'through a series of casual, short-term, or temporary jobs, have none of the forms of labor security that the working class and the salariat acquired in the welfare-state era, and have relatively low and insecure earnings' (Standing 2012, p. 590).

Not all experience the casualisation of the workforce in negative ways. Exact levels and reasons for undertaking 'non-permanent' work and casualisation in Australia are hotly contested. It is argued, for example, that '[c]asuals do not want to lose their flexibility or their casual loading', or that casual work is preferred 'as it allows [casual workers] to take part in the workforce and balance family responsibilities or study commitments' (Willox 2012). The evidence in relation to young people suggests something more nuanced and complicated.

A key feature of this debate is whether the fluidity of the workforce creates opportunities for greater flexibility or whether something more troubling and precarious is taking place. Returning to our two cohorts from the Life Patterns Project, there is evidence that young people value flexibility in employment more than previous generations, but not at the expense of job security. Although around 60 per cent of participants in both cohorts of the study noted that a job being 'secure' was very important when deciding whether to take a job in the future, individuals from Cohort Two who left school in 2006 were less concerned whether the job was full-time (approximately 42 per cent versus 55 per cent) and more interested in having access to flexible hours compared with individuals from Cohort One who left school in 1991 (approximately 23 per cent versus 18 per cent) (Cuervo et al. 2013).

Fluid work arrangements loom large amongst the young people in this study, with three-quarters working irregular hours, and a high proportion not in permanent employment. This is not an issue that disappears with age; around one-quarter of Cohort Two, aged in their mid-30s, were involved in working irregular hours (Cuervo et al. 2013). As Furlong and Kelly (2005, p. 209) observe, there is a distinction 'between flexibility and precarity' that needs to be better understood – particularly in relation to perceptions of choice. They suggest that the difference between them is marked by 'a classic social division, in which the nature and character of choice is intensely problematic, and is structured by patterns of social disadvantage...choices, in terms of economic activity and labour market participation, are profoundly influenced by the complex relationships between social class, gender, ethnicity, and geography' (Furlong & Kelly 2005, p. 209). The examples of Indigenous young Australians and those more broadly from low SES backgrounds and living in regional and remote areas described in the previous chapter highlight these patterns and influences.

There is no doubt that some young people prefer casual/part-time work because of the benefits that flexibility offers. The demands for greater flexibility in working life are not necessarily a problem for some young people, but rather it is the impact that this fluidity has on other aspects of life that is significant. In his research on the Life Patterns Project, Dan Woodman (2012b) describes how some young people employed in retail and hospitality (huge employers of young people) have to work a variety of hours, including late or irregular shifts, and experience challenges in developing and maintaining stable and intimate relationships.

Many can maintain a social life through media such as Facebook to connect with friends at irregular hours or at short notice. But working at unplanned or short notice makes it difficult to plan for things as elementary as a regular meal with family or the occasional birthday. For others, obtaining a mortgage is difficult because they do not have a stable income to qualify for a bank loan. As the markers of maturity, transition and security are reconfigured and pushed later in life, these challenges have potentially profound implications for work, family and social wellbeing as the rhythm of life and family changes. An opinion piece published in the *Guardian* in 2014 gives one frustrated voice to the concerns of young people. Reflecting on the lack of home affordability, unemployment and broader casualisation of the workforce, the author, Eleanor Robertson, writes: 'This data makes my fertile friends look like the demographic equivalent of a two-headed unicorn. For most people our age, participation in the job-marriage-mortgage-kids pathway is a virtual impossibility. We live with our parents or in sharehouses. Our jobs are often crappy, if we're lucky enough to have one rather than being on the dole or having our work exploited for nothing by dodgy internship merchants' (Robertson 2014).

While part-time work (and internships for that matter) provides flexibility, valuable life experiences and material gains, it may not be a stepping stone to full-time work. There is a widely perceived but erroneous long-term benefit of part-time work. The 2009 House of Representatives *Inquiry into Combining School and Work: Supporting Successful Youth Transitions* pointed out that work experience is valuable and viewed as a step to permanent (HOR 2009). But notably, teenagers in part-time jobs are statistically only slightly more likely to move into full-time employment than those who are unemployed (Robinson et al. 2011). A major concern is for those who are discouraged by the inability to get sufficient work and give up looking. Combine this with significant levels of long-term youth unemployment (notably that following the GFC – between 2008 and 2011 the percentage of young Australians without a job for a year or more nearly doubled [Robinson et al. 2011, p. 11]) and this concern is intensified considerably.

Getting full-time work is not just about job security. Many casual workers (of all ages) must forgo other benefits of secure full-time work. In industries such as rental, hiring and real estate services, 97.2 per cent of all full-time workers in Australia choose their holidays compared to only 69.7 per cent for casuals. Only 18.9 per cent of casuals have access to flexible time off, in contrast to nearly 56 per cent of full-timers (Stacey 2013).

As we have seen, underemployment is significant – even for those with qualifications. A question arises as to whether secure work awaits those seeking full-time employment at the end of young people's post-school study and training. Since the latter half of the 1980s, the age at which young people enter full-time work has increased. In the overarching context of labour market change, while things do get better past the age of 25, it would appear that for many, the option to pursue full-time work is out of reach. Increasing levels of education amongst young people overall mean that those with poor education outcomes are likely to struggle in the labour market. Disengagement and ongoing social exclusion is, for these people, not a stage in life but a *way* of life.

These challenges are not confined to Australia. During a discussion on youth employment arising from the 2012 UN World Youth Report, young participants raised a number of concerns in relation to job insecurity. These included 'the prevalence of short-term contracts; low wages, amidst rising costs of living; difficulties in obtaining adequate practical work experience, with some youth calling for such requirements in educational institutions; few opportunities for workplace advancement; debts, including student loans; and family well-being' (UN 2012b). Another area of concern raised during the discussion related to a widespread feeling that education was not adequately preparing young people for the contemporary labour force, noting a disconnect between the level of academic qualifications and jobs.

The promise of getting desirable work at the end of a university degree decreasingly holds for some graduates. There are a number of reasons for this. On the supply side, in 2014, around 1.2 million Australians were undertaking full-time study. This number is almost double full-time enrolments in 1996 (Universities Australia 2014). The resultant competition, Ortlieb (2015) suggests, 'seems to be manifesting itself in credential inflation – the value of academic credentials decreases over time, along with the expected advantage given a degree holder in the job market . . . Jobs that high school graduates used to fill are being reserved for university graduates.' Employers, as we have seen, are demanding higher qualifications (Bradley et al. 2008; Foster et al. 2007; Modestino 2010). Today, Ortlieb (2015) writes, 'Postgraduate degrees are what bachelor degrees represented a generation ago – an upgrade from the status quo.'

Credential inflation has been identified as a key issue in Europe (European Commission 2010). There is an increasing requirement for employees to have high-level qualifications, with skills shortages identified across the EU. In 2010, less than one-third of EU citizens (31 per cent) had a higher education degree, compared with over 40 per cent in the

US and over 50 per cent in Japan (European Commission 2010). In Australia, around 44 per cent of 25- to 34-year-olds had attained a tertiary education in 2010 (OECD 2012a). But the growth in jobs – and more specifically jobs typically associated with university qualifications – is not keeping pace. As a result, credential inflation appears to be taking place in other areas of the workforce. In the US, for example, the number of employees in sales, customer service and management workers with an undergraduate education increased by 10 per cent over five years (Ferguson et al. 2013; Ortlieb 2015). The study from which this figure came from also found that 58 per cent of employers said they can get degree holders 'because of the tight labor market', while 55 per cent said 'skills for my positions have evolved, requiring higher-educated labor'. One effect of this is a widening gap in wage levels between those with and without degrees. In the US, the wage gap between college and high school graduates has grown from 35 per cent to 50 per cent (Allen 2014). The glut of graduates relative to slow labour market growth is intensifying global competition.

As mentioned above, a characteristic of this competitive labour market is a delay in university graduates getting a full-time job. It has been reported that in some Australian courses, as many as two-thirds of graduates did not secure full-time employment within four months of completing their study (Dodd & Tadros 2014). This trend has been increasing in severity in recent decades and is impacting on most fields of study. A decrease of 16 per cent in the employment of university degree holders has taken place over the past 14 years (Employment Data from Graduate Careers Australia surveys cited by Ortlieb 2015). In some areas, this leads graduates to pursue postgraduate qualifications (Dodd & Tadros 2014). A 2013 survey of graduates in Australia found that 61.2 per cent of all postgraduates perceived that their advanced degree was either 'required' or at least 'important' (Guthrie & Bryant 2014). And so the upward inflationary pressure to gain higher qualifications continues.

Policy responses to precarity

By the time that the European Commission (2010) outlined its post-GFC *Europe 2020* strategy in 2010,[1] the rate of youth unemployment in the EU had reached nearly 21 per cent. Broadly speaking, efforts often focused on matching labour supply to demand through supply-side initiatives. These included up-skilling young workers through increasing their participation in vocational education, training and higher education by widening mobility across member states. Increasing participation in secondary education was another notable plank of the plan. Goals, for example, included increasing the percentage of people who completed tertiary or equivalent education to 40 per cent by 2020, while reducing early school leavers to 10 per cent by 2020. Data from 2009 showed that 14.4 per cent of people in the EU aged 18–24 had attained less than an upper secondary education and were not in further education and training (Eurostat, cited in European Commission 2010, p. 2).

Demand-side proposals included possible subsidies for employers taking on young people and a 'Youth Guarantee' for school leavers (in which member states could guarantee young people a job within four months of leaving school). However, funding and implementing demand-side initiatives were deeply constrained by the downward turn in economies across the EU. Other proposals included legislative initiatives, such as implementing single employment contracts and addressing the segmented nature of labour markets. A goal of the strategy was to have 75 per cent of individuals aged 20–64 in employment by 2020 (European Commission 2010) – a goal that today seems difficult to achieve given the persistent and extreme levels of unemployment in parts of Europe.

Consistent with these goals, Australia continues to work towards lifting participation in education to boost employment, with an emphasis on higher education participation. While incentive-based approaches have been proposed (Walsh 2013), in recent years, the discourse of policy proposals related to young people has adopted a complex double taxonomy of deregulation (e.g. higher education and labour markets) and control (e.g. how young people spend their welfare payments). Upon being elected into government in 2013, the Liberal–National Party Coalition proposed a suite of methods and ethos that drew inspiration from government approaches in the UK and the US. From the US, measures were proposed to deregulate higher education and reintroduce Work for the Dole. A wider ideological narrative was repurposed from the severe austerity measures in the UK alongside a broader shift in social and political responsibility from the state to individuals. These approaches shed light on the attitudes of recent federal governments to young people and their place in contemporary worlds of work. Policy proposals made by the recent Liberal–National Party Coalition, for example, are indicative of an emergent strand of neoliberalism that have adopted a particularly punitive and infantilised view of young people who are not in school or work. Australia is a unique case study in that its recent government has shown an active interest in austerity measures despite the fact that Australia is one of the wealthiest countries in the world.

These conservative, neoliberal responses elicited disapproval amongst the public and news media. Many unpopular ideas never reached legislation; however, they signal a willingness of elected representatives to radically reimagine transitions policy and reflect a particularly virulent (though not necessarily effective) manifestation of neoliberalism in Australian policy.

A brief overview of neoliberalism

In his brief history of neoliberalism, David Harvey defines it 'in the first instance a theory of political economic practices that proposes that human well-being can best be advanced by liberating individual entrepreneurial freedoms and skills within an institutional framework characterized by strong private property rights, free markets, and free trade. The role of the state is to create and preserve an institutional framework appropriate to such practices' (Harvey 2005, p. 2). Harvey continues: 'It holds that the social good will be maximized by maximizing the reach and frequency of market transactions, and it seeks to bring all human action into the domain of the market' (2005, p. 3).

Emerging most visibly in the policy of governments in the UK and the US at the end of the 1970s and 1980s during the Thatcher and Reagan governments, neoliberalism is characterised by privatisation, market deregulation, a focus on individualised responses to social and economic challenges, which has as its corollary a 'withdrawal of the state from many areas of social provision' (Harvey 2005, p. 3). Its roots are typically traced back to the works of Friedrich von Hayek, Milton Friedman and the Chicago school of economics. But as Treanor (2005) suggests, 'Neoliberalism is not just economics: it is a social and moral philosophy.' Neoliberalism places a high value on market exchange 'in which the existence and operation of a market are valued in themselves, separately from any previous relationship with the production of goods and services, and without any attempt to justify them in terms of their effect on the production of goods and services; and where the operation of a market or market-like structure is seen as an ethic in itself, capable of acting as a guide for all human action, and substituting for all previously existing ethical beliefs' (Treanor 2005). Processes of neoliberalisation have profoundly impacted on 'divisions of labour, social relations, welfare provisions, technological mixes, ways of life and thought, reproductive activities, attachments to the land and habits of the heart' (Harvey 2005, p. 3). They are also intimately tied to processes of globalisation (Quiggin 1999).

The manifestation of neoliberalism within different national and cultural contexts varies considerably. While maintaining the basic tenets described above, neoliberalism in Australia has distinctive localised characteristics. It has shaped the policies of both Labor and Liberal governments since the 1980s. The following discussion will focus on the particular approach of the recent Liberal–National Coalition (2013–present), although it must be noted that the critique of neoliberalism that is woven throughout the remainder of this book does not exclusively apply to the policy proposals of the Coalition government; its seeds were planted long before this government came into office.

Neoliberal responses to young Australians in and out of work

Just prior to the 2013 Australian Federal election, the soon to be elected Liberal–National Party Coalition presented a 'contract to the Australian people' (Abbott 2010). This leaflet placed a high emphasis on building a stronger and more diversified economy, as well as growth in income. But while the 250,000 or so young people who leave school each year account for a significant proportion of the workforce and will play a major role in Australia's future economic development, young people were strangely absent from the Coalition's election campaign, except by loose association. The exceptions to this were the proposed Job Commitment Bonus offering payments to long-term unemployed young people to get and keep secure work; an assurance that Commonwealth schools funding committed by the previous Labor government for the 2014 school year would flow to all states and territories; and as outlined in the previous chapter, a redevelopment of the Colombo Plan, which seeks to boost the transnational engagement of university students across the region and beyond. Once elected, the Liberal–National Party Coalition promised to generate one million new jobs over the following five years (1.7 per cent a year) and two million new jobs over the next decade (1.6 per cent increase per year) (Abbott 2012). The methods and ethos chosen by this government proved to be controversial, and they appear to draw inspiration from recent experiences and approaches in the UK and the US.

In 2010, the UK's newly elected Coalition government sought to slash the budget deficit as a national priority. In a twist on the Thatcher years, the government sought to move from 'no society' to 'the big society', in which policy sought to favour, as the conservative government implied, 'strivers' not 'skivers' and 'scroungers' (Grice 2013). The Australian government followed a similar pathway. Announcing its first budget in 2014,

Australia's conservative Coalition government immediately attempted to slash the budget deficit as a perceived matter of emergency. The treasurer declared that the age of entitlement was over and that the age of opportunity had begun. This policy discourse reflected a view by the government that 'we need to be lifters, not leaners' (The Australian 2014).

The Job Commitment Bonus proposed by the Coalition prior to the election offered payments to long-term unemployed young people to get and keep secure work. The scheme, which was implemented in July 2014, provides a AU$2,500 bonus to those aged 18–30 who have been unemployed for 12 months or more if they find a job and stay off welfare for a continuous period of a year. An additional AU$4,000 is paid should they stay in work and stay off welfare for a 24-month period (Department of Employment 2014a). When looking at broader labour market trends, relying on incentive-based approaches like these has some limitations. One challenge, for example, is whether the beneficiaries of this scheme can stay employed. Another concern is for those who are discouraged by their inability to get sufficient work and give up looking. Providing an incentive such as Job Commitment Bonus might go some way towards addressing this, but if the work is not there then its impact will be limited. These kinds of incentive-based proposals were quickly overshadowed by a more punitive approach.

The Coalition then announced a series of responses and proposals that sought to shift the burden of debt from the state to young people. It adopted a language of austerity as a basis for public policy. Throughout their campaign, they had evoked a perceived national economic crisis, characterised by what they argued to be excessive spending of the previous Labor government resulting in a budget deficit 'black hole'. Building on the foundational idea that work builds 'a sense of self', the Coalition government announced a raft of neoliberal proposals to restrict the social safety net, and in so doing, make individuals more responsible for managing their own risk by seeking work. Speaking to community organisations, Treasurer Hockey asserted: 'If we don't start living within our means the people who are the most vulnerable in the community will suffer the most' (Browne 2014).

Amongst the 'learn or earn' rules announced in the 2014 budget was a proposal to reduce welfare payments to the unemployed. Unemployed people under the age of 25 would no longer qualify for the Newstart Allowance of AU$510 a fortnight, previously available to young people once they turned 22. Instead, these people under 25 would have to apply for a lower Youth Allowance, worth AU$414 a fortnight at the full rate (Karvelas 2014a). Furthermore, most of those in search of work under the age of 30 would be forced to wait six months before receiving unemployment benefits, depending on their work history (McLintock 2014). The government attempted to extend markers of transition from 'youth' to 'adulthood' to the age of 30, with potentially serious consequences, which will be explored below.

It was also initially suggested that unemployed young people would be required to submit 40 job applications per month to qualify for benefits, while participating in a Work for the Dole scheme.[2] This approach also echoes austerity measures in Britain, which have targeted the long-term unemployed in similarly punitive ways. Regulations introduced in Australia in 2014 made it a requirement for those on benefits to attend a job centre daily (rather than fortnightly), undergo training, or commit to six months of 'voluntary' unpaid work. Those failing to comply would have the allowance docked for four weeks (The Independent 2014).

Other aspects of the social safety net were withdrawn. For example, funding was removed from organisations that typically supported young people seeking work and further training, such as Youth Connections and the Local Learning and Employment Networks (in Victoria). These organisations also provided other forms of transitions support, such as career counselling. Combined with controversial proposals to extend fee payments for higher education and the replacement of Tools For Your Trade (financial assistance to apprentices) with the Trade Support Loans Programme, these measures reflected a governmental strategy for managing risk by shifting responsibility onto young people (and presumably their families) as a means of addressing the budget deficit.

Amongst the many implications of these proposals in Australia, the location of young people at risk is particularly salient to the neoliberal approach adopted by recent governments. As noted earlier in this book, young people most vulnerable to risk of marginalisation from earning or learning live in regional and remote areas (Robinson et al. 2011). Geographic location, as we have found, is an important predictor of risk to marginalisation from opportunities to undertake work or further study and training. Policy measures have attempted to compel young people to move to where the work is through the kinds of punitive measures outlined above (Cox 2014).

Recent policy in this regard has also appeared to be contradictory. In some rural areas, such as the Murray–Darling Basin, from which the exodus of young people in search of work is higher than elsewhere in Australia (ABC PM 2013), measures to relocate young workers could have a profound impact. These proposals suggested that young people would be forced to leave family and support networks to search for scarce jobs in unfamiliar places on a minimum wage or with no social benefits. It ran counter to the existing National Stronger Regions Fund, which seeks to increase regional employment.

A deeper set of techniques for managing risk is at play here, as policy narratives have adopted a double taxonomy of responsibilisation and control in relation to the management of risk. The backdrop of this taxonomy is market competition. Stephen Ball (2004, 2010) has shown how the global marketisation of schooling has introduced logics of competition to public education through the introduction of league tables and the intensified measurement of student performance through standardised tests. These also serve as instruments of control, 'alongside the shift of responsibility to teachers, young people, parents and communities to work on an ever increasing list of social problems' (Bottrell 2013). As Peter Kelly (2001) has pointed out, the individualisation and responsibilisation of young people is now a standard feature of managing risk. This policy discourse constructs young people as responsible for aspects of their lives that are shaped by national and global forces beyond their control or influence.

On the one hand, this responsibilisation takes the form of compelling 'leaners' to become 'lifters'. On the other, the conditions attached are a form of governmentality that seeks to regulate some forms of transition as a basis of risk management. For example, then Minister for Social Services expressed interest in supporting the incorporation of 'income management' within a suite of support services available to job seekers. This 'income management' would determine how young people spent their welfare payments, presumably to prevent them from frittering these payments on 'non-necessities', such as alcohol (news.com. au 2014). The view of young people as 'suspect' that is clearly evident here contains another contradiction: while espousing the importance of personal responsibility and choice, it seeks to enforce control over the life choices that young individuals can make.

Two further implications of these kinds of policy proposals arise. Firstly, by compelling people under the age of 30 to wait six months before they can access Newstart or Youth Allowance, it consigns young people to an extended period of transition. Taking into account the flow-on effects to key life decisions such as buying a house or starting a family, the link between youth and futurity effectively relegates young people to an extended state of transition.

Secondly, by transferring responsibility for risk to young people, these proposed policy measures have their own risk of exacerbating a 'failure of the self'. Evidence from previous Work for the Dole schemes in Australia and the US, for example, suggests that compelling people to work may reduce their job-searching activities because they feel fully occupied, as well as stigmatise them in the eyes of some employers (Borland & Tseng 2003). As Mitchell (2015) has argued, Work for the Dole 'forces people to work at below legal hourly pay rates [as] just a compliance measure designed to extract menial effort in return for miserly income support. It does not provide a pathway to permanent work or develop productive skills.' This risk of failure is heightened for those living in regional and remote areas of Australia, where jobs are often already scarce. The stigmatisation of those marginalised from work as 'leaners' is not new. In the past, leaners have gone by different pejorative names, such as 'dole-bludgers', 'cruisers' and 'job snobs' (Mitchell 2015). The difference today is that in pursuit of a budget surplus, contemporary governments have shown a reluctance to invest in the creation of large-scale programmes stimulating job creation, and appear to have dropped any meaningful aspiration to promote full employment (Mitchell 2015).

This responsibilisation of individuals implies that parents would also have to carry a greater burden. Two in three 12- to 19-year-olds live at home with two parents with a further 20 per cent living with one parent (Muir et al. 2009, p. 32). This suggests that the significant proportion of teens living away from home could face additional challenges. The data also suggest that young people are residing for longer periods of time with their parents (Muir et al. 2009). The fluid and insecure nature of the workforce may begin to explain why they do.

Where previous policy sought to mitigate risk by building pathways to work, training and study and other support services for young people, this neoliberal policy generically treats individuals as capable of lifting themselves out of conditions leading to their marginalisation. Risk is reformulated as a motivator through the punitive policy measures outlined above. Social structures and government-funded safety nets have been hollowed out and replaced by one in which the young person is largely responsible for his or her mobility.

Many of the labour market challenges faced by young people are not unlike those experienced by other demographic groups – particularly those experiencing marginalisation in the latter stages of life. What makes the experiences of young people more compelling is their link to risk, failure and the future. Elsewhere, Rosalyn Black and I have discussed this relationship in detail (Black & Walsh 2015), and I would like to briefly revisit that discussion here. Paralleling the transition from school to work is the widely perceived transition to adulthood. This transition is seen to be a process of 'becoming' and one that is a major step along the life course. It is about 'becoming an adult, becoming a citizen, becoming independent, becoming autonomous, becoming mature and becoming responsible' (Kelly 2011b, p. 48), particularly when viewed through the eyes of policy makers. Writing in response to the harsh measures proposed in the 2014 Australian Federal budget (more about this below), Wyn and Cuervo (2014) strikingly warn: 'The harms that are done [at this stage of life] cannot be retracted. Young lives cannot be relived.' The step to adulthood cannot be undone or relived, which gives this period of transition a particular salience. Moreover, it has a wider significance because young people are so strongly associated with the future. This association of young people with the future is 'axiomatic', evocative and powerful (Foster & Spencer 2011, p. 128). It can be imbued with hope as well as concern, and again, policy reflects both of these, but with a punitive tone.

With regard to hope, it is not uncommon to see this ideal expressed in policy (e.g. see MCEETYA 2008, p. 9). This in and of itself is not a bad thing; however, it becomes problematic when located within broader discourses of young people within the neoliberal policy of recent governments in the US, UK and Australia. In Australia, the last 25 years has been a time in which this ideal has underpinned a belief that young people should be able to – as individuals – reflexively navigate the kinds of labour market challenges highlighted earlier in this book. This belief forms the bedrock of recent government agendas to dismantle the welfare state and shift responsibility to individuals so that they themselves can respond to the changing nature of the workforce. Again, taking individual responsibility for one's life is not inherently negative; however, it becomes problematic when we look at the deeper structural problems highlighted in Chapters One and Two, in which individuals from lower socio-economic backgrounds, or living in regional and remote areas, or who come from Indigenous backgrounds face additional challenges when seeking to gain work. Others may be a victim of extraordinary, unforeseen circumstances (such as illness).

In light of the trends outlined in the previous two chapters, the view of young people as an object of concern predominates much of the thinking about young people and their transition to working life, and it is generalised beyond these 'at-risk' groups to young people in general. They are characterised as being at risk of marginalisation and the associated behaviours and negative impacts on wellbeing that are associated with disengagement from working life. Policy is driven by a risk-factor analysis that is now so central to public policymaking in general (France et al. 2010). This type of analysis seeks to understand the current conditions and behaviours of individuals and groups to predict, prevent and/or minimise future problems. Young people are a particular 'site for anxiety' (Woodman & Wyn 2011, p. 7) because of what they might become as adults who are 'productive' or 'unproductive' members of society and the economy. As suggested above, in the neoliberal context that dominates public policy, young people are both seen to be 'at risk' (Kelly 2000), while simultaneously expected to be responsible for minimising or avoiding risk. Responsibility, it has been noted, 'is attached to risk' (Lupton 2006, p. 12). In 'the globalised, risky labour markets of the liberal democracies' (Kelly 2011a, p. 7), young people are 'at risk' of failing to reach conventional markers of adulthood, such as securing full-time employment or buying a house (Wyn 2009). Where the neoliberal ideal promotes the idea that individuals are responsible for their own life success, employment is a key marker of this success (Fejes 2010). As Wyn and Cuervo (2014) observe, '[M]embers of Generation Y have largely accepted that it is up to the individual young person (and their family) to invest in education and learn how to navigate increasingly insecure labour markets.' To not achieve this success is equated with a 'failure of the self' (Bansel 2007, p. 286). It is no coincidence then that government policy frequently targets young people who experience workforce insecurity and unemployment, as young people are seen to be at risk of this failure. But as Judith Bessant (2009) has pointed out, '[T]oo many times in the past three decades, governments are treating the unemployed, in this case young people, as the problem – rather than addressing the real need, which is for more jobs.' She argues that while governments have evaded addressing the boarder structural problems of unemployment described in Chapter One, they have simultaneously inflamed public anxiety about 'unemployed youth'.

A view from business: employer perceptions of young people

This anxiety also arises from a perception that many young people are not adequately prepared for working life. Concern over the readiness and ability of young people to work is shared by parts of the business community. Surveys of business related to young people's employability and the perceptions of employers of their readiness for the 21st century workforce suggest a mismatch of skills and training to available work and a dissatisfaction by some employers with their younger employees (Stanwick et al. 2013). This perceived mismatch between skills and jobs is by no means confined to Australia (*The Economist* 2013a). In a review of America, Brazil, Britain, Germany, India, Mexico, Morocco, Saudi Arabia and Turkey, McKinsey found that only 43 per cent of the employers indicated that they could find employees with sufficient levels of skill at the entry level (Mourshed et al. 2012; *The Economist* 2013b). A survey of 542 employers of various sizes and from various sectors in the UK found that 71 per cent believed that schools and colleges could be doing more to develop employability skills (CBI 2012, p. 6).

Concerns by employers over a lack of foundation skills, such as literacy and numeracy, mirror concerns expressed by the Australian elite 'Group of Eight' universities that many new students entering higher education are underprepared for working life. For example, basic-level maths is now the most commonly completed maths course at Year 12, while the study of intermediate maths has declined (Go8 2012).

In addition to a more competitive job market, many young people face the challenge of overcoming employer preconceptions of youth. Employers have expressed concern in relation to the preparedness and attitudes of their young staff. Research by the Chamber of Commerce and Industry Queensland (2011), for example, identified dissatisfaction by some employers with young people's business and customer awareness, self-management skills and problem solving abilities, as well as their literacy and numeracy skills. Other research by Mission Australia found that employers rated poor reliability, immaturity and a lack of long-term commitment as their top reasons for negative experiences with young workers (Mission Australia 2013). Similarly, a 2012 survey of 300 bosses found that they had difficulty retaining young people. It also found that young people had high expectations for career advancement and made particular demands around work-life balance (King 2012).

Why might this be the case? One possible explanation relates to Australia's extraordinary economic performance. A benefit of higher levels of education and economic prosperity for some Australians has led to the formation of a 'post-materialist view', whereby aspirations seek for both interesting and well-paid work that does not become the centre of life at the expense of other lifestyle choices. Other priorities and values take place over material concerns. Parents seek a better life for their children, so when young people ask more of life than being a 'mortgage slave' or tied to one career, should we be surprised? This is arguably one of the benefits of prosperity.

Another explanation might be that as stable, secure work becomes more difficult to come by in a casualised labour force, young people are reciprocating by rejecting conventional loyalty to employers. For example, a journalist from the *Australian Financial Review* argues that this reflects the 'adaptive behaviours' of young people rather than changes to the labour market: '[o]ver the last few decades, young workers have started to "keep their options open" not from choice but out of necessity – no one will offer them a real job' aside from short-term positions, internships, contract and back fill positions without the associated benefits. 'So if young people are the lion's share of casuals, and their job conditions carve them out as a virtual underclass, what realistically do you expect them to do?' (Stacey 2013). The possibility of a lifelong stable career may be neither desirable nor possible.

These policies and business arguments for a mismatch of skills and jobs are to some extent misleading and misguided. They echo the limitations of neoliberal responses seeking to affect transitions policy in Europe, where Stein, Stauber and Walther have argued that 'many policies that are intended to "lead" towards gainful employment, adult status and social integration, are in fact "misleading" in terms of reducing social integration to labour market integration, thus neglecting young adults' subjective perspectives and leading to a "waste" of motivation; not considering the change of labour societies and reducing the "mismatch" between supply and demand to an individualised "pedagogisation" of labour market problems' (2003, p. 4). There is also a question of whether employers are doing enough to invest in the development of their staff. The evidence suggests that some employers are not investing enough in training and retaining employees. In the context of the Science, Technology, Engineering and Mathematics workforce, Deborah Corrigan argues that it is, for example, 'cheaper to employ a new graduate than [to] educate a current worker' (Corrigan, cited in Benderly 2015). We shall return to this later in this book.

But beneath these issues is a genuine concern as to whether schooling and further study are aligned with the fluid and changing demands of working life. The problems experienced by businesses outlined above are not entirely baseless.

The preparedness of young people to participate in a changing workforce

While post-school qualifications are not a guarantee of gaining satisfying work, qualifications still matter. Those who complete school fare better across a range of indicators, from economic to broader measures of wellbeing. But levels of qualification and skill can have mixed effects on employment outcomes. For example, depending on the type of qualification, it is more difficult to get a good job at a particular level of education (Stanwick et al. 2013). In addition, the evidence suggests that those who were over-skilled in the past are more likely to be over-skilled in the future (Mavromaras et al. 2012; Stanwick et al. 2013). While over-skilling is lowest among university graduates, it has a greater impact on their wages. The policy focus in recent years on getting more young people through university (e.g. through the uncapping of university places) is admirable in its intent but becomes problematic if desirable jobs and favourable incomes do not lie at the end of study.

Another challenge relates to accessing meaningful hands-on work experience. Many young people have the qualifications, but lack experience for certain jobs on offer. Business can play a greater role here. Innovative, cross-sectoral responses are needed, which are explored in Chapter Six.

With other pathways to employment being vulnerable to fluctuations in the economy, such as apprenticeships, the role of vocational training as a pathway to work has become uncertain or inadequate in preparing young people for labour market changes. Apprentices were amongst the first to feel the full force of the GFC as they were the first to be let go by employers. The steady rise in the proportion of young people doing apprenticeships and traineeships from the 1990s to 2008 reversed in 2009 back to the 2003 level (Robinson et al. 2010). The effect of exchange rate fluctuations on local industry, combined with a tectonic shift in the manufacturing sector (such as the collapse of the car industry) and a potential decline in mining activity reflect a wider shift in the nature of the Australian economy. A question arises as to whether young people who work in these sectors are adequately prepared in terms of skills and knowledge for the changes to come. This question is explored in the next chapter.

Conclusion

This chapter has explored neoliberal responses to youth transitions. It has highlighted a prevalent and occasionally punitive sensibility in recent proposals to get young people into employment. While neoliberal responses are pervasive in the UK and Australia, they should not be treated as totalising in their effect. A case will be made in the next chapter that there are spaces and opportunities to develop responses to neoliberalism and to the contemporary challenges of working life in general.

The disjunctures and disconnections outlined in this chapter feature elsewhere in this landscape and will be explored in coming chapters. Other ways of working are proposed to address some of these or at the very least, to think about them in potentially new ways.

Schooling remains a critical site in which these responses can be developed. But we need to push the boundaries of how schools and the teachers and school leaders within them operate. This argument begins with an understanding of schools as located within a wider ecology of actors, policies and forces. Part Two of this book starts by looking at how resilience can be harnessed and developed in young people to respond to change. There are debates about whether contemporary notions of resilience are reflective of – and captive to – dominant neoliberal ways of thinking. A case is made for a more sophisticated and nuanced view of resilience that incorporates a social ecological view beyond the individualised, responsibilised approaches favoured by neoliberal policy. This case is the basis upon which adversity capital can be developed in young people to respond to and navigate workforce change and precarity. A key component of this is the development of skills, literacies and competencies that enable young people to navigate uncertainty and sometimes hardship, which is discussed in Chapter Four.

The discussion then looks to other key actors and organisations within the ecosystem of schooling. These include teachers and school leaders, careers advisers and actors beyond the school gates seeking to improve education outcomes, such as business, the third sector and parents. It also highlights tensions that emerge between these actors and forces, as well as between schools and policies seeking to shape them.

Part II

Young People, Teaching and Schooling in Transition

4
Adversity Capital

Introduction

In this chapter, we turn to the question of how prepared young people are to participate in a changing workforce. It has been suggested that there is a need to examine whether the relevant skills are being developed for contemporary working life beyond 'the basics' of numeracy and literacy (Kahn et al. 2012). Changing conditions of learning, work and life compel a need to develop better ways of harnessing broader skills, capabilities and literacies in young people as important resources for resilience. The growth of precarious and rapidly changing conditions of work has made it imperative that young people, to quote Johanna Wyn (2009, p. iii), 'become skilled at navigating a sea of uncertainty'. A combination of a changing youth labour market, long-term unemployment and persistent marginalisation experienced by certain groups reinforces the need to address the issue of how well young people are prepared for increasingly fluid worlds of work.

These skills involve 'doing' as well as 'knowing'. As the OECD's Andreas Schleicher suggests, the 'world economy doesn't pay you for what you know, but what you can do with what you know' (Schleicher 2013). They form the building blocks of lifelong learning, which will be important if young people are to adapt to a shifting workforce. In a fluid economy requiring adaptation, learning how to learn is particularly essential.

In Chapter Two, we explored some of the big issues shaping the shifting terrain of the workforce in a world shaped by globalisation, economic uncertainty, demographic shifts, technology, and cultural and political change at international and local levels. As the challenges, concerns and lifestyles of young people have become enmeshed in the global, so too is a need to foster the literacies necessary for them to understand and participate in the contemporary workforce. Where some young people are no longer 'bound to a single place' or nation-state (Arvanitakis & Sidoti 2011, p. 14), these literacies assume greater significance beyond the ways by which we rely on 'local knowledge' and networks that have been traditionally relied on to get work. Local knowledge remains extremely important; however, the need to think and engage globally requires practical ways of addressing the increasing virtual and actual mobility of young people. A renewed international interest in foundation and soft skills in young people and their capacity to navigate uncertain and fluid worlds of work are examined.

The theoretical concept of adversity capital is then proposed as a basis for critically understanding and responding to a visible disconnect between policy, business expectations and wider trends affecting young people outlined in previous chapters. Adversity capital, which draws upon soft skills as a resource for navigating labour force fluidity, enables young people to be more adaptive and resilient. The discussion locates the notion of adversity capital and related soft skills and resilience within broader conceptualisations of youth subjectivities in which reflexivity and responsibility feature prominently as a basis for governing young people. A critical question is asked as to whether the development of these skills as a form of adversity capital reflects a shift in focus of education towards developing the 'entrepreneurial self', in which subjectivity is characterised by individual self-management and responsibility (Farrugia 2009; Kelly 2001, 2006). But it is argued that this form of capital also offers scope for resistance to the responsibilisation of young people as a basis for their regulation and provides the capacity for them to critically engage and resist the domination of certain economistic, neoliberal ways of thinking and being.

A return to foundational and soft skills

The promotion of soft skills is not a novel idea. The need to develop skills relevant to the labour market has, for example, been a pillar of European strategies such as the European Commission's *Youth Opportunities Initiative* (European Commission 2011). In Britain, calls to grow the 'skills for success' and the need for schools to prioritise self-discipline reflect a need to elevate the development of these skills (Roberts 2009). The Young Foundation in the UK has done some important work on furthering their identification via its Skills for Effective Engagement Development (SEED) skills framework, which incorporates social intelligence, emotional resilience, enterprise and discipline (Roberts 2009).

Reflecting on both the Australian and global context, Kahn et al. (2012, p. 5) have noted:

> Across the developed world, employers report frustrations that all too often young people are ill-prepared for life in the workplace. The consequence for young people is often a struggle to find meaningful or lasting employment. Governments too acknowledge that these skills are not just useful for the workplace but help to build cohesive communities with active citizens playing a role in civic life.

In Canada, during the late 1980s and early 1990s, for example, the significance of these skills was recognised as important to the contemporary economy. The Economic Council of Canada suggested that 'the nature and level of skills required in the labour market were being transformed by a combination of three factors: growth of the service sector, technological innovation, and changes in the way work was being organised' (Andres & Wyn 2010, pp. 48–49). This proposed reorientation of the relationship between education and the workforce towards the emergent *knowledge society* has rightly been received with caution; namely, that it should involve more than a narrow vocationalism, and should also take into account forms of lifelong learning that would enable employees to adapt to the changing workforce during their lifetimes (Andres & Wyn 2010).

These soft skills – also referred to as literacies, 'generic and basic skills' (Roberts & Wignall 2010, p. 1) – include social intelligence and emotional resilience (Roberts 2009). Increasing attention is given by educators and other service providers to develop problem solving, oracy and self-discipline to equip young people to navigate fluid labour markets (IYF 2013). They are also sometimes referred to as 21st-century skills and competencies, 'to indicate that they are more related to the needs of the emerging models of economic and social development than with those of the past century, which were suited to an industrial mode of production' (Ananiadou & Claro 2008, p. 5). These skills, attitudes, and dispositions include critical thinking, communication, creativity, information literacy, ICT literacy, global awareness, financial literacy and environmental literacy (Partnership for 21st Century Skills 2009). They are seen to be essential not only for workplace readiness but also for participation in other areas of life and for the cohesion of communities more generally (Kahn et al. 2012).

Hannon et al. (2011) suggest that changing environmental conditions require new kinds of competency and literacy, such as information literacy, cross-cultural literacy, and ecological literacy. Literacies are 'areas in which we need to be able to both comprehend and express ourselves fluently' (Hannon et al. 2011, p. 5). Information literacy moves beyond the notion of basic competence in using digital technologies to a more advanced and creative level of digital competency (Walsh et al. 2011). Ecological literacy arises from a recognition 'not only that our understanding of ecosystems is severely limited, but also that we are incapable of seeing ourselves as part of a complex, interconnected, and interdependent system within which our actions have unpredictable consequences across the globe' (Hannon et al. 2011, p. 6).

Zhao (2009, p. 173) defines cross-cultural competency as 'the ability to move across cultures comfortably and fluently'. Hannon et al. elaborate further: 'As well as understanding other cultures, developing global competence offers up for scrutiny our sense of our own identities, core values, and cultural practices' (2011, p. 4). This global competence arises from the need for young people to interact, cohabitate and work with people from across the world (Zhao 2009). In the context of transnational labour market mobility in the EU, language skills have particular significance (European Commission 2011). But the same can be said in Australia given its increasing regional focus in the Asian century described in Chapter Two. This competency is already reflected in the preamble of the Melbourne Declaration, which identifies the importance of students being 'Asia literate' (MCEETYA 2008, p. 4). The connection between schooling in Australia and engagement with Asia is also explicitly made in the Australian Curriculum (ACARA 2014a). Asia literacy seeks to build 'the skills to communicate and engage with the peoples of Asia so they can effectively live, work and learn in the region' (ACARA 2014a). In the Asian century, the need for global competence based on new knowledge, skills, literacies, dispositions and awareness becomes all the more pronounced in the Australian context. But as we have seen, progress in teaching Asian languages in schools has been extremely limited. The wider development of these soft skills in Australian education has arguably also been patchy and uneven. Nevertheless, the inclusion of Intercultural Understanding in the Australian Curriculum as a General Capability to 'promote recognition, communication and engagement with the different countries and cultures within Asia' is a positive step forward (ACARA 2014b, p. 3).

Over a decade ago, during the Howard government, a report by the Department of Education, Science and Training, Business Council of Australia with the Australian Chamber of Commerce into 'employability skills', recognised the changing nature of work and a growing need for foundation skills 'required by enterprises to ensure long-term economic growth' (ADEST, ACCI & BCA 2002, p. 12). But this assessment was confined primarily to the 'adult' population, despite the fact that these skills are equally relevant to young people.

Historically, beyond schooling, one of the main non-school avenues of soft-skill development has been in the area of employment services for unemployed Australians. For-profit providers have assumed much of the responsibility for this development since the Commonwealth Employment Service was privatised in 1998. But these networks of providers have received substantial criticism, such as the Productivity Commission's *Independent Review of the Job Network* in 2002 (Mitchell 2015; Productivity Commission 2002). Criticisms include fraudulent activity by providers, a failure to get the majority of clients into secure jobs and a lack of development of skills required to get work (Mitchell 2015). Government data from 2014 show that less than half of those who had received help from Job Services Australia during the previous 12 months got work. Around half of those working wanted more work and 57 per cent of jobs gained were 'casual, temporary or seasonal' (Department of Employment 2014b; Mitchell 2015). As Mitchell (2015) notes, cries by the private sector of skills shortages are not new and billions of dollars in government funding have been spent on developing them through for-profit providers such as the Job Network. The point he makes is that investment in this area will be wasted while opportunities to work do not exist. (We will return to this problem later in the book.)

Many of these soft skills are already developed in Australian-based education and training programmes such as vocational education and training (VET) in schools and curriculum such as the International Baccalaureate; however, they need to be more widely and explicitly adopted across schooling in general. So while recognition of the need to develop these skills is not new, the need to revisit, build upon and expand their development in young people has assumed greater urgency in light of the economic conditions outlined in Chapter One.

In response to the Bradley Review of Australian higher education (Bradley et al. 2008), the federal government uncapped the number of university places, heralding a growth of participation in higher education. It has been suggested that a proportion of these additional students may be less academically prepared than was expected in the past (Go8 2012). As noted earlier in the previous chapter, there is a perceived deficit of foundational skills such as literacy and numeracy. Other skills are also absent.

Soft skills in the Australian Curriculum

These soft skills are not foreign to schooling in Australia. They are routinely developed (but perhaps less explicitly) in schools throughout the country and are implicit in policy aspirational documents, such as the Melbourne Declaration, whose second goal is for all young Australians to become successful learners, confident and creative individuals and active and informed citizens. Successful learners develop their capacity to learn and play an active role in their own learning; have the essential skills in literacy and numeracy; and are creative and productive users of technology, especially ICT, as a foundation for success in all learning areas; and are creative, innovative and resourceful, and are able to solve problems in ways that draw upon a range of learning areas and disciplines. Confident and creative individuals develop personal values and attributes such as honesty, resilience, empathy and respect for others. Active and informed citizens act with moral and ethical integrity and are able to relate to and communicate across cultures, especially the cultures and countries of Asia (MCEETYA 2008, pp. 9–10). As part of 'promoting world class curriculum and assessment', the Melbourne Declaration states that the curriculum will 'enable students to build social and emotional intelligence, and nurture student wellbeing through health and physical education in particular. The curriculum will support students to relate well to others' (MCEETYA 2008, p. 13).

The Australian Curriculum has consequently sought to incorporate the development of these skills and capabilities. During consultation for the development of the Australian Curriculum, discussion focused a view that 'the gap between education and the work readiness of young people is widening. Early and intense educational intervention is needed to help young people develop the work readiness, career development and work knowledge' (ACARA 2013b, p. 4). Echoing the surveys of business outlined above, this approach urged the development of skills and capabilities to prosper in new knowledge economies that 'differ from those of the past. Young people will need a set of personal and interpersonal capacities, wide-ranging global awareness and the flexibility to manage rapid change and transition' (ACARA undated). These general capabilities and non-technical work-readiness skills and knowledge reflect a wider interest amongst education systems in developing soft skills to enable young people to be responsive and adaptable to changing global labour markets.

The Australian Curriculum emphasises general capabilities in the form of an interrelated set of knowledge, skills, behaviours and dispositions that students are expected to develop and draw on both within the context of the school environment and beyond. Consequently, the emphasis of these general capabilities is on transcending specific content areas and contexts. It is contended that general capabilities are forged through active and full participation in a range of curricular, extracurricular and non-school activities and experiences. Moreover, it is assumed that students will require these general capabilities in a variety of different contexts in order to flourish in our complex and changing world. Nevertheless, it is also acknowledged that some of the specific 'general capabilities' (e.g. numeracy) are more likely to be both fostered and demonstrated in a particular learning area (e.g. mathematics) (ACARA 2013a).

Aside from literacy and numeracy, there are five other general capabilities in the Australian Curriculum that are relevant here, which overlap and interrelate. Firstly, ICT capability refers to the process by which students learn to use ICT effectively, appropriately and safely. It is noted that the use of ICT is not fixed, but necessarily responsive to a rapidly changing environment in which both the nature and potential uses of technologies are evolving (ACARA 2013a). Students are expected to use ICT for a wide variety of purposes: from accessing, managing, creating and presenting information to communicating and collaborating with peers to problem solving and empirical reasoning. The importance of ICT skills reflects wider recognition in other countries, such as recent EU policy in the form of the Europe 2020 *Digital Agenda* (European Commission 2011, p. 7).

In a similar manner to numeracy and literacy, the Australian Curriculum emphasises the importance of providing authentic contexts for ICT learning across different learning areas, and provides guidance for teachers as to how this might be achieved. Therefore, the ICT capability is based on the assumption that technologies are digital tools that can support a variety of forms of learning in many different contexts. Part of this process involves the student coming to understand that a given machine will have strengths and limitations, and will vary in its fitness for use in a particular learning situation. This active stance is encouraged to prevent students from mindlessly following procedures and themselves becoming 'tools of the machine' (Maas cited in ACARA 2013a, p. 59).

Another capability – critical and creative thinking – seeks to develop students' ability to learn to produce and assess knowledge, explain and explore ideas and concepts, and to generate and analyse alternative solutions as they endeavour to solve problems (ACARA 2013a). This capability is connected to a general set of dispositions and behaviours that are, according to the curriculum's authors, at the core of contemporary education. These include the use of reason and logic, and the capacity to imagine and innovate. Critical and creative thinking are related, but not interchangeable. Whilst critical thinking is predominantly focused around developing and dissecting arguments and supporting or refuting these arguments based on evidence, creative thinking involves the generation of novel ideas and applying existing ideas to new contexts. Despite these distinctions, it is argued that critical and creative thinking can be encouraged simultaneously through activities that require students to integrate the more critical proficiencies in reason and logic with the more creative flairs of imagination and innovation. A key aspect of developing students' capability to think critically and creatively involves encouraging them to share their thinking with others, while learning to give and receive feedback constructively (ACARA 2013a).

A third area – personal and social capability – is developed by students as they learn to understand both themselves and other people (ACARA 2013a). This capability encompasses a range of practices including emotional awareness, self-regulation, persistence and the ability to emphasise and build positive relationships with others in a variety of contexts. It is argued that such practices are critical for developing a positive sense of self and getting on in the world, and they serve as a foundation for both learning and citizenship.

As students gain insight into their emotions and behaviour, it is proposed that they will be better able to regulate how they respond to a given social situation and therefore be better equipped to build positive, meaningful relationships with others. Given how integral this particular capability is to all aspects of a school environment, it is not surprising that it is expected that personal and social development be addressed across all learning areas. Having said this, it is noted that some of the relevant practices and skills may be most explicitly addressed in specific learning areas, such as Health and Physical Education (ACARA 2013a).

Developing the fourth capability of ethical understanding involves students learning to develop a strong personal and socially oriented ethical outlook (ACARA 2013a). Such an outlook is expected to assist students to better manage conflict, cope with uncertainty and understand the impact of their values and behaviours on others. Moreover, through encouraging collaborative inquiry into the ethical dimensions of their learning, students can come to understand how ethical decisions are forged in a democratic, pluralistic society. This particular capability has a global dimension. As cultural, social, environmental and technological changes transform the world, students are increasingly exposed to a range of complex issues with which they must engage. For example, issues such as our human rights and responsibilities, the rights of animals, environmental issues and global justice are identified as being pertinent to this current generation of students. It is suggested that a focus on ethical understanding across all stages of schooling will better prepare these students to navigate this increasingly integrated and multifaceted world.

The final capability, intercultural understanding, refers to students developing an appreciation for their own particular cultures, languages and beliefs, as well as those of other people (ACARA 2013a). Students are expected to engage with a diverse range of cultures, and develop insight into commonalities, whilst respecting points of difference. By encouraging students to view culture through an analytical lens, students can come to understand the role of culture in forging individual and collective identities. In a similar manner to the capability of ethical understanding, an emphasis on intercultural understanding is thought to be particularly necessary in an increasingly interconnected, complex world. Intercultural understanding also overlaps with personal and social capability, as developing greater appreciation for different cultures is expected to foster empathy, and offers critical insight into the students' own beliefs and assumptions. Intercultural understanding is likely to be more relevant to learning areas concerned with people and societies; it is perhaps most relevant to the three cross-curriculum priorities: Aboriginal and Torres Strait Islander histories and cultures, Asia and Australia's engagement with Asia, and sustainability.

These capabilities reflect a positive step forward in developing the skills, literacies and competencies to navigate the challenges outlined so far in this book. Currently, however, activities seeking to foster such skills are less likely to take place within the school context than outside it, which is far from perfect or even adequate.

There is also a strong suggestion that schools and school systems operate in a way that enables some students' participation over others, with the least confident and engaged students also the least likely to be heard (Black 2012; Walsh & Black 2009). This has important implications for the development of the capabilities and represents a missed opportunity for schools and systems seeking to engage young people in learning as well as to build their soft skills. Young people who play an active role in their schools demonstrate better levels of social and emotional competence, a greater sense of autonomy and better communication and collaborative skills (Halsey et al. 2006). They also have a stronger sense of themselves as learners (Fielding & Rudduck 2002).

One closely related area that remains undervalued is oracy, which is a feature of effective teaching and learning in early childhood and primary settings (Alexander 2010). Though implied in personal and social capability, the ability to express oneself through speech could be more specifically developed as a foundation for developing other capabilities outlined above in the Australian Curriculum. Oracy, for example, already plays an important part of formal assessment in some countries. Oral exams, or 'vivas', are widely used in Europe. In Norway, 16-year-olds must take an oral exam on a subject that is decided on the day of the examination. It has been argued that they should be used within NAPLAN testing to assess communication skills as a basis for workplace readiness (Williams 2014).

In summary, while there are some positive developments in the development of soft skills, there is a need to prioritise their development in a more systemic and considered way. As tools for adaptation and negotiating change in different contexts, they form the basis of what I call 'adversity capital'.

Adversity capital

The sociologist Zygmunt Bauman has rightly observed that '[w]e live in a world of universal flexibility [. . .]. Safe ports for trust are few and far between, and most of the time trust floats unanchored vainly seeking storm-protected havens' (Bauman 2000, pp. 135–136). 'Work', he writes, 'can no longer offer the secure axis around which to wrap and fix self-definitions, identities and life-projects' (Bauman 2000, p. 139). Martin Jay also notes how contemporary life is characterised by 'precarious uncertainty, short-term planning', 'ephemeral relationships' and 'struggles to manage risk' (2010, p. 97). Consequently, Bauman suggests, 'In a life ruled by the precept of flexibility – life strategies, plans and desires can but be short-term' (Bauman 2013, p. 113).

The fluid nature of the contemporary workforce suggests a renewed need for young people to harness soft skills and competencies to navigate this uncertainty. They are a kind of toolbox that can be used by young people to navigate precarity and the fluidity of working life. Serving as a kind of adversity capital that enables young people to be more adaptive, flexible and resilient, they also reflect the need to prepare young people for more fluid working lives in which the conventional notion of a career is obsolete. Building on Pavlidis's (2009) use of the concept of 'adversity capital' elsewhere in youth sociology, these skills reflect an extension of this idea to the area of education, and whose development could be useful to teachers and policymakers seeking to develop in their students a wider range of soft skills.

This notion features elements of social and cultural capital. Bourdieu expanded Marx's concept of capital to include non-material and material aspects (Svendsen & Svendsen 2004). But this notion of adversity capital moves beyond Bourdieu's definition of cultural capital as the 'instruments for the appropriation of symbolic wealth worthy of being sought and possessed' (Bourdieu 1977, p. 488). While adversity capital may be used to generate forms of cultural capital, it has more material concerns in the form of social capital, which includes 'the sum of the resources, actual or virtual, that accrue to an individual or a group by virtue of addressing a durable network of more or less institutionalised relationships of mutual acquaintance and recognition' (Bourdieu & Wacquant 1992, p. 119).

The type of capital here has more in common with Lareau and Weininger's approach to cultural capital, which 'stresses the importance of examining micro-interactional processes whereby individuals' strategic use of knowledge, skills, and competence come into contact with institutionalised standards of evaluation' (Lareau & Weininger 2004, p. 135). But given the current absence of formal institutionalised standards of evaluation related to the skills and competencies of adversity capital, it widens the field of strategy to encompass processes beyond education to social and economic domains of living. The challenge here is that 'institutionalized standards of evaluation' still matter and dominate the measurement of student outcomes – particularly with the rise of standardised testing through NAPLAN and Programme for International Student Assessment (PISA). This challenge suggests a need to extend and develop more sophisticated measures of educational success that are aligned with post-school life, social and economic norms and expectations.

In her use of the term of adversity capital, Pavlidis writes that 'an individual's ability to negotiate risk depends on their ability to distance risk from themselves and their body – to overcome or negotiate the structures of society – and depends on their reflexive capacity' (2009, p. 9). The development of soft skills that is proposed here explicitly seeks to build reflexive capacity. They include a critical knowledge and capacity to navigate everything from rights at work to challenging wider norms related to working life and life in general. This includes the knowledge and ability to question predominant discourses such as neoliberalism.

The term 'adversity capital' is deliberately loaded; it suggests that young people should develop personal assets that promote economic mobility in a world in which work is characterised by increasing levels of insecurity. It also promotes an ability to critically move across different cultural, mediated and non-mediated contexts. It signifies that not only will these skills help young people to get a job but also describes them as subjects potentially confronting a life of vulnerability and precarity. It is a form of capital that can be productive of other forms of capital upon which young people can critically confront and navigate precarity and potentially build a better life.

There are long-standing debates over the degree to which soft skills can and should be taught. Ananiadou and Claro (2008) summarise the most prominent debates in relation to 21st-century learning, which I will address in turn. Firstly, debates around whether the emphasis should be 'on content and a broad liberal arts curriculum rather than the teaching of skills such as critical thinking or learning how to learn. The main argument advanced by this approach to teaching is that, although such skills are very important, they cannot be taught independently, i.e. outside a particular knowledge domain such as those designated by traditional academic subjects, nor will students be able to apply such skills if they lack the appropriate factual knowledge on a particular domain' (Ananiadou & Claro 2008, p. 6). I wish to make it clear upfront that the case for adversity capital made in this book does not see these distinctions as neatly distinct. There is a very strong and valid case for teaching the liberal arts, and, moreover, soft skills are arguably best taught in relation to rich content areas and experiences.

A good example is the fostering of oracy in the International Baccalaureate's Personal Project, which is taught in the Middle Year's Programme. Students develop a proposal for a project, which they then design and deliver in the form of 'a product or developing an outcome evaluating the product/outcome and reflecting on their project and their learning' (IB 2015). Students plan their time and materials, record development of the project, develop understandings and solve problems, and communicate with their supervisor and others. The projects are student-led and explicitly seek to develop attitudes and skills such as communication, problem solving and communication.

Another criticism is that 'the rhetoric of 21st century competencies is seen as yet another facet of an economist approach to education according to which its main goal is to prepare workers for knowledge-intensive economies or even in some cases for particular firms. Instead of putting the emphasis on a harmonious development of all human abilities, the discourse on competencies overstates the relevance of work-related competencies' (Ananiadou & Claro 2008, p. 6). For this discussion, as I wrote in the introduction to this book, it is important to locate these skills and competencies within a richer and wider context. Moreover, the notion of adversity capital explicitly seeks to challenge and question forms of domination and prevailing discourses, such as neoliberalism.

The individualistic nature of the discourses of soft skills described above is also problematic. Returning to the policy discussion in the previous chapter, responsibility for navigating flexibility and uncertainty is increasingly located in the individual. Beck has highlighted reflexivity and individualisation as a form of social integration in contemporary life (Beck & Beck-Gernsheim 2002). The neoliberal policies outlined earlier suggest youth workforce participation as a reflexive practice in which young people individually seek to navigate complex economic, cultural and social circumstances. During the last three decades, these policies have been predicated on the idea that young people are themselves expected to reflexively navigate the risks arising throughout contemporary life (Aldenmyr et al. 2012), and to be 'intelligent, wise, happy, virtuous, healthy, productive, docile, enterprising, fulfilled, self-esteeming, empowered' (Black & Walsh 2015; Rose 1998, p. 12). Through this individualisation, it is promised that 'people will be set free from the social forms of industrial society – class, stratification, family, gender status of men and women' to choose an identity of their own (Beck 1992, p. 87). But as we saw in Chapters One and Two, choice can be elusive and illusory for those from disadvantaged backgrounds facing structural forms of marginalisation. Consequently, adversity capital is dependent on the recognition by others of its value, as well as the provision of support mechanisms where structural barriers to participation predominate. For young people experiencing marginalisation due to factors such as their ethnicity or geographic location, interventions by government, business and others are as important as ever.

A related criticism is that many of these competencies 'are not within reach of all young people, firstly because not all today's students are going to become knowledge-intensive workers even in developed countries, and secondly because this rhetoric forgets the needs of the vast majority of the world's population in developing countries. The discourse on 21st century competencies is therefore hardly relevant in all contexts and there is a risk of enlarging socio-economic disparities when promoting such competencies among the world's elite' (Ananiadou &

Claro 2008, p. 6). However, the notion of adversity capital incorporates skills and competencies that are routinely taught in non-formal learning contexts within developing countries, such as Indonesia (UNESCO 2006). The assumption here is not to exclusively prepare young people for knowledge economies but to engage wider contexts of precarity and fluidity.

Furthermore, adversity capital not only applies to those who are visibly disengaged, but takes into account people who may do well in school but do not have the competencies, motivation and predispositions to become active self-directed lifelong learners post-school. As Hannon et al. (2011, p. 5) argue, '[F]ocusing on dropouts masks a bigger issue, because it only takes account of the visibly disengaged.' In his work on England's Learning Futures project, Price (2010) refers to this group as 'disengaged achievers'. Adversity capital needs to be developed in these young people too.

There is another related area in which adversity capital may be problematic. On one level, the idea of adversity capital may seem to further responsibilise young people when situated in the wider governmental discourses of responsibility and reflexivity described above. The development of these skills, as a form of adversity capital, may reinforce a shift in the focus of education towards developing the 'entrepreneurial self' described by Kelly (2001, 2006). The overarching neoliberal policy discourses described in the previous chapter shift responsibility onto individuals, while dismantling broader social and economic safety nets. It could be argued that this approach further responsibilises individuals, while deflecting responsibility from bigger social, political and economic interests and institutions. These, however, are not discrete. An argument will be made in the following chapters of this book for wider social, economic and institutional change that provides support to young people. And the case for building adversity capital in young people does not seek to locate young people to be responsibilised, compliant and passive. Though developed in individuals, adversity capital challenges individualised 'pedagogisation' of labour market problems. Skills such as social capability and emotional intelligence reinforce the powerful role of community and the social in young people. 'Similar to other forms of capital such as cultural capital and symbolic capital, adversity capital is only valuable if it is valued by others' (Pavlidis 2009, p. 11). As suggested above, this question as to whether adversity capital is valued by others – particularly employers and educators – is an important one within the context of global markets and the dominance of forms of economic capital.

As also implied above, the notion of adversity capital risks being an economistic way of understanding the social. But the project of the self is about a subjectivity that is not fixed and not reduced to the economic and individualistic notions of self and society. Therefore, adversity capital is at its core a critical reflexive project that accounts for relational practices rather than individualised and responsibilised ones. It acknowledges young people's 'subjective perspectives as a powerful basis for navigating change, insecurity and uncertainty. Rather than dismiss young people's experience of adversity as only of negative consequence, the concept of adversity capital can be used to empower young people to value their own experiences and life courses as valuable and meaningful, in this way developing the reflexivity needed to negotiate and mediate risk.' Adversity capital is therefore used 'where those young people who have experienced adversity use these experiences and understandings of the world to effectively deploy themselves in an increasingly risky and fluid society' (Pavlidis 2009, p. 10). It includes the development of resilience that incorporates individual and social dimensions.

Adversity capital, neoliberalism and resilience

As Ungar (2008) suggests, there are numerous ways that resilience is conceptualised. For this discussion, resilience refers to 'competence when under stress. Resilient children may show competence dealing with threats to their well-being' (Ungar 2008, p. 220). The way it is used here also acknowledges that 'resilience is not a condition of individuals alone, but also exists as a trait of a child's social and political setting' (Ungar 2008, p. 220). Resilience includes social policies and structural deficiencies beyond individual-level factors and is 'a culturally and contextually sensitive construct' (p. 234). And to paraphrase Ungar, resilient young people 'need resilient families and communities' (p. 221). The second half of this book examines these dimensions in further detail.

But viewed in the wider political context outlined above, resilience, 'broadly defined as positive adaptation despite adversity' (Bottrell 2013; see also Garmezy & Rutter 1983), is arguably itself a problematic concept. Dorothy Bottrell's critique of responsibilised resilience in neoliberal social policy is salient here. In the current political environment, neoliberalism valorises a certain kind of individual – one who is either blamed or takes the credit for their failures and successes (Rigsby 1994, p. 93). In doing so, it relegates to the periphery the importance of social structures, collective action and values, economic safety nets and the state. According to a neoliberal view, the state's function is to preserve processes, practices and institutional frameworks that enable the pursuit of 'well-being . . . by liberating individual entrepreneurial freedoms and skills within an institutional framework characterized by strong private property rights, free markets and free trade. The role of the state is to create and preserve an institutional framework appropriate to such practices' (Harvey 2005, p. 2). As Bottrell suggests, 'We see these processes in the policy text of resilience as it articulates the neoliberal ideology of entrepreneurial individualism and repositions young people, families and communities in terms of the capacities relevant to this ideal.' Importantly, she argues, 'In this way, it takes them out of their everyday lives, actual concerns and the social organisation of ruling relations that give rise to them' (Bottrell 2013). This dislocation exacerbates the kinds of structural and deeply embedded inequities and forms of disadvantage identified earlier in Chapter Two: 'Indigenous people, people of colour, the poor and working-class carry the burden of historical inequalities that have been exacerbated by neoliberal economic policies driving the new institutional framework of individualised resilience and responsibility' (Bottrell 2013). But where Bottrell argues that this 'emphasis on individuals, their skills and attitudes' is attached to 'an outmoded notion of resilience that decontextualises it from cultural contexts, social structures and political processes', there is space here for the critical and communitarian aspect of adversity capital that draws on a notion of resilience which acknowledges that 'whether a young person, parent or community endures, copes or thrives is dependent on the resources of the community that are accessible and culturally meaningful' (Bottrell 2013). Adversity capital relies on these resources alongside the active intervention of states and other actors to support, develop and enhance these resources. Moreover, it challenges the dominance of neoliberalism by actively linking the development of resilience in individuals with the importance of community-based responses to navigate and, where necessary, actively challenge dominant paradigms that work against the interests of those communities.

Resilience is a positive response to vulnerability, such as 'economic shocks and turbulences'. These approaches start with the question, 'When we experience adversity . . . how shall we respond?' (Rose 2014). Resilience suggests a perception that futures are not predictable or calculable. It is applied to a variety of contexts, including 'the raising of children to meet the demands of the future' (Rose 2014). Resilience entered the vernacular in this way in the 1970s. It is a way by which people can 'optimise themselves' to respond to adversity. If vulnerability is the 'problem', developing and harnessing existing capacities for resilience is one possible response. If total security, such as the objective of full employment in 20th-century policy or gaining secure work in the 21st century for many people becomes 'a fantasy', then resilience is seen as a means of navigating and responding to adversity and uncertainty. It is possible to develop capacities in young people to 'bounce back' (Rose 2014) from conditions of adversity, such as precarity in the workforce. 'Resilient strategies', Rose suggests, 'seem highly light, mobile and translatable ways of dealing with contingency.' Resilience is innate and can be developed, even amongst high-risk children and young people.

Research into resilience in relation to children seldom frames it a capacity to be instilled in the individuated subject. It is not exclusively an individual capacity but is grounded in other relations, such as family, through schooling and through socially responsible activity. Rose (2014) highlights that 'compensating experiences outside of home' are important for a range of reasons, such as to build self-esteem (e.g. working while at school). The work of Ungar and others draws on research that 'has shown that the resilience of individuals growing up in challenging contexts or facing significant personal adversity is dependent on the quality of the social and physical ecologies that surround them, as much, and likely far more, than personality traits, cognitions or talents' (Ungar 2013, p. 1). These ecologies are investigated in Chapter Six.

As Rose (2014) points out, critics of resilience argue that it is another form of neoliberalism that relegates people to either manage their own insecurities or abandoning them to their fate. But because resilience has no single form of logic, it cannot be reduced to this neoliberal view. Neoliberalism should therefore not be understood as a totalising ideology or force. The 'polyvalence of resilient strategies' resists the simple reduction of resilience to the individuated notion that is ascribed to neoliberalism (Rose 2014). It can grow out of protective solidarity within communities and in turn generates sociality. Research into resilience in children has shown a capacity for solidarity and community resilience to emerge particularly during adversity, rather than dysfunctional individualised responses, as would be expected according to the neoliberal critique of resilience (Rose 2014). Ungar suggests that the problem with this individualistic view of resilience is 'partially the result of a dominant view of resilience as something individuals *have*, rather than as a *process* that families, schools, communities and governments facilitate. Because resilience is related to the presence of social risk factors (we can only speak of resilience in the presence of at least one stressor), there is a need for an ecological interpretation of the construct that acknowledges the importance of people's interaction with their environments' (Ungar 2013, p. 1).

Following the suggestion of James Côté, there is an opportunity to develop a political economy of youth that challenges the contradictions and consequences of neoliberalism, such as 'the current prolongations of youth, the deterioration of youth living conditions and their diminished economic prospects later in life' (Côté 2013, p. 3). Adversity capital is the basis for what Côté identifies as a '"critical emancipatory" position that helps those who might be accepting their exploitation as "normal" to see how they can overcome their false consciousness' (Côté 2013, p. 3), and critique 'free-market logics as the root of many social problems and seeking radical alternatives to correct capitalism's dehumanising tendencies' (p. 3). While recognising the material consequences of the contemporary market, it also challenges a belief that the conditions in which young people find themselves are 'normal'. Adversity capital therefore offers scope for resistance to responsibilisation. Critical thinking is in particular a vital soft skill, which when used in combination with others can be a powerful source of agency. Pavlidis's notion of adversity capital 'is a resource that people can use to transform adverse life experiences into an asset' (2009, p. 11).[1] My use of the term differs, in that resilience is enhanced by the development of these soft skills and is something that can be developed as a form of prevention in schools and other community, educational and workplace settings. It also situates these skills and competencies in a wider social, economic and cultural context.

As Rose's (2014) approach highlights, discourses of resilience are neither exclusively individualised, nor 'negative' per se. Individuals typically reside in a variety of communities that can bolster forms of resilience, such as family and support networks. They draw from various resources (e.g. families, social networks and non-government support services) to navigate, participate and deal with marginalisation. As we see reformations of the make-up of 'families', for example, the social fabric is changing. But within these changes are 'moments' of relational agency and possibilities for solidity. Families (in their various forms) have enduring relevance in young people's lives (Wyn et al. 2011). They continue to serve as havens, as does education as a means of shoring up young people's capacity to engage changing worlds of work. And where young people lack these forms of support, adversity capital can provide the basic tools to navigate contemporary working life. These tools do not operate in isolation. They are ideally embedded in social structures and frameworks as suggested above.

Conclusion

The Melbourne Declaration suggests: 'Globalisation and technological change are placing greater demands on education and skill development in Australia and the nature of jobs available to young Australians is changing faster than ever' (MCEETYA 2008, p. 4). There is need to build the skills, competencies, literacies and intelligences in young people that are relevant to these changing conditions (Kahn et al. 2012). As the places where young people are potentially first exposed to the possibilities of adversity capital, schools are a good place to start developing these critical skills as a core component of adversity capital.

Skills and competencies beyond literacy and numeracy are important for developing resilience in young people to deal with changing labour force conditions, as well as broader challenges in life. While we routinely assess and report on young people's basic academic skills, such as their literacy and numeracy, we lack mechanisms to assess or recognise a wider group of skills and attributes necessary for navigating employment and life in general. Meeting the challenge of a changing economy, a more fluid workforce, the impact of technology and Australia's engagement with the Asian region, require young people to have a wider set of literacies, competencies and employability skills. They are also important to developing resilience in young people.

In a 2014 lecture, Rose describes a shift from 'risk to resilience' (Rose 2014). In the governmental policy discourses of risk that emerged during the late 20th century, individuals were expected to make calculations about the future as a basis of shaping what they do in the present. At the end of the 20th century, the involvement of actors such as the Job Network reflects a multi-agency approach to managing workforce risk. However, labour market uncertainty renders this kind of risk calculation to be problematic. Governing through risk continues to take place, but the assumption that risks are calculable, predictable and manageable is being called into question. Contemporary approaches to resilience rework risk in a way that recognises that people are vulnerable to uncertainty and change in ways that make determining risk factors incalculable (Rose 2014).

Where risk is predicated on an anxiety about the future, resilience is imbued with a certain optimism. The notion of adversity capital described here builds on Rose's (2014) suggestion that

> the logic of resilience is a hopeful one . . . to foster resilience is not to create disciplined subjects whose conduct is fixed by norms and

judged in terms of good and bad. It doesn't require some all-seeing government agency that seeks to know and regulate everything in a territory but nor does it seek to devolve all responsibilities to isolated, autonomous individualised subjects seeking to live their life as entrepreneurial selves, maximising their utilities and responding to market incentives. In its imagination, strategies of resilience seek to make use of the natural capacities of living human beings to come to terms with adversity when they are a part of supportive networks of community affiliation.

Resilience, formulated here as both natural and which can be taught, 'is suited to our problematic present' (Rose 2014). As Rose (2014) suggests, 'innovative action whether by loving parents, inspiring teachers, resourceful communities, cannot merely enable survival but flourishing . . . by maximising resilience'. Collective, infrastructural dimensions of resilience are important. The development of adversity capital as a basis for resilience therefore seeks to harness certain skills, capabilities and competencies in individual young people, while acknowledging that its efficacy depends on it being supported by adequate resourcing (e.g. of schools, teachers and community-based support). It represents one means of refocusing responses to precarity to the kinds of social ecological dimensions of resilience proposed by Ungar (2013) and Rose (2014).

The concept of adversity capital developed here is also a means of not only addressing certain concerns of business by promoting the development of soft skills but also providing a critical basis upon which young people navigate the pervasive and choppy seas of global labour markets. The challenge is to develop adversity capital that can be converted into other forms of social, economic, political and cultural capital. So what does this look like in practice?

A challenge for educators is to provide a means for developing these literacies in ways that meaningfully connect with the everyday lives of young people and the contemplation of their current and future working lives. This is not the responsibility of career advisers and councillors alone: all teachers and educational leaders play an important role in ensuring that the development of these literacies are embedded in all parts of the curriculum and in ways that purposefully engage all students and school staff. There are examples of where schooling has sought to develop a wider project of the self. Educational curriculum has incorporated soft skills as part of a wider development of the self, such as the Personal Project in the International Baccalaureate's Middle Years Curriculum described above.

A deeper question arises as to whether conventional models of teaching are equipped to prepare young people for fluid worlds of work. These soft skills also need to be present in our teachers and school leaders. At a deeper level is the question of whether key conventional schooling is capable of doing this. These are the central themes of the remainder of this book.

A final observation is that developing adversity capital depends on a range of economic, social and political support structures to be effective. However, the neoliberal policy trajectories described in this chapter are deeply problematic and divisive – not only in the notional separation of lifters and leaners but also in the practical ways that it understands and seeks to locate young people as objects of contemporary policy. Ideally, adversity capital should not be developed in young people *in response* to the kinds of punitive policy proposals outlined above. Practical, systemic responses to workforce fluidity and precarity should be aligned in the best interests of young people, as we will explore in the following chapters.

5
Teachers in Transition: Current Challenges

Introduction

So far, we have traced the impact of the GFC on young people's pathways to work and unemployment. The effects of that economic downturn are layered on top of longer-term employment trends in which there are fewer full-time jobs for teenagers. For many young adults, secure work comes later in life. These trends are enmeshed with wider developments related to globalisation. International labour markets offer opportunities for those who are willing and able to travel, while others seeking lower-paying work in Australia must compete with temporary migrants from overseas, as well as older Australian workers. These are just a few of the labour market dynamics.

Labour markets are changing in other ways. As Beck (2000) suggests, economic activity within 'developed' societies is increasingly focused on knowledge-based services, rather than primary and secondary production. Labour markets are less regulated and more fluid. Occupational structures are changing. And as we saw in Chapter One, these changes impact different social groups in variety of ways (MacDonald 2009).

In Chapter Three, various disconnects were identified between policy aspirations, business expectations and young Australians in the labour market. In Chapter Four, it was highlighted that soft skills continue to have significance in this changing landscape as part of a wider need to develop adversity capital in young people – particularly those facing precarity in relation to work. In light of the need to develop adversity capital in young people, the next two chapters ask: what are the implications for educators and schools in response to shifting regimes of youth transitions and the need to prepare young people for increasingly fluid worlds of work? At a deeper level is a key question: how aligned is schooling to young people's expectations and the fluid realities of worlds of work and global change? We continue to rely on an industrial model of schooling in a post-industrial society. This chapter explores the question: how ready are teachers to prepare young people for contemporary working life?

In an increasingly post-industrial society, preparing young people requires new approaches. Realigning schooling to the fundamental shifts outlined in Part One of this book is a major challenge. This part of this book therefore focuses on the teaching profession and schooling. It seeks to provide ideas for change and to start a discussion about how we might approach the challenges of educating young people in the 21st century.

It should be noted that the purposes of schooling are by no means exclusively focused on making young people 'work-ready' – the benefits of education on personal, social and economic development are far wider and richer; but in the context of the challenges outlined in Part One, this discussion focuses on the role of teachers and schooling in developing young people for workforce participation.

From a wider perspective, the teaching profession and the pre-service initial teacher education (ITE) programmes that prepare new teachers face the challenge of addressing the needs of 'unprecedented diversity among school students' (Caldwell 2012, p. 16). As we saw in Chapters One and Two, while performing well on some indicators, persistent challenges remain in outcomes and transitions for students in particular contexts, such as those from low SES backgrounds, those living in regional and remote areas, and those from Indigenous backgrounds (Bentley & Cazaly 2015). Stubborn challenges also emerge in lifting levels of literacy and numeracy – challenges that are by no means confined to Australia. Low levels of achievement in literacy and numeracy have been strongly linked to unemployment among young adults (Marks & Ainley 1999).

Beyond parental background, teachers can have a profound impact on the life outcomes of young people. It is for this reason that governments perennially review the teaching profession and the institutions tasked with preparing teachers, such as universities. On 13 February 2015, for example, The Teacher Education Ministerial Advisory Group (TEMAG) report was released. The Australian Federal Government established TEMAG in 2014 'to provide advice on changes needed to the training of our teachers' (DET 2015a, p. 3). The Report focused on ITE in five areas:

- Stronger quality assurance of teacher education courses
- Rigorous selection for entry to teacher education courses

- Improved and structured practical experience for teacher education students
- Robust assessment of graduates to ensure classroom readiness
- National research and workforce planning capabilities (DET 2015b).

The review implied that a greater shift was needed in the locus of teacher preparation towards in-school training, while boosting the quality of teacher education in universities. It came on the back of a wave of investment in resources and thinking about where the teaching profession is heading. This is a historically important point in time to reflect on the teaching profession for several reasons, including the development of standards for the teaching profession by the Australian Institute for Teaching and School Leadership (AITSL), a wider reappraisal of teacher education and where it should take place, and current discussions on how to improve teacher quality as mentioned above.

Current challenges to developing teachers reveal certain tensions and contradictions in how we think of the profession in relation to the greater workforce in general. Issues such as the role of financial incentives and rewarding the profession, management of unsatisfactory performance, evaluation in teacher quality, casualisation of the teaching workforce and the general mobility of teachers highlight these tensions, challenges and contradictions. The casualisation and fluidity of the teacher workforce (particularly for new teachers) suggest that insecurity in the workforce is by no means confined to young people. The teaching profession – particularly teachers just starting out – features forms of precarity.

This chapter critically examines teaching as a profession. While there is now a broad consensus about the importance of teachers as one key influence on student outcomes, what goes into creating and developing quality teachers and the challenges facing the profession is often poorly understood. These challenges have a bearing on how well equipped teachers and schools are to address the issues raised in Part One of this book.

We begin with a critical snapshot of the recent policy environment in Australia. Starting with the Melbourne Declaration on Educational Goals for Young Australians, the discussion outlines recent influential reports and policy statements, such as the National Partnership Agreement on Improving Teacher Quality (COAG 2008); AITSL's Standards for Teachers and School Leaders; the Australian Curriculum; the Productivity Commission's (2012) Schools Workforce research report, *Realising Potential: Businesses Helping Schools to Develop Australia's*

Future (DEEWR 2011); and the Henry White Paper Australia in the Asian Century (Australian Government 2012). It also looks at the work of key actors such as AITSL and various state and territory authorities as well as influential non-government actors such as the Grattan Institute. The discussion then examines a range of challenges facing the teaching profession across key points of development in the teacher life cycle, from those entering the teaching profession to teachers in senior leadership roles. It also includes an overview of the importance and challenges of developing a national approach to the teaching profession in Australia.

Drawing from the experiences of other high-performing systems, this discussion provides a snapshot of contested debates of how to best prepare teachers for working life and investigate whether these approaches are appropriate to the demands of what Bauman (2000) has characterised as 'liquid modernity'. Looking at current approaches to developing good teachers, this chapter offers some exploratory questions about where the profession is heading and how it might engage the challenges outlined in the first half of this book.

Teaching at front and centre

The potential impact of the teacher on student learning is widely recognised. But amongst policymakers, academics and education professionals, there is fierce debate over what 'makes' quality teaching. It is argued that '[d]ifferences in teacher effectiveness account for a large proportion of the differences in student outcomes . . . Outside of family background teacher effectiveness is the largest single factor influencing student outcomes' (Jensen & Reichl 2012, p. 5). According to measures such as those used by the OECD, the achievement of students with effective teachers three years in a row will be 49 percentile points higher than that of students with less effective teachers (Jensen & Reichl 2012, p. 5). But it is important to keep in mind that comparative measures on student outcomes, such as PISA and NAPLAN, are only a proxy of student outcomes and that success in school requires more comprehensive measures to encompass other forms of learning (e.g. of soft skills) that seek to incorporate a holistic view of the young person within her/his social ecological settings.

By extension, it is worth considering how relevant the teaching 'profession' *is* – both in the context of the contemporary labour market and in how well the profession is equipped to understand and prepare young people for fluid worlds of work.

The current policy environment

The 2015 TEMAG review mentioned above follows a longer policy trajectory seeking to improve the teaching profession in Australia. The Improving Teacher Quality National Partnership Agreement, for example, was established 'to drive and reward systemic reforms to improve the quality of teaching and leadership in Australian schools' and 'deliver system-wide reforms targeting critical points in the teacher "life cycle" to attract, train, place, develop and retain quality teachers and leaders in our schools and classrooms. It also has a specific focus on professional development and support for principals' (COAG 2008, p. 4). This policy trajectory reflects, in part, an effort to define teaching as a profession, or perhaps more specifically its *status* as a profession.

I remember once being asked what I did for a living. Answering that I worked in an education faculty of a university was insufficient: 'what do you *do* in that faculty?' was the next question. 'We prepare teachers for teaching.' The person was surprised that teaching was something that was *taught* in a university. Perhaps this reflects a wider lack of understanding about what goes into making good teachers, or, possibly, a belief that teaching is a profession unlike others, and yet it requires specialist knowledge, learning and development just like other professions. The status of teaching routinely receives attention in the media – particularly negative attention, which has been heightened in recent years following the growing use of performance measures such as NAPLAN.

Worthy efforts to articulate and benchmark what it means to be a good teacher and the teaching profession in general have positively assisted discussion about what it means to be a good teacher, and the means by which good teaching can be achieved. This discussion is important here as in the remainder of this chapter, I wish to explore ways by which the profession could be further improved to meet the challenges of young people in the 21st century. It is useful to briefly examine some key aspects of this recent discussion.

One notable starting point is the formation of AITSL in 2010. Funded by the Australian Government, AITSL was established to develop and maintain rigorous professional standards for teaching and school leadership. It has also sought to implement a national approach to the accreditation of pre-service teacher education courses and foster high-quality professional development for teachers and school leaders through professional standards and professional learning.

The National Professional Standards for Teachers define 'the elements of high-quality, effective teaching in 21st century schools that will improve educational outcomes for students'. They have been developed based on the 'broad consensus that teacher quality is the single most important in-school factor influencing student achievement' (AITSL 2011a, pp. 1–2). They draw from the experience of local and international education systems to outline what teachers are expected to know and be able to do at four career stages: Graduate, Proficient, Highly Accomplished and Lead. The Graduate Standards underpin the accreditation of initial teacher education programmes. Graduates from accredited programmes qualify for registration to teach in each Australian state and territory. In addition to this, AITSL consulted with school jurisdictions and key stakeholders to develop, trial and validate a process by which teachers can undertake voluntary certification at the highly accomplished and lead levels. Efforts were made to align the Standards with existing standards and programmes, such as those offered by the New South Wales (NSW) Institute of Teachers and the Victorian Institute of Teaching (SiMERR 2012b).

Pilot testing of the Standards was considerable (SiMERR 2012a). These pilots were beneficial in providing a 'voice of the profession'; building a framework from which teachers can 'self-reflect' to engage in ongoing professional learning; to provide high-quality teaching and learning experiences; and 'to build a positive public profile of the profession' (Pegg et al. 2010, p. 16).

The development of the Standards follows international practice. Standards are used in Ireland, Northern Ireland, Scotland, England, Finland, the US, Poland, Singapore and New Zealand. They describe 'what student teachers and teachers need to be able to do to be considered competent professionals'. Approaches vary across countries. Where Finland's standards provide a 'light touch' in detail, for example, England is, by contrast, more prescriptive (Caldwell 2012, p. 24).

The Australian Standards provide the basis for a common language about the profession between teachers, teacher educators, teacher organisations, professional associations and the public (AITSL 2011a, p. 2). As one pilot study of teachers in Tasmania found, 'In a national context where the use of Standards over many years has been largely ad hoc ... teachers are ready to embrace a consistent and professional teaching language that can guide teacher, school and system development and planning' (SiMERR 2012b, p. 28). They also reflect a continuum of professional expertise from undergraduate preparation through to being a leader in the profession (Pegg et al. 2010, p. 2). School leaders across sectors noted that the development of Standards helped 'focus their conversations with staff about professional growth. They also felt that this would complement their current processes and that it would be possible to align the standards with their current expectations for staff . . . . It was also seen as a useful beginning for further conversations about teaching practices' (SiMERR 2012b, pp. 32–33).

In developing these standards, a question arises as to how well they reflect the role of teaching in 21st-century contexts. Though important and valuable, it is possible that they perpetuate a view of the profession that is internally focused; that is, they are predicated on a view of teachers and schooling that is to some extent inward looking, without sufficiently engaging changes in the wider landscape of learning and work. (This will be explored in more detail in the following chapter.) Nevertheless, they provide a useful foundation upon which to think about the teaching profession in light of the challenges outlined in Part One of this book. A keystone of this foundation is ITE.

Initial teacher education

The functioning and quality of ITE have been subject to numerous debates about appropriate entry requirements, models of practicum, ITE programmes and alternative programmes that provide entry points into teaching, such as Teach for Australia. There is ongoing discussion of whether universities are exclusively best placed to develop teachers. In its crudest terms, a big part of the discussion concerns whether teachers should be 'trained' in school settings as a form of apprenticeship, and what role (if any) universities should play in the professional education of teachers. The challenge here is to identify and prepare teachers for what my colleagues Simone White and Rachel Forgasz refer to as 'teaching for the future' (White & Forgasz in press). As we shall see, preparing for teaching through practical experience in schools is incredibly valuable but has potential constraints in developing teachers for the changing landscape of schooling and the demands made upon young people post-school. Schooling tends to focus on getting students to completion of Year 12 or equivalent,[1] but could be doing more to develop young people for life beyond the school gates (and beyond higher education). The continuum set out in AITSL's Standards, for example, culminates in the completion of schooling, but to what extent do they take into consideration what happens beyond school? And how well are the dynamics and needs of the contemporary labour market understood by teachers?

In 2011, AITSL specified new standards and procedures for the accreditation of ITE programmes, requiring a minimum two-year qualification for graduate entry programmes throughout Australia (AITSL 2011b).

The Standard, which echoes that used in high-performing systems such as Finland, marks a change in approach to accreditation that phased out the existing model of one-year accreditation. The two-year qualification for graduate entry has been adopted for some time in Finland. Widely recognised internationally for its high-performing education system, Finland has demonstrated success in addressing 'the issues now being faced in Australia such as closing the gap between high- and low-performing students, with observers invariably citing the length, quality and standing of its program' (Caldwell 2012, p. iv). In Finland, teacher education for primary and secondary schools involves a combination of a three-year bachelor's degree and a two-year master's degree. Primary teachers must obtain a master's degree in educational studies, while secondary teachers obtain a master's level qualification in their chosen subject speciality. Finland was an early adopter of the two-year programme, and the master's degree has been required for its teachers since 1979, following reform of its higher education system. Every year of study includes a practicum supervised by university teachers in the first year of study, university-trained school teachers in the second and third years of study, and supervision by local school teachers in the last two years (Niemi & Jakku-Sihvonen 2009).

The one-year graduate approach previously used in Australia was developed over 50 years ago and suited 'an earlier era when most who completed them were intending to become secondary teachers in schools where retention rates to upper levels were low and failure rates high' (Caldwell 2012, p. iv). With Australian teachers working in diverse environments characterised by a range of educational, cultural, social and economic challenges and opportunities, the need to develop richer and more flexible opportunities for ITE is arguably significant in Australia where there is considerable diversity amongst students. The gap between high- and low-performing students according to international measures is also relatively high, despite Australia's relatively good performance overall. As the demands of teachers have become greater and more sophisticated over time, the value of condensing professional knowledge and field study into one year was seen to be untenable (Caldwell 2012). In other parts of the world, such as the US, short-term programmes have been shown to be ineffective. This is not to suggest that alternative routes to teaching do not have value – particularly those offering opportunities to attract recruits to teaching at different stages of life and from a variety of professional backgrounds. But experience in countries such as the US has found alternative certification programmes to be highly variable in quality (Darling-Hammond

2010, p. 37). In addition, research has shown that 'teachers who entered as "lateral entry recruits" without prior teacher preparation, those who lacked certification in the field being taught, and those who were inexperienced' had negative effects on student achievement (Darling-Hammond 2000, p. 39).

Nevertheless, the length of programmes varies considerably throughout the world. The broader practice and research findings on the effectiveness of teacher programmes show them to be highly variable in quality and design (Caldwell 2012; Darling-Hammond 2010). Research has also shown that there is no greater or lesser impact on student achievement if a teacher's academic background has been in education specifically or the subject area taught in school. Linda Darling-Hammond (2000, p. 4) points out that 'comparisons of teachers with degrees in education vs. those with degrees in disciplinary fields have found no relationship between degree type and teacher performance'. Nevertheless, 'research indicates that on average, the distribution of outcomes – in terms of teachers' preparedness, effectiveness, and retention – is significantly more positive among preservice programs than programs that offer less preparation prior to entry' (Darling-Hammond 2010, p. 37).

A wide variety of models for ITE exist in Australia, with about 450 courses offered by 48 institutions in 2014 to around 80,000 teachers (DET 2015a, p. 3). The Australian government mostly funds these. They are diverse but share similar features – aside from recent changes to their duration. They typically include general core units about the practice of teaching, as well as opportunities for developing subject-area knowledge in certain disciplines. They feature opportunities for hands-on experience through in-school practicums, although these have been criticised as being insufficient or inadequate. The 2015 TEMAG report, for example,

> makes it clear that practical in-class experience should give teacher education students the opportunity to connect what they learn at university with real world practice. However, it shows that there is a high degree of variability in the quality of practical experience available. The quality of the placement is influenced by the relationship between universities and schools, as well as the supervising teachers selected to guide and assess teacher education students and how well these teachers are prepared for the role . . . Placements must be supported by highly-skilled supervising teachers who are able to demonstrate and assess what is needed to be an effective teacher. (DET 2015a, p. 7)

The Advisory Group also strongly argued for improved partnerships between universities and schools to enable better practical experience. This kind of approach sees schools and universities as the main repositories of ITE. How adequately placed these institutions are as the central providers of teacher education in the 21st century is discussed in the following chapter.

Why do people want to become teachers? A survey of staff in Australian schools found that early career teachers (i.e. who have been in the profession for less than five years) tend to enter the profession because of a love of teaching, to work with young people, and a desire to contribute to society (McKenzie et al. 2014). The majority of early career teachers are aged 30 or under (64 per cent in primary, 62 per cent in secondary). They enter the profession early in life, often without significant experience in the wider workforce. The largest proportion of survey respondents said the decision to become a teacher was typically made while in school, although significant proportions of early career teachers made the decision while in other employment (28.3 per cent in primary, 31.2 per cent in secondary). It could be argued that entering the workforce at an early stage of working life may influence their outlook and awareness of the wider workforce, shaping not only their perceptions of what is happening post-school but also the kinds of experience that they bring to school settings. That said, a significant proportion of early career teachers are over 40 years of age (13.5 per cent in primary, 16 per cent in secondary) (McKenzie et al. 2014, pp. 89–91).

There have been calls to attract a wider pool of potential teachers from different stages of life and careers. These calls have included the development of more flexible entry requirements for teacher 'training' in Australia by the Productivity Commission (2012, p. 2). In recent years, following approaches developed in the UK and the US, programmes such as Teach for Australia have taken a different approach to ITE. In the Teach for America programme, from which Teach for Australia is derived, high-achieving graduates who have not studied education are recruited and placed in teaching positions after just a few weeks of training. This is based on the premise that subject-area knowledge developed during the other university study is sufficient, and that practical knowledge about the methods of teaching can be taught on the job. But studies have challenged the efficacy of these teachers compared to those who have undergone certified training. One study found that '[o]n all tests, and in both years, the certified teachers out-performed the under-certified novice teachers from Teach for America [TFA]. Our results contradict claims made by TFA advocates that the enthusiasm and subject-matter knowledge, as well as a general education in a prestigious university, prepare these recruits to teach adequately in America's classrooms. The TFA teachers are no better able to teach than any other under-prepared teacher' (Laczko-Kerr & Berliner 2002, p. 41). In some areas, TFA teachers perform worse than teachers educated via traditional university pathways, although they have also been shown to perform relatively well in some areas, while some 'start worse but roughly catch up in later years' (Boyd et al. 2005, p. 24; 2006, p. 202). TFA recruits who gain certification after two to three years fare similarly to their certified counterparts in supporting gains in student achievement; however, most leave within three years (Darling-Hammond et al. 2005; Heilig & Jez 2010). High attrition rates have also been reported within the Australian version of this programme, Teach for Australia. It has been found that around 55 per cent of Teach for Australia associates continued teaching into their third year with an additional 20 per cent pursuing advanced degrees in education (Walters 2012).[2]

Despite this evidence, there is something appealing about learning through hands-on experience, as well as the life-experience that these student teachers bring to classrooms. Teach for America and its equivalents arguably have a role to play in attracting recruits to teaching 'across life stages from various life paths' (Darling-Hammond 2010, p. 37). There is enormous potential here to develop teachers who bring wider experience and knowledge to the classroom, although the research suggests that these models need considerable improvement, particularly in developing teachers who end up staying in schools.

Professional learning and collaboration

Schools are often resistant to new ideas, collaboration and cultures of openness required to reap the benefits of sharing and professional teamwork. Data from the 2008 Teaching and Learning International Survey (TALIS) found that while teachers in Australia reported a relatively common practice of exchanging and discussing teaching material, discussing the development of individual students, attendance at team conferences and ensuring common standards; in contrast to this, professional collaboration through practices such as team teaching, observing other teachers to provide feedback and engaging in professional learning activities was far less common (Jensen et al. 2012, p. 85).

There are also persistent challenges related to the ongoing professional development and learning of teachers. These are arguably significant in understanding how teachers can adapt and evolve to meet the demands of economy and society. Engaging in professional learning 'will be the primary vehicle for ensuring that the practices of schools, school leaders and teachers are continually refreshed in ways that ensure their ongoing effectiveness in promoting the learning that today's and tomorrow's young people will value and need' (Cole 2011, p. 3). Good professional learning involves continuing inquiry into teaching practice, challenging problematic discourses and providing opportunities to interact collaboratively within communities of colleagues and other professionals, including engaging external expertise and professional learning partnerships (Doecke et al. 2008; Mayer & Lloyd 2011; Timperley et al. 2007).

Why do teachers undertake professional learning? Another survey of teachers in schools across all Australian states and territories found that teachers participate in professional learning based on a personal choice from available options (55.2 per cent), a decision by school administration (34.8 per cent) or school administration influenced by external priorities (24 per cent), or a school-based committee (21.7 per cent) (Doecke et al. 2008, p. 88). In terms of the location of the activity, just over 61 per cent respondents did not mind whether the professional learning occurred in school or off-site, but 30.9 per cent preferred the latter. Doecke and colleagues' study found that 'other work priorities taking precedence in the time available' mainly inhibited participation in professional learning, while cost, distance issues and lack of available activities suited to needs also hindered participation (Doecke et al. 2008, p. 112). Most troubling of the findings in this survey was that the change in practice as a result of professional learning was rated as 'significant' by only 23.2 per cent of respondents, compared to 'a bit' by 62.6 per cent and not really by 12.5 per cent (Doecke et al. 2008, p. 109).

While one of Doecke and colleagues' key principles of professional learning is that 'teachers engaged in rich professional learning tend to work together with other teachers to build more dynamic and rigorous learning communities, in which everyone – teachers, students, and parents – can participate' (2008, p. 28), there is arguably wider scope for other actors in the not-for-profit and business sectors to be more involved. But within schools, certain cultural constraints sometimes prevail. Despite the benefits of collaborative working, inherent in schooling is a privatisation of teaching that is characterised by solitary working practices. Cole (2011, p. 13) argues, 'One of the biggest challenges on the road to establishing the school as a rich environment for teacher learning is to "de-privatise" the work of teachers and the results of this work' within schools. This could arguably be extended to how they engage professionals in other sectors.

Professional learning needs to be fostered in schools in a deliberate, focused and systemic way. Schools tend to allocate funds for professional learning in response to individual teacher's requests to attend externally provided professional learning events. Because teachers 'often consider that it is their prerogative to decide whether or not they will participate in professional learning and if they so decide, it is also up to them to determine the focus for their professional learning' (Cole 2011, p. 5). The implication of this is that too often, professional learning is not linked to the broader strategic goals and needs of schools or broader socio-economic contexts in a systematic way. Professional learning is privatised to the detriment of the benefits arising from collegial exchange of ideas and practice, as well as engagement with the wider community. Professional learning needs to address the individual needs of teachers, but within the context of a school's overall priorities and improvement strategies (Cole 2011). Whole school approaches to professional learning are important because 'it is not highly effective individual teachers or pockets of effective practice that change schools, but consistent application of effective teaching practice across the school' (Cole 2011, p. 5). Building on this, linkages of teachers to other professions outside of schools are, however, the exception rather than the norm.

Processes of teacher performance and development, including teacher reviews, also tend to be school based and the responsibility of the school principal. Typically, there is no involvement of external actors in these processes (Marshall et al. 2012). Schools and teachers could be doing much better in linking with the community to provide hands-on and timely, real-world experience to the daily work of teaching and learning.

Valuable approaches to professional learning and development, such as mentoring by more experienced teachers, are important for both new and experienced teachers. But approaches such as mentoring could also be further widened to include community members, such as from the private sector and not-for-profit organisations, which can provide hands-on learning opportunities for teachers. While it is acknowledged that quality hands-on learning experiences are valuable for many students both within school and beyond, these experiences could equally apply to and be extended to teachers. These include the development of soft skills and competencies required by teachers to understand and actively prepare students to navigate contemporary worlds of work.

There is a wider issue of the nature of schools as places that can dynamically respond to change. Reflecting on the challenges of implementing performance measures, for example, Jensen and Reichl suggest that 'the culture within most schools, and school systems, is a long way from one of openness and sharing, continuous learning and high performance – changing this culture will not be easy' (Jensen & Reichl 2012, p. 1).

Teaching for diversity

The macro-challenges outlined in Chapter Two have implications for teachers and their capacity and ability to develop soft skills in students. As Cole observes, 'Globalisation and technological, environmental, social, demographic and economic change and rapid and continuing advances in information communication technologies will place greater demands on, and provide greater opportunities for, young people. These changes will also place greater demands on and opportunities for teachers and school leaders' (2011, p. 3). We shall now briefly examine some of these in relation to teachers.

The diversity of students and their needs poses challenges to the implementation of professional standards such as those provided by AITSL. 'One of the challenges in writing standards for principals', Dinham notes, 'is to capture the sheer diversity of the contexts in which Australian principals can operate – from teaching principals to those heading multi-campus schools, low to high SES, low to high NESB, urban to regional to isolated, struggling to successful schools, government to other systems to independent schools, and so forth' (2011, p. 4).

The need to recognise and respond to the diverse needs of young people is evident throughout the key policy documents such as the *Melbourne Declaration on Educational Goals for Young Australians*, which, for example, recognises that 'Australian students from low socioeconomic backgrounds are under-represented among high achievers and over-represented among low achievers . . . there is room for improvement in Australia's rate of Year 12 completion or equivalent' (MCEETYA 2008, p. 5). Goal one of the Melbourne Declaration includes that Australian schooling promotes equity and excellence, and states that all Australian Governments and school sectors must 'ensure that schools build on local cultural knowledge and experience of Indigenous students' (MCEETYA 2008, p. 7). The National Partnership Agreement on Improving Teacher Quality includes amongst its five outcomes that 'schooling promotes social inclusion and reduces the educational disadvantage of children, especially Indigenous children' (COAG 2008, p. 3).

Social inclusion encompasses a diverse group of young learners. Australians aged 12–24 comprise a richly varied group of people. As we saw earlier in this book, young Australians who were born overseas make up one-fifth of the total population aged 12–24. One in five speaks a language other than English at home. Indigenous young people account for 3.6 per cent of young people aged 15–19 and just under 3 per cent of all people aged 20–24 (Muir et al. 2009, p. 12). Young people have a wide range of abilities and needs and come from diverse socio-economic contexts.

Following on from Chapter Two, demographic change is also having significant impacts on the teaching profession. Many countries currently face a high replacement rate of teachers, with teachers recruited in the most expansive phases of the education system retiring or near retirement (OECD 2008). This trend has been evident over the last 15 years. Countries such as the US, New Zealand and the UK have also experienced significant shortages of teachers in general. In countries such as the US, the issue is not so much that of supply but retention: 'In 2000–01 there was a 15.7 per cent annual turnover of teachers, with 7.3 per cent moving schools and 8.4 per cent leaving the profession. Of those teachers who moved or left the profession, 22 per cent indicated that dissatisfaction was the primary motivating factor, and 40.3 per cent listed "school staffing action", such as lack of professional support, poor leadership as the main factor' (Lonsdale & Ingvarson 2003). The impact of Australia's ageing workforce is pronounced in certain areas of the profession, such as in the area of special needs education (Thomas 2009). Shortages of special education teachers, and teachers in general, are particularly pronounced in rural and remote areas (Hudson & Hudson 2008). These particular areas of shortages are significant in light of the persistent marginalisation from work experienced by young people with disabilities and young people in general who reside in regional and remote areas as discussed in Chapter Two.

In the previous chapter, it was argued that meeting the challenges of a changing global economy and the impact of technology require our students to have a wider set of competencies and employability skills, ranging from problem solving and communication skills (especially oracy) to digital and cultural competencies. These literacies form the building blocks of lifelong learning, which are important to the ability of students to adapt to a shifting workforce in which more than one career will often be undertaken. These skills, as suggested previously, involve 'doing' as well as 'knowing'. In a changing economy, learning how to learn formation is particularly essential to adaptability. A corollary of this is the ability to navigate the vast and often overwhelming amount of information available on the World Wide Web. With the profound impact of technology on young people, some teachers struggle to keep pace with change and expectations of young people about how and where it is used. Consequently, developing digital literacy continues to be central to teachers as well as students.

How we think about proficiency in the educational use of technology by educators is important here, alongside the institutional and cultural barriers they face on a daily basis in educational settings. As with young people, teachers may be competent in using technology, but they are not necessarily *digitally literate*. Where competency involves being able to basically use a device such as a tablet, computer or app, digital literacy involves higher-order skills to critically navigate and evaluate information and technology. It moves beyond basic competency to becoming *creative* in the use of information and a range of digital media and being able to manipulate and use media in new ways.

From my experience as an educator, there appears to be a significant generational difference at times. Worryingly, this difference is characterised by low levels of competency amongst some educators, who continue to grapple with the basic use of platforms like Moodle, and who struggle to integrate digital media into their learning environments. Despite the ubiquity of technology in our society, educators often lack digital literacy in the sense described above. Being able to critically and creatively use digital media opens up all kinds of opportunities, such as through the use of 'flipped classrooms' and the engagement of students with other people across geographic and cultural contexts. It is not suggested that technology should drive teaching and learning – good pedagogy, curriculum and providing rich and diverse learning experiences should always be drivers – but there are many powerful, freely available and relatively easy-to-use tools out there that are arguably underutilised. Sometimes, limited technology usage is in part attributable to factors such as a lack of exposure to effective practice and professional learning, as well as lack of access to suitable and up-to-date equipment, technical support and assistance in a rapidly changing environment. Another delimiting factor goes back to professional learning and development: there needs to be greater emphasis on developing digital literacy during the initial development of educators. Universities and training providers could be doing better at this, although there are undoubtedly pockets of good practice. Given the high degrees of access and relatively inexpensive availability of tools, apps and devices, there is no longer an excuse for educators to be complacent about digital media. The choice *not to use* these tools should be a conscious and deliberate one based on what works best in educational settings. And schools should be aiming for digital literacy to be the base standard – not digital competency.

Cultural and linguistic diversity poses additional challenges to teachers. In Chapter Two, a case was made for improving the development of cultural competencies to navigate this diversity. For teachers, AITSL's

Standards state that a core component of professional knowledge is that '[t]eachers know their students well, including their diverse linguistic, cultural and religious backgrounds' (AITSL 2011a, p. 4). The National Professional Standard for Principals further proposes that they recognise 'the multicultural nature of Australian people', 'foster understanding and reconciliation with Indigenous cultures', 'recognise and use the rich and diverse linguistic and cultural resources in the school community' and 'recognise and support the needs of students, families and carers from communities facing complex challenges' (AITSL 2011c, p. 42). But the challenges of growing up in the Asian century outlined in Chapter Two suggest that much more explicit work needs to be done in not only developing awareness but also in basic areas, such as language instruction. Cultural competency is not only valuable for international engagement; it is also valuable within Australia, particularly in addressing racism in schools and how teachers 'foster engagement with, and partnerships by, local Indigenous communities, and will build positive learning relationships with Indigenous children' (Buckskin, cited in Foley 2013, p. 156).

Teaching for diversity is linked to student achievement in high-performing systems. One dimension of this, native language instruction, is seen as important in countries such as Finland, in contrast to parts of Australia – most notably in the Northern Territory – where changes to policy around the native language instruction continues to be a highly charged issue. In 2009, the Northern Territory government sought to 'dismantle bilingual education by making it mandatory for schools to teach the first four hours in English' (Human Rights Commission 2009, p. 70). By contrast, in 1999 the Indigenous people of Finland Saami (or Sami) gained the right to receive native-language instruction in their comprehensive schooling from Grades 1 to 9. This type of policy reflects the positive research findings that when educating Indigenous children, 'the mother tongue should be the main teaching language for the first eight years' (Caldwell 2012, p. 23). The promotion of intercultural understanding through the development of teachers' knowledge of history and cultural backgrounds is a key focus in Finnish pedagogical studies, as described by Niemi and Jakku-Sihvonen (2006; Caldwell 2012, p. 24). With regard to navigating the challenges of diversity, such as racism in schools, research has suggested that teachers can sometimes be inadvertently part of 'the problem' due to lack of cultural awareness and competency (Mansouri et al. 2009). But contradictory policy inhibits the development of cultural competency and language instruction. This domestic inhibition goes hand in hand with the decline of the instruction of languages relevant to Australia's regional engagement outlined in Chapter Two, in which the teaching of languages such as Indonesian have stagnated or, in some cases, declined. Language instruction provides a core basis for building cultural competency. The problem here is systemic, which in part relates to current curriculum priorities.

Curriculum

Curriculum plays a major role in setting the agenda for what goes on in classrooms and beyond. As discussed in Chapter Two, the Australian Curriculum[3] recognises the need to respond to the labour market conditions outlined in Chapter One. The Australian Curriculum: Work Studies Years 9–10, for example, seeks to address the fact that 'Australian industries and enterprises face unprecedented global competition and pressure for increased productivity. This, in turn, contributes to an unpredictable work future for young people, where routine job opportunities are limited, and outsourcing, contract work and flexible work arrangements are the norm. School leavers can no longer anticipate a single job or single-track career for a lifetime and will be encountering jobs which currently do not exist' (ACARA undated). In response, Work Studies Years 9–10, an applied learning curriculum, was developed to adapt discipline-based learning to work contexts (ACARA 2013a).

The delivery of curriculum by teachers in classrooms is where 'the rubber hits the road'. As Allan Luke (2010, p. 59) has argued, curriculum 'comes to ground via an enacted curriculum of teaching and learning events "lived" by students and teachers'. Luke rightly argues for 'visible connections of school knowledge to everyday civic, cultural, political and social life' (p. 61), which has salience here as the true value and impact of the Australian Curriculum's capabilities reside in how teachers provide opportunities for enabling these connections to be made in relevant, efficacious ways. As I will argue in Chapter Six, there is greater scope for making these connections beyond the school walls. Making these connections is important to the development of adversity capital.

Insecurity in the teaching workforce

Insecurity in the workforce is by means confined to young people. Alongside the challenges to the teaching workforce outlined throughout this discussion is the precarity experienced by many qualified teachers. In 2014, for example, it was reported that over 44,000 qualified teachers were not able to secure a permanent job in New South Wales alone

(McDougall 2014). Many of those who are employed – particularly new teachers – are on fixed-term contracts. A 2014 survey of new teachers found, for example, that two-thirds of Victorian government school teachers were employed on short-term contracts in their first five years of teaching. There are signs of improvement: though 65 per cent were on fixed contracts, this figure reflected an increase of 10 per cent on the previous year (AEU 2014).

This insecurity is global in nature. An OECD analysis of TALIS in 2008 notes, 'A concern in many countries is the contractual status of new teachers' (Jensen et al. 2012, p. 89). While just under 85 per cent teachers enjoy secure and even permanent employment across TALIS 2008 countries, 11 per cent of teachers were employed on contracts for one school year or less, while 4.5 per cent were on contracts for more than one school year. The analysis identified 'a concern for many teachers who lack the job security that is prevalent throughout the teaching profession. Short-term contracts can affect teachers' effectiveness not only through heightened anxiety from being employed on fixed-term contracts but also from the practicalities of having to seek new employment on a continual basis. Job searching is a time-consuming activity that can detract from teachers' responsibilities and reduce their commitment and attachment to their school' (Jensen et al. 2012, p. 89). Echoing the Australian experience, far more new teachers were employed on fixed-term contracts than experienced teachers – 45 per cent of new teachers on average compared to 88 per cent of experienced teachers (Jensen et al. 2012, p. 89).

This demoralising trend has potentially profound implications. Teachers are driven by a deep moral purpose in what they do (Hopkins 2008, p. 33). They want to make a difference in their students' lives. The moral purpose of teaching underpins the working life of teachers. Leaders have a critical role in defining and shaping this purpose in school settings. Citing Canadian research, Timperley (2011, p. 15) writes: '[T]he strongest leaders had an expansive view of the kind of education they wanted for young people in their schools and all their activities were accompanied by an intensive moral purpose in achieving this.' Teachers' development and professional learning involves 'the process by which, alone and with others, teachers review, renew and extend their commitment as change agents to the moral purposes of teaching and by which they acquire and develop critically the knowledge, skills and emotional intelligence essential to good professional thinking, planning and practice with children, young people and colleagues through each phase of their teaching lives' (Day & Sachs cited in Mayer & Lloyd 2011, pp. 2–3).

But what happens if the moral purpose of teaching is challenged by a profession that is undervalued, underpaid and sometimes precarious? Moreover, school leaders are constrained by regulatory frameworks in determining the contractual length of their staff. Additionally, what if the profession is misaligned with the needs of students in an increasingly fluid world? The development of adversity capital is consequently as important in teachers, not only to shape how they teach students but also to prepare themselves for working life as a teacher.

Conclusion

Schools and teachers often have near-impossible demands made upon them. They are not only responsible for striving for excellence in teaching and learning but also for a range of other social and cultural challenges. Teachers routinely simultaneously assume the role of counsellor, mentor and parent-by-proxy. They are tasked with addressing wider societal challenges of equity, social cohesion and inclusion. In cash-strapped settings, they must be increasingly entrepreneurial, adaptive and responsive to change.

Positive steps have been taken in recent years in how we think about teaching as a profession, and the ways in which teachers develop and learn across the professional life cycle. In connecting ITE and the professional learning and practise of teachers to the wider challenges faced by young people, this chapter has attempted to push even further how we think about teaching and professional learning beyond conventional settings (i.e. schools and classrooms). The challenge for the profession going forward is to move beyond a historical frame in which conventional approaches are based on industrial models of schooling and particular ways of working within schools that inhibit ongoing professional learning and collaboration.

Commensurate with broader changes to the workforce, teaching for post-industrial economies as a profession will be characterised by the need for greater flexibility, adaptive practice and working beyond the conventional boundaries of the school gates. As Timperley argues, 'Traditional notions of professionalism based on industrial models have been replaced by more flexible notions of successful teachers and leaders being adaptive experts who work in schools which have a high adaptive capacity.' Adaptive experts 'are flexible in their responses to new challenges' and 'constantly review their practice for its effectiveness in a given circumstance and seek new knowledge and skills to meet emerging challenges . . . Teachers need to develop a diverse range of capabilities which they can bring to bear to address the specific needs of particular individuals and groups of students to master new curriculum, new technology, new environmental, social and economic understandings and the intersections and interconnections between them' (Timperley 2011, pp. 1–3). These capabilities are not dissimilar to the features of adversity capital outlined in the previous chapter.

By extension, it is argued that school leaders 'need to create schools that foster inquiry in ways that lead to high levels of adaptive capacity' (Timperley 2011, p. 20). Again, adaptive capacity is a core feature of adversity capital, which needs to be developed in leaders and teachers, as well as students.

And while there is no single 'what works' approach to professional learning and development across diverse settings (Mayer & Lloyd 2011), pushing the boundaries of what constitutes these and where they take place may be necessary to make schooling more relevant and aligned with contemporary challenges and opportunities. With a deepening understanding of young people's wellbeing and the need for broader metrics around student outcomes beyond literacy and numeracy, a shift also has to take place in how professional development impacts the intellectual, spiritual, physical, moral, social and cultural wellbeing of students. Accordingly, 'It is no longer acceptable for professionals in schools to do their individual best. Rather, it is expected that they will engage collectively with what is known to be effective in improving outcomes for all students' (Timperley 2011, p. 1).

The growing complexity of the role of teachers and school leaders raises the question of whether their tasks and expectations can be articulated within a single profession. Commensurate with this shift towards a post-industrial architecture of schooling is the reality that '[t]he world is also no longer divided into specialists and generalists' (Schleicher 2012, p. 34). Schleicher (2012, p. 35) describes a key implication of this shift:

> The goal of the past was standardization and conformity, today it is about being ingenious, about personalising educational experiences; the past was curriculum centred, the present is learner centred, which means that education systems increasingly need to identify how individuals learn differently and foster new forms of educational provision that take learning to the learner and allow individuals to learn in the ways that are most conducive to their progress.

These challenges suggest a need to rethink the professional identity of teachers. It could be that, in future, the profession as a whole will undergo significant changes in its composition, with new areas of expertise forming in areas such as school partnership brokers. In the longer term, it is not difficult to imagine that all schools might have the equivalent of a dedicated chief operating officer who is skilled in bringing the organisational pieces together within school communities of the 21st century. Some may feel discomfort at this kind of corporatised model; however, as complex organisations with equally complex expectations, different organisational models will need to be developed to meet the challenges confronting schools and society.

It is also argued here that adversity capital needs to be more explicitly taught in schools. Schools routinely promote certain graduate attributes. These invariably feature some soft skills and competencies implicitly taught – but more systematic and explicit efforts are arguably needed. And how aligned and purposeful are teaching and learning in those institutions to developing those attributes? Are they measured? Should they be measured? And can they be measured?

A final point is given that young people value hands-on learning, in what ways can we embed opportunities for hands-on learning of these skills through meaningful and sustainable community and industry partnerships? Schools could more explicitly engage with developing these skills and providing opportunities for teaching and learning in the community, with industry and within the world at large. Where some are doing this well, we need to find ways of making good practice, common practice. These themes are explored in the next chapter.

6
Beyond the School Gates: Are Our Education Institutions Obsolete?

In Chapter Four, an argument was made for a more explicit development of soft skills, such as problem solving, communication and cultural competency. One challenge for educators is to more explicitly develop these literacies, alongside numeracy and literacy, in ways that meaningfully connect with the everyday lives of young people and their contemplation of current and future working lives. This is not the sole responsibility of career advisers and counsellors: all teachers and educational leaders play an important role in ensuring that the development of these skills is embedded in all parts of teaching and learning and in ways that purposefully engage students and school staff.

In the previous chapter, it was argued that thinking about teachers and teaching tends to be confined to the learning that takes places within schools. Schools often operate in isolation, and the professional learning of teachers is in some ways scattered and disconnected from the realities of contemporary working life. At a deeper level is the question of whether key conventional schooling in its current forms is capable of meeting the challenges of 21st-century working life. The fluidity of labour markets suggests a need to re-examine schooling and its connection to what happens post-school in equipping young people with the knowledge, skills and dispositions to learn and adapt to the challenges of the contemporary labour force.

As suggested in Chapter Five, with conventional pathways from school to the life beyond relying on industrial models of education, much of what takes place in schools has not significantly changed during the last century. In an increasingly post-industrial society, preparing young people requires new approaches and relationships with external actors, alongside existing approaches that seek to build capabilities relevant to the 21st-century workforce.

There is a diverse range of programmes, organisations and individuals seeking to develop these soft skills, although they generally operate across a range of locations and often in isolation from each other. Some work within the existing curriculum frameworks, while others provide alternative education programmes. Non-governmental organisations are doing some important work to develop approaches that integrate support with soft skills, vocational training and work experience, aimed at highly disadvantaged groups. These approaches could be generalised or 'mainstreamed'.

This chapter argues that schools still tend to concentrate on learning within classroom settings, rather than taking a wider view of learning that takes place formally, informally and non-formally beyond the school gates. In addition, schooling tends to focus on getting students to completion of Year 12 or equivalent without sufficient understanding of, and alignment with, what comes after school. Despite widespread recognition of the importance of lifelong learning, schools could be doing more to prepare young people for life post-school. They could also be doing more to connect learning to worlds of work beyond the school gates. This is becoming all the more significant as the world of work for young people is changing in relation to previous generations.

The following discussion looks at recent efforts to reappraise where learning takes place. It argues for deepening and extending professional dialogue between teachers, school leaders and wider professional communities. Following on from Chapter Five, the emerging landscape requires a rethinking of how teachers engage both local and global environments. This applies not only to how they respond to learner-centred approaches but also to how they are trained both to enter the profession and across the teaching life cycle as discussed in Chapter Five.

A driving question throughout this final part of the discussion is: how relevant is teaching, learning and schooling to current thinking about how we best prepare young people for working life in the 21st century? Within the context of schooling in Australia, there have been a number of recent efforts to better connect students to worlds of work, but it is argued that more systemic approaches could be developed. Through these connections, young people need to be encouraged to harness these soft skills and literacies actively throughout school and other contexts. Just as importantly, they should foster meaningful connections between these contexts inside and outside of school.

This chapter explores how schools could better facilitate these connections. Partnerships with corporations and not-for-profit organisations are seen as a way of providing more direct links. With governments seriously considering greater corporate involvement in public schools, this chapter outlines some cautionary tales to highlight both the benefits and potential challenges to the public purposes of schooling. Opportunities for such participation could better equip young people for working life. The development of essential literacies and competencies through these connections could improve their capacity to navigate changing worlds of work and life in general.

Reappraising where learning takes place

Throughout the world, there has been a renewed shift towards thinking about where and how student learning should take place in ways that enable students to link conceptual thinking to their own experiences, and through learning that relates to the individual learner and her or his needs.

European policy has suggested a need 'to extend and broaden learning opportunities for young people as a whole, including supporting the acquisition of skills through non-formal educational activities' (European Commission 2010, p. 4). According to the European Commission, 'Smart and inclusive growth depends on actions throughout the lifelong learning system, to develop key competencies and quality learning outcomes, in line with labour market needs' (2010, p. 3). Exploring avenues of non-formal and informal learning have been seen to be increasingly important in addressing the challenges of youth employment following the GFC. The recognition of skills acquired through learning activities within these contexts has been a priority in recent years. Volunteering and the promotion of 'apprenticeship-type vocational training and high quality traineeships as workplace learning experiences, [and] building bridges to the labour market' form part of a wider push to connect learning to 'real-world' experiences (European Commission 2010, p. 4).

The OECD has argued for greater attention to educational practice in which

> the learning environment recognises that the learners in them are the core participants. A learning environment oriented around the centrality of learning encourages students to become 'self-regulated learners'. This means developing the 'meta-cognitive skills' for learners to monitor, evaluate and optimise their acquisition and use of knowledge . . . It also means to be able to regulate one's emotions and motivations during the learning process. (Dumont et al. 2010, p. 14)

The Centre for Educational Research and Innovation's (CERI) Innovative Learning Environments project explored the role of emotions, technology, collaborative learning and organisational routines as a way of embedding learning in daily practice (OECD 2012b). It is argued that effective learning environments encourage student engagement and where learners come to understand themselves as learners. That learning is social and often collaborative is emphasised in this approach, as well as being attuned to learners' motivations and recognising the importance of emotions (Istance 2011, pp. 5–6). Learning environments are learner-centred, that is, highly focused on learning as the principal activity and personalised with the learning environment acutely sensitive to individual and group differences in background, prior knowledge, motivation and abilities. The Innovative Learning Environments project also worked from the assumption that learning is effective when it takes place in group settings, where learners can collaborate and when there is a connection to community (Istance 2011, p. 6). This connection to community is important, as we shall see below.

This focus on learner ownership is not new and is evident in high-performing systems. That learners have strong agency and influence in learning and learning environments has, for example, been promoted by The Finnish National Board of Education (Finnish National Board of Education 2011). It has also been promoted in other conceptual approaches such as Cisco's 'Education 3.0' approach, which seeks to draw from

the insights of learners themselves who, for the most part, have [previously] been treated as the objects rather than subjects in the process of learning. It takes into consideration the progressive development of the learner through stages of schooling and beyond, as well as different levels of understanding. Meta-cognitive skills are central so that learners can identify, challenge and understand the preferred ways of learning. Emphasis is placed on skills and concepts rather than specific content. It is argued that learning needs to be purposeful and provide depth of understanding and application whilst not being crowded by content. Nevertheless, while a significant part of learning is skills/thinking based, content of course, remains important. Learning opportunities involving co-construction and deep engagement by learners pay enormous dividends in terms of improved outcomes. (Hannon et al. 2011, p. 13)

Hannon et al. (2011, p. 3) provide the characteristics of learning ownership: 'Schools which harness the power of learner ownership to transform their approach to teaching and learning are likely to feature more project- or enquiry-based learning, greater and more meaningful student voice, and peer-to-peer teaching and mentoring.'

Soft skills are implicit in these approaches. Cisco Global Education, for example, recognises the importance of thinking skills, such as problem solving, synthesising evidence and constructing an argument and non-cognitive ones, such as resilience and persistence, which are often developed beyond school gates (Cisco Systems Inc 2010).

This work is largely speculative, but points to an *attitude* to learning that places the learner at the centre alongside a potentially more outward-looking ethos, in which non-school actors play a larger role in education. It suggests an expanded landscape of schooling and education that urges educators to find ways to work more in partnership with community and non-school actors, such as business and not-for-profit sectors, to address entrenched problems and improve student outcomes.

As with mass education systems elsewhere in the world, Australian schools have to do more with fewer resources, and partnerships are seen as a way of leveraging opportunities to build capacity. They can also provide work experience and develop skills in schools to more effectively get work (CCIQ 2011; FYA 2014; in the US context, see Casner-Lotto & Barrington 2006).

These approaches suggest possibilities for an extension of the educational landscape beyond conventional institutions, such as schools. To understand this landscape, it is useful to think of schools and school systems as ecological in nature; that is, that they are made up of numerous factors, discourses and forces that interact in complex ways to influence the nature of school practice. One approach proposes an analogy of mass education as a kind of platform or reef upon which a range of actors and stakeholders interact in a learning ecology or ecosystem (Hannon et al. 2011). According to this model, the conventional notion of the school as an organisation that works in isolation gives way to one in which the school becomes a 'base-camp' from which educators engage with other key actors and stakeholders to improve student outcomes, adopting more flexible and adaptive modes of practice and building their school's capacity to work beyond the conventional boundaries of the school gates. Within this model, 'system leaders need to reposition themselves so that rather than being primary providers of education, they provide a platform for a diversity of providers' (Hannon et al. 2011, pp. 2–3).

Schools can be understood as the products of both macro- and micro-ecologies. As Eggleston (2012, p. 109) suggests, 'The ecology of the school and the creation, distribution and use of resources that determines it is clearly a partnership between all who live and work within it.' Vertical and horizontal forces shape these ecologies. Vertical forces and discourses include state, national or international policies and initiatives that are transmitted through education systems, such as AITSL's Australian Professional Standard for Principals. The model included in the Standard describes the context in which leaders operate across school, sector, community and education systems at local, regional, national and global levels respectively. It also emphasises the importance of school leaders being 'always fully interdependent, integrated and with no hierarchy implied' (AITSL 2011c, p. 5). The Standard recognises that excellent leaders 'engage with families and carers, and partner, where appropriate, with community groups, agencies and individuals, businesses or other organisations to enhance and enrich the school and its value to the wider community' (AITSL 2011c, p. 11).

Central to these practices are school community partnerships. In Australia, the importance of school community partnerships has received increasing interest by recent federal and state governments. The Council of Australian Governments (COAG), for example, promoted the National Partnership Agreement, which sought to empower local schools and improve school leadership through community engagement. Some 1,000 government and non-government schools were invited to participate in Phase One of the National Partnership Agreement on Empowering Local Schools in 2012 and 2013 (DEEWR 2013). Another initiative commissioned by the former Gillard government, the Business–School Connections Roundtable, sought input from a range of actors including the Australian Business and Community Network; IBM Australia; Microsoft Australia; Rio Tinto Australia; Principals Australia; Woolworths; the Foundation for Young Australians and Macquarie Group Foundation. It identified a number of opportunities for businesses to contribute as a partner with education institutions at a strategic level through 'more significant school–business relationships'. Other forms of engagement proposed included 'adding value' to the implementation of the Australian Curriculum and supporting improved school retention through work experience (DEEWR 2011, pp. 34–40).

Vertical engagement is also increasingly visible at the state level. In Victoria, for example, the Department of Education and Training (formerly the Department of Education and Early Childhood Development) identified 'the importance of partnerships in the learning community and commits to removing barriers and facilitating such arrangements in future' (DEECD 2013, p. 8). In the Australian Capital Territory, the Department has undertaken a range of community engagement activities through community consultation processes, stakeholder relations and community partnership programmes aligned with the government's *Community Engagement* initiative (ACT Government 2011).

Policy initiatives such as these and AITSL's Standards reflect a broader international recognition of the need to elevate the capacity of schools to engage in *horizontal* engagement through partnerships with other actors beyond the classroom. Such partnerships feature in high-performing systems. Schooling policy in Finland, for example, identifies parent and community engagement as a priority and the development of new partnerships is recognised as a key component of educational innovation (Finnish National Board of Education 2011). As part of teacher development, pedagogical studies include 'how to cooperate with other teachers, parents and other stakeholders' (Niemi 2011, p. 46), and there is a wider value placed on the 'ability of teachers to communicate with . . . families and other stakeholders . . . as an essential part of teacher competence' (Niemi & Jakku-Sihvonen 2006, p. 57). Caldwell notes the complexities in teachers' communication with parents and the community within Finnish schooling: 'They have to be aware of opportunities and ways to work together with other partners and stakeholders in formal and non-formal educational contexts in order to provide learning opportunities to learners at various age levels. They also need to be aware of value contradictions in society and educational institutions and they should be prepared to deal with moral and value-based issues' (Niemi & Jakku-Sihvonen 2006, cited in Caldwell 2012, p. 23). The quality and degree of community support for schools in Finland has been linked to its high performance in student achievement (Caldwell 2012, p. 18).

At the micro-level, these horizontal relationships and discourses generally arise within the specific context of the local community (although technology potentially enables them to take place anywhere). These depend on the nature and needs of the community served by the school, and may include business, parents and carers. They also include brokers, funders, social entrepreneurs and other actors and stakeholders who are seeking to work with schools and teachers to improve student outcomes. Examples of brokers in Australia include organisations such as National Australia Bank's (NAB) *Schools First* programme, the Australian Business and Community Network and Social Ventures Australia (SVA). Providers include organisations such as Asia Education Foundation, The Smith Family, Beacon Foundation, High Resolves Initiative, The Song Room, Ardoch Youth Foundation, Hands on Learning, the International Baccalaureate and Teach for Australia. Funders include not-for-profit organisations such as the Business Working with Education Foundation, the Foundation for Young Australians and the R.E. Ross Trust. Partnerships such as 'Assessment and Teaching of 21st Skills' (jointly enabled by Microsoft, Cisco and Intel) have also been increasingly influential, as are research organisations such as the Australian Council of Educational Research and the Grattan Institute.

All of these organisations are part of the complex ecosystem in which schools increasingly operate. A growing number of schools are forming partnerships with or through such organisations, both to improve student outcomes and for the benefits that they bring in the form of knowledge, human and capital resources. These include in-kind support in the form of business expertise, opportunities for teachers to increase their skills through professional placement and collaboration and the provision of facilities. For many of these schools, a major incentive to undertake these partnerships is the reality that, as suggested above, they have to 'do more with less'. This necessity arises throughout the world in comparable education systems, such as those in the UK.

One immediate area in which partnerships could be better used is in careers education. Career advisers at school can help with successful transitions, and informed advice is seen by students to be useful (Rothman & Hillman 2008). However, careers education tends to be variable in quality and accessibility (Tatham & McIlveen 2009). Within schools, career counselling has had limited effect for a number of reasons. Firstly, it is often located at the periphery of school life and is often an 'add-on' to the curriculum. This can be seen physically in the ways that careers education is often located within schools. I have seen schools in Victoria in which the space provided for students to learn about work is physically located out of the way from daily school traffic, often in areas occupied by final year students. This can be intimidating to younger students and sends a message to the wider school population that thinking about work happens towards the end of schooling. Any chance for students (arguably at any age) to see the possibilities for what lies beyond schooling can be valuable, and yet this is often deferred until subject-area pathways have already been determined. Careers advisers themselves may lack a wider awareness and experience of the current workforce and assume the demanding role alongside regular teaching duties. The work of advisers is typically internally focused and based within schools, delimiting opportunities for students to see what worlds of work look like. It is here that non-school actors such as not-for-profits and business could play a greater role. They can provide practical and relevant advice and experience to students and teachers. That schools could benefit from external partners is not confined to careers education. There are wider benefits and challenges, which are outlined below.

Recent policy efforts to address to address some of these issues include the National Career Development Strategy of the ALP government (2007–13), which directed AU$6.1 million funding to support *Making Career Connections* projects, aimed to 'equip students with the skills and knowledge to make effective career decisions' (Garrett 2013, p. 1). These projects sought to connect young people to working environments and develop the skills required to navigate them. The Liberal National coalition government that succeeded the ALP government proposed a different approach, as examined in Chapter Three – we shall return to this in the Conclusion.

Opening the school gates

In countries such as Australia, the landscape of schooling is shifting towards an environment in which schools are increasingly seeking ways to work with community actors and stakeholders to address entrenched challenges to improve student outcomes. As Michael Fullan (2000, p. 5) suggests, 'Schools need the outside to get the job done. These external forces, however, do not come in helpful packages; they are an amalgam of complex and uncoordinated phenomena. The work of the school is to figure out how to make its relationship with them a productive one.'

As discussed in the previous chapter, the culture of teachers in schools can also inadvertently be a powerful barrier to change. We have seen that the culture within many schools and school systems is not necessarily characterised by openness, professional co-operation and continuous learning (Jensen & Reichl 2012; Jensen et al. 2012). The privatisation of teaching practices echoes the ways that schools are often inward looking. Schools face a number of challenges and constraints in opening their gates to the wider community, which will be discussed below.

The vertical misalignment of policy and practice

There is arguably a misalignment of some education policy to school practice. Where education policy may be concerned with universal, national and international issues and priorities, schools tend to be shaped by and concerned with their specific local context, including the school culture, history and community context (Rawolle & Lingard 2008; Thomas 2008; Thomson 2009). This local context is typically less stable and more complex and nuanced than the policy field that seeks to shape it (Ball 1994; Blackmore 2010). These need to be more closely linked; however, instability between these contexts can create challenges and disconnections between macro-(vertical) agendas and the more dynamic (horizontal) microcosm of daily school life. And education policy is not necessarily 'delivered, in tablets of stone, to a grateful or quiescent audience' (Ozga 2000, p. 1). It is subject to an ongoing reinterpretation and recontextualisation at the level of the school through which school leaders interpret policy in the light of their own knowledge, values and daily experience.

Leaders also face an increasing responsibility to manage a range of policies, actors and stakeholders. While the need for schools to increase capacity through engagement with the community is now recognised as a key feature of the 21st-century education landscape, the capacity of many schools to do this is limited by a lack of experience in working with these wider actors. There is a case here for rethinking what constitutes 'school leadership'. School leaders not only include those who hold formal leadership positions but may also include 'those who exercise influence within and across schools' (Timperley 2011, p. 4). They consciously intermesh leadership within the school community (Fullan 2005; Levin 2008; Timperley 2011). Leadership is predicated on the notion that 'an education leader promotes the success of every student by collaborating with faculty and community members, responding to diverse community interests and needs and mobilising community resources' (Dempster et al. 2011, p. 16). Many also actively incorporate input from students (Walsh & Black 2011). Despite recognition of the importance of this broad leadership approach, there is a real need to develop a better understanding of how school leaders need to be equipped in order to work effectively with the community and the range of other stakeholder groups now involved in schooling (Dinham 2011).

Opening up the business of schooling

Challenges also arise outside of the school. At the level of horizontal engagement, the need for greater involvement of sectors not traditionally involved in the shaping or delivery of formal education creates challenges around the different ways that schools and external organisations work and their differing expectations of the purposes and outcomes of education. The recent history of business involvement and engagement in schools, for example, has suffered from a mixed and sometimes contradictory set of purposes. The idea of corporate engagement with public schools in Australia is not new. It has been on government agendas and practised by individual schools for some time. But a few cautionary tales from the last 20 years are worth noting.

A 2012 report by the Productivity Commission on the Schools Workforce identified the need to develop strategies to enhance engagement between schools and the business community. 'In particular', suggested the Commission, 'equipping teachers and principals with appropriate skills and giving them the scope and incentive to employ those skills, will go a considerable way to meeting the engagement goals enunciated . . . by the Business–School Connections Roundtable' (Productivity Commission 2012, p. 323).

As outlined above, that Roundtable identified opportunities for business to contribute to education reform as a partner with education at a strategic level by 'adding value' to the implementation of the Australian Curriculum, through trade cadetships and trade-training centres, work experience and via new pathways into teaching by 'adding value' to Teach for Australia and Teach Next. Success to date has been mixed. Teach Next, a Commonwealth-funded programme intended to bring the expertise of non-teaching professions into the schoolroom, was notable for initially attracting more than 500 applicants, but reportedly managing to recruit only 14 new teachers during a two-year period (DEEWR 2011).

At the micro-level of horizontal engagement, individual-level school–business partnerships have been around for some time. In Victoria, for example, Coles Supermarkets ran a promotion in conjunction with Apple during the 1990s in which students and their parents who amassed a certain amount in purchases from the supermarket chain were eligible for a 'free' Macintosh computer. More recently, the National Australia Bank's *Schools First* programme attempted to recognise school community partnerships seeking to deliver improved educational outcomes for students. This corporate rewarding of public schools and teachers (who seldom get national recognition) was unprecedented and the level of financial investment by the bank was substantial.

Perhaps the most ambitious initiative was the AU\$47 million per year Schools–Business Community Partnership Brokers programme – which acted as an intermediary to foster links between schools and business. An evaluation of the programme by SVA identified a range of benefits. Schools could, for example, take advantage of external skills and resources to free up existing school resources. They could also broaden professional networks to provide career opportunities for students (SVA 2013).

But some efforts to forge school–business partnerships have led to dubious practices. For example, during the 1990s, McDonald's restaurants sponsored sports activities in schools across New South Wales. The restaurant displayed its logos at sports events, and the schools were encouraged to establish personal relations with local store representatives by inviting them to speech nights and fairs. Students, school staff and parents were encouraged to eat at certain outlets during 'McHappy hours'. In return, ten per cent of earnings were given to the school. At that time, *Time* magazine reported that a hoax letter was allegedly sent around schools advising principals that all school names would have the prefix 'Mc' and teachers would henceforth be referred to as 'crew members' (Cole-Adams 1993, p. 53).

Other cautionary tales of business involvement in schools include Whittle Communications, which provided resources to the US public schools such as TV and satellite dish sets through corporate advertising. In return, over 90 per cent of the nearly eight million students attending these schools were required to watch a news programme each day that included advertising by Snickers and Burger King. Reportedly earning $630,000 a day, this advertising was, by contract, required viewing (Kozol 1993).

Around the same time during the 1990s, Burger King Academies – quasi-private and fully accredited high schools – operated in at least 14 cities of the US. Companies such as Education Alternatives also ran public schools for profit. The corporation's president observed that 'it's open season on marketing' (Kozol 1993, p. 8). Critics at that time rightly asked: what is more dangerous, the products advertised or the brand of attitude that is espoused? Kozol is wary of a corporate inclination to sell 'predictability instead of critical capacities. It sells a circumscribed, job-specific utility' (Kozol 1993, p. 10).

On the other hand, another benefit of partnerships identified by the SVA evaluation cited above was that partnerships could align school activities with industry needs. This claim echoes the concerns by the International Labour Organisation of a global mismatch between skills and jobs, as described in the Introduction of this book and Chapter Three. While education systems are seen to be failing to adequately prepare students for changing job markets, the question again arises as to whether an emphasis on skills-alignment to industry could risk schools becoming too focused on meeting market demand. Schooling should be about the development of well-rounded individuals capable of critical thinking, but focusing too much on labour force readiness might reduce education exclusively to 'training'. Nevertheless, businesses could be doing more to train young people on the job. Post-school and in work, businesses in the US are offering fewer training opportunities than in the 1970s and as we saw earlier in this book, it is argued that this is a key area in which skills development could be improved in Australia as well (Cappelli 2012; *The Economist* 2013b).

There is also a question of whether business strategic plans can be aligned to the long-term goals of schooling. In June 2014, Australian Prime Minister Abbott mooted the idea that Australia could follow one American model of schools partnering with major companies. He had recently visited the Pathways in Technology Early College High School in New York, which in partnership with IBM enables students to graduate with a high school diploma and an associate's degree (Hurst 2014). Forming direct links between companies and school/training facilities, and deciding which areas of industry are worthy of partnerships, is challenging given the changing nature of industry in Australia. The closure of major car manufacturers in South Australia and Victoria during the last several years stands as an example of how significantly an industrial base can change.

Business strategies, like policy agendas, are subject to change in ways that delimit the kinds of long-term investment required to impact upon educational ecologies. For example, the final Schools First awards were given in 2014, and following the 2014 Federal Budget, funding of the School–Business Community Partnership Brokers programme ended later that year. There is a related issue of matching the life cycles of policy with those of business. It has been reported that

> Companies are constantly redesigning work – for example they are separating routine tasks (which can be automated or contracted out) from skilled jobs. They are also constantly redesigning themselves by 'upsizing', 'downsizing' and 'contracting out'. The life expectancy of companies is declining, as is the job tenure of chief executives. Policymakers are finding it more difficult to adapt their labour-market institutions quickly enough. (*The Economist* 2013b)

Another challenge is to ensure that equity is maintained where there is no market incentive to do so. That said, there is a wealth of expertise that business can offer schools. Businesses can provide opportunities for hands-on learning – for both students and teachers. But in the longer-term, there is a need for greater consistency of quality in the role of business in schooling, requiring mechanisms to improve the compatibility and fit between what schools need and what business offers, and to match appropriate companies with schools.

Where recent practice has been dominated by businesses making occasional forays into schools for specific activities, longer-term and sustainable commitment has yet to be demonstrated. Such commitment would need a regulatory framework to ensure that the public good of schooling is maintained. Part of this framework could ensure that schools in high-need areas and circumstances have access to the support of business. These schools tend to lack the readiness and internal capacity for business involvement. Any strategy to deepen or extend the role of business in schools should include a better mechanism for the distribution of this involvement; otherwise, it could inadvertently serve to reinforce existing discrepancies and inequities in disadvantaged communities. Better training to schools in selecting and establishing corporate partnerships that meet ethical guidelines and avoid overt commercialism would also need to be developed. More broadly, training for both schools and companies in bridging the cultural gaps that exist between the sectors and, in particular, for companies in working with schools in high-need areas, would also be valuable (Walsh et al. 2009). In recent years, frameworks have been developed to guide business–school relations that emphasise the importance of alignment between the goals and practices of business–school partnerships (PhillipsKPA Pty Ltd 2010), but there is some way to go in moving from aspiration to material reality.

The third sector

As we have found, the not-for-profit sector has also brokered and directly enabled opportunities for schools and their students to develop soft skills and be exposed to working life. Programmes by organisations such as the Foundation for Young Australians' Worlds of Work,[1] Ardoch Youth Foundation, Beacon Foundation, the Australian Business and Community Network and Hands on Learning are examples of how a range of actors can enable schools, teachers and students to be more closely connected to labour force developments in the wider world. They offer programmes that provide young people with hands-on experience and skills to navigate the contemporary labour force. But evidence of their long-term impact and wider scalability is scarce and much needed.

The philanthropic sector could also play a greater role in funding innovation and research. Research conducted in Australia during the last 15 years suggests a burgeoning will amongst foundations to support multi-component policy solutions (Black 2008, 2009). These may include solutions with a strongly place-based focus. The sector also has an innate independence from the policy sphere that could make it suitable to fund 'risky' or change-leading projects. Similarly, it has the capacity to create a politically neutral space within which diverse or even adversarial groups can be drawn together in pursuit of common causes.

Parents

Parents, and their engagement with their children, are incredibly powerful influences on student outcomes (Gemici et al. 2014). The incremental impact of parental education levels, for example, is striking. In 2009, the early leaving rate for 15- to 24-year-olds whose both parents had completed Year 12 was just 15 per cent. Where only one parent had completed Year 12, the rate of early leaving more than doubled to 33.8 per cent. Where neither parent had attained Year 12, more than three times as many young people (45.1 per cent) left school early. Perhaps unsurprisingly, a similar pattern emerges in relation to the employment status of parents. Where both parents were unemployed, the 2009 rate of early school leaving was much higher (35.4 per cent) than in families in which both parents were working (24.7 per cent) (Robinson et al. 2010, p. 42).

Efforts to engage parents in the daily work of schools and in building adversity capital could have a powerful impact on young people and the schools in which they learn. The testimonies of young people themselves illustrate family influences that, at times, cut across normative trends. In one report, a young woman describes a home environment that encouraged her engagement in higher or further education despite her parents' experience: 'My mum didn't finish high school, she dropped out in about Year 10. Dad finished high school and that was all. My dad always said he wished he'd studied further and he never did, so he wanted us to have the opportunities that he didn't, I suppose' (Robinson et al. 2010, p. 43). A young man in the same report describes a family experience that not only echoes the data in relation to young people but also shows educational mobility amongst their parents, which suggests that normative assumptions about adult education patterns may also overlook variations in individual experience:

> My parents both left school before they completed their schooling, but that was almost the expected thing in their generation. Dad worked in a factory, Mum was a stay-at-home mum. Dad had a disc explode in his back about 18 years ago now, so went back to uni and got a degree and is utilising that. Out of my siblings, there's five of us altogether of which I'm the second-youngest, and I'm the only one

who went on to complete tertiary education. So there wasn't really an expectation from family about having to go to uni. It was 'do with your life what you would be happy to do with it'. (Robinson et al. 2010, p. 42)

The findings of other studies (e.g. Savelsberg 2010; Wyn et al. 2010) indicate how important family is as a source of support for young people's educational and employment aspirations and experiences. These studies further highlight the unequal familial resources available to different groups of young people. They demonstrate the poorer outcomes experienced by young people who receive little or no support from their families in relation to their education and employment. Following on from the discussion in Chapter Three, they raise important questions about the potentially harmful impact of current education and labour policy in making young people and their families responsible for their educational and economic outcomes. By overlooking these disparities in familial resources, these policies could exacerbate the marginalisation of the most vulnerable young people.

Parents can also inadvertently inhibit wider reform. A recent OECD study found that a reason comparatively few educational reforms are evaluated is that '[p]arents are a very conservative force . . . Everybody wants the education system to improve, but not with my child' (Schleicher, cited in Ware 2015).

Teaching parents about the 'language of schooling' can have a powerful effect on engaging parents in their child's education. Hattie (2009) cites the Flaxmere Project in New Zealand, which was designed to engage parents of low socio-economic students to support their children in schools by sharing with parents, who may be unfamiliar with education, the language, approaches and concepts used in the education of their child. Bentley and Cazaly (2015, p. 22) propose this as 'an example of co-production by both school and family, using common understandings of learning to support the student together'. It is further possible to draw parents more deeply into the wider context of schooling and post-school possibilities. This dialogue could be a two-way street, on which parents from different working backgrounds could provide valuable advice on the career development of students in schools.

Getting young people more involved

The capacity of schools to listen to young people themselves could also be improved to better understand their needs. As suggested earlier, many young people are very aware of the importance of wider social and economic issues and have opinions about what they might need to engage the world after leaving school. The 2012 Mission Australia Youth Survey of over 15,000 young people cited earlier in this book showed that young people rate the economy and financial matters as topmost areas of concern (Mission Australia 2012). And yet, schools provide limited opportunities for young people to actively participate in shaping these issues, despite the pre-eminence placed on young people's participation in Australia's overarching educational goals (ACARA 2012). The role of young people's participation in their learning and in determining the conditions in which they learn is significant, but arguably underdeveloped.

Mobility, demography and technological access in the 21st century

The big issues discussed in Chapter Two also directly and indirectly shape the nature of schooling and its development. One major driver of change that was not discussed was climate change. The first officially reported environmental refugees began to depart from the Pacific atoll of The Carteret Islands in 2009 (Morton 2009). Following further environmental change, while some people will be forced to relocate, others will experience restrictions in actual mobility as the costs of travel rise and the regulatory mechanisms for migration are changed. Environmental changes may place new pressures on education systems; consequently, ecological literacy is increasingly important in light of the challenges potentially posed by climate change.

Virtual mobility will undoubtedly be greatly enhanced by the diffusion of ICT, but the dynamic of physical mobility is shifting and may radically transform in coming years. This dynamic will be characterised by new global modalities of exclusion defined by resource scarcity, which could in turn place profound challenges on education. The potential impact of environmental degradation on the mobility of all people could place new demands on schooling and its capacity to harness the knowledge and skills of young people to develop responses to change.

Demography is another modality that could dramatically shape the wider purposes of schooling. As suggested in Chapter Two, shifts in population and migratory flows will present new challenges and approaches to social cohesion, such as how younger and older members of the population support each other as the population ages. As we have seen, it is already affecting the constitution of an ageing teacher workforce, which itself exhibits some signs of precarity.

Given the emphasis on technological innovation, the ongoing challenge of ICT access remains significant. Access is skewed a number of ways, including a strong correlation with educational attainment and urban population development and access. Access, alongside digital literacy, remains uneven. A problem with the notions of learner ownership discussed at the start of this chapter is that they often do not account for gaps in technological access and literacy that continue to arise amongst learners in Australia and throughout the world. Despite the explosive growth of ICT, digital inclusion remains important. Following the discussion in Chapter Two, while access to the Internet has grown significantly in Australia, for example, there are still significant gaps in both the access and the digital literacy of learners and educators. In particular, these gaps heighten the risk of exclusion to those in regional and remote areas. Exclusion from access to the necessary technological architecture has been an ongoing problem for some time, and Australia lags behind many other OECD countries.

Conclusion

The initiatives described throughout this discussion and the previous chapter affirm the need to deepen and extend professional dialogue, engagement and collaboration between teachers, school leaders and wider professional communities. The wider policy landscape outlined here requires a rethinking of how teachers engage both local and global environments. This applies not only to how they could extend learner-centred approaches and learner ownership, but also to how they are trained to enter the profession and develop and learn across the teaching life cycle, as discussed in Chapter Five.

The findings of the TEMAG review outlined in that discussion suggest that improvement needs to be made in the quality and quantity of in-school experience provided in ITE programmes offered by universities. There is considerable evidence to support this kind of vertical reform; however, more effort needs to be made to develop at least three areas of horizontal engagement. Firstly, the wider reform agenda implicitly posits the school as a central place in which hands-on experience can take place. While schools continue to be a central, vital and valuable context, this approach to improvement could be widened to bring in other actors beyond the school who can bring valuable knowledge, resources and professional experience to school settings. As discussed in Chapter Five, we need to be thinking more widely about how teachers are prepared for schooling. The profession is currently inward looking and these trends risk reducing teaching to 'training' without sufficient attention to teacher 'education' as a profession that requires much more to be effective and relevant to the contemporary challenges of education. For example, 'many of the teaching practices currently used in schools are not informed by evidence' (DET 2015a, p. 9). Another part of this involves teachers understanding the wider issues arising from a fluid and more competitive labour force and how students are best prepared to meet the challenges of post-school working life. There is a need to ensure that career advice and ongoing professional development of teachers in general is aligned to changing environments of learning and work. In addition, we have seen that the teacher workforce itself shows signs of precarity. Many newcomers will struggle to find secure work and may well go on to work in other sectors, such as government. Teachers, therefore, require adversity capital as employees themselves.

As a corollary of the school-centric approach of current reform proposals, universities themselves could widen their scope of activity to more meaningfully engage in other cross-sector partnerships to enrich the ITE programmes offered. Like schools, many universities are inward looking and could do significantly more to ensure that the knowledge and graduate attributes developed are more relevant to the needs of contemporary communities and life post-university. Schools, universities and other service providers could both benefit greatly by more explicitly developing and harnessing the value of horizontal engagement with other actors in the community.

At the systems level, there is an appetite for the reform of schooling. As Hannon et al. (2011, p. 3) point out, 'across the developed world, governments face the challenge of transforming education systems built for the 19th and 20th centuries, while cutting spending'. Major education reforms throughout the world are, in different ways, seeking to address the kinds of challenges raised in this book. Bringing about the kinds of systemic changes proposed in this chapter will require dedicated thought and new forms of practice in response to the challenges outlined above. Hannon et al. note that 'some innovators in education are questioning the very idea of schools as the right (or the exclusive) solution to the challenge of educating their young people' (2011, pp. 2–3). Third-sector actors, private and other community actors seeking to drive social innovation could play a greater role in the daily lives of schools and in shaping how young people are educated, and how resilience is harnessed and developed.

These various actors can play an important role in developing adversity capital. Resilience, as we have seen, is not something that is developed

exclusively within individuals. As suggested in Chapter Four, social ecological factors such as schools, parents, community services and other
cultural factors 'are as influential as psychological aspects of positive
development when individuals are under stress' (Ungar 2013, p. 1).
Focusing on the wider ecology of education also includes this sociological dimension in which resilience can be positively developed in young
people within the context of their communities.

But, in contrast to the relatively rapid changing cycles of many businesses and some policies outlined above, efforts to reform and transform
education systems are at best glacial. Those education systems that have
sought major reform during the last 40 years have dedicated considerable time and resources. Writing in the context of developing Standards
for the Australian teaching profession, Jensen and Reichl make the point
that 'high performing systems in East Asia undertook a deep analysis
of learning and teaching at the start of their reforms. Hong Kong, for
example, began with a 20-month investigation of the state of learning
and where it needed to be . . . The findings of that investigation determined all subsequent reform efforts' (Jensen & Reichl 2012, p. 4). When
the Singapore Ministry of Education rolled out major reforms to the
teaching profession in 2001, it did so after considerable planning and
development. Systemic reform requires virtually aligned, well-resourced,
long-term policy approaches that foster innovation at the ground level
through greater horizontal engagement. These could, for example,
open new forms of teacher development and practice, while opening
up schooling to worlds of learning beyond the classroom and enabling
greater opportunities for students and teachers to experience and better
understand worlds of work.

Internationally, efforts have been made to forge better relationships
between schools and local business, as well as improving vocational
education and pathways to apprenticeships. Countries such as South
Korea have developed vocational schools targeting the development
of skills shortages and for which tuition and board are funded by the
government (*The Economist* 2013b). It is argued that 'countries with the
lowest youth jobless rates have a close relationship between education
and work' (*The Economist* 2013b). Germany, for example, has maintained vocational education and training pathways that, to some extent,
have offset the effects of slow economic growth. By contrast, it is argued
that schooling in countries such as France has low levels of connection
between school and work and that this may be related to its high levels
of youth unemployment (*The Economist* 2013b).

A 2014 report by the Foundation for Young Australians argues: 'To
navigate more complex careers pathways, young people will . . . need to

learn careers management skills and get work experience through their schooling' (FYA 2014). Schools need to be reconfigured to enable greater opportunities for learning beyond the school gates. Opportunities for practical experience outside the classroom are by no means abundant (or new), but have enormous scope for improvement and extension.

The types of approaches to learning discussed in this chapter, such as Education 3.0, have yet to be practically operationalised on a large scale, so the evidence on how they work in practice is sparse. An OECD questionnaire survey published in 2009 shows that while most countries or regions develop soft skills[2] 'in their regulations, guidelines or recommendations for compulsory education . . . , there are few specific definitions of these skills and competencies at national or regional level and virtually no clear formative or summative assessment policies for these skills' (Ananiadou & Claro 2008, p. 4). In addition, evaluation of the teaching of these skills and competencies 'is often left to external inspectors as part of their whole school audits. Similarly there are few teacher training programmes that target the teaching or development of 21st-century skills, although there exist several teacher training initiatives that focus on developing teachers' ICT pedagogical skills, most of them optional' (Ananiadou & Claro 2008, p. 4).

Nevertheless, the approach to learner ownership promoted here could be problematic. There is a danger, for example, that this focus on learner ownership and 21st-century learning may privilege certain learners, such as those who are predisposed to learning independently.

While this chapter has explored how schooling could be improved to benefit the needs of young people in the 21st-century labour force, what is greatly needed is *evidence*. In general, there is a striking lack of research into the impact of reforms through evaluation in education systems throughout the world. A review published in 2015 by the OECD found that since 2008, only one in ten of education reforms carried out around the world have been analysed by governments for the impact they have on students in schools (OECD 2015). The review looked at 450 reforms carried out by the OECD's 34 member countries between 2008 and 2014. Schleicher suggests that some of the reasons why so few are evaluated for impact included the lengthy trajectories of reforms and complexity of measuring their educational outcomes (Schleicher, cited in Ware 2015). A related challenge here is that more research needs to be done on the efficacy of soft skills, their relationship to numeracy and literacy and the best ways of embedding their development in schooling.

Conclusion: Where to for Young People?

This book has sought to highlight five challenges related to how young people are prepared for the contemporary labour force during their school years. It started by highlighting the greater fluidity and precarity of working life in relation to young people. It located this within a wider context of domestic and global macro-drivers of change, ranging from migration to demographic, cultural and technological factors. Australia was compared to international trends and was analysed as a useful case study given that recent government proposals to address young people's transitions have adopted a neoliberal tone of austerity, despite the fact that Australia has fared relatively well since the GFC. It then critiqued recent neoliberal policies and provided the theoretical concept of adversity capital as a way of understanding and navigating these changes. The second part of the book explored how the teaching profession may be constrained to respond to these contemporary challenges, before outlining ways in which schools could be more outward-looking in their daily operation. Threaded throughout this discussion was consideration of whether schooling could be more relevant to the needs of young people working in post-industrial society by challenging conventional institutions of teaching, schooling and youth transitions.

In the current climate of public debates dominated by ideology, lack of hard evidence and misperceptions, this final discussion revisits some of the key issues identified throughout this book and critiques ten perceptions upon which recent governments have proposed policy to improve young people's transitions from school to work, further study and training.[1] These perceptions are not confined to the Australian context and will resonate across other contexts internationally.

Perception 1: schools are the default sites for learning

Debates about teacher quality highlighted in Chapter Five, though important, have sometimes inadvertently hijacked the discussion of other approaches that target student need, such as those identified by the Gonski Review, which also explicitly recognised the importance of extending and improving school community partnerships as a key approach to improving student outcomes (Gonski et al. 2011). New approaches are needed to provide young people with the skills needed to negotiate the contemporary labour market. This could start a more robust national approach to career pathways. Within schools, career advice has taken place at the periphery of school life and arguably failed to keep in step with changes to the workforce and to the expectations of young people themselves. A reimagined career-development strategy could contribute to the more explicit building of skills and capabilities that are not sufficiently developed in school. This strategy could be more explicitly implemented across the life course (K-12 and beyond) as a means of harnessing and building adversity capital in young people, as well as providing the tools to engage in study, work and life more deeply than in current career-development approaches.

Greater investment of time, resources and innovation is needed in preparing young people for work and for developing adversity capital in and out of school. Quality teaching remains important; what is further required are new types of teachers and learning experiences in school contexts, as well as beyond the classroom. We need to think more about engaging external actors, such as those in the workplace, parents and mentors, for example, in the active development of teachers and students. This starts with moving beyond the current status placed on school completion. Educators need to be thinking beyond graduation from secondary school. Where 'employers are increasingly seeking those with postgraduate qualifications as proof of their ability to think, analyse, solve problems, communicate effectively and improve outcomes' (Ortlieb 2015), there is a further need to more explicitly develop these during schooling as a basis for what happens to young people post-school. These should not be developed in isolation from literacy and numeracy. And while we routinely rely on, assess and report on these basic academic skills, we lack a robust means of assessing or developing a wider group of skills and attributes necessary for navigating employment and life, in general, which are key to the development of adversity capital. Efforts to improve rates of literacy and numeracy should continue as baseline measures; but a more explicit approach to developing adversity capital is required alongside these.

Perception 2: young people are reluctant to work

In Chapter One, we saw that youth underemployment is a major issue. Many young people want more work but cannot get it. For example, ABS (2013c) data show that nearly a third of underemployed part-time workers aged 15–19 had experienced insufficient work for one year or more. Secure work has dwindled for teenagers and competition for jobs is increasing as a result of factors such as migration and demographic change, as we found in Chapter Two.

Perception 3: secure work is available if young people want it

The value of school completion is not in dispute. It continues to be the case that, in general, those young Australians who complete Year 12 or equivalent fare better in life. Engagement in study tends to lead to better educational outcomes and increased wellbeing amongst young people. It is particularly critical for young people aged 16–24 moving from school education to employment or further training (Lamb & Mason 2008; Robinson & Lamb 2009). There have been solid gains in this area – the national apparent retention rate for students from Year 7/8 to Year 12 reached 81.6 per cent in 2013 (ABS 2013b) – but more needs to be done to develop a wider set of skills and competencies.

With increasing levels of educational attainment, more young people eventually get 'good' jobs after the age of 25. Young women have been particular beneficiaries, with around 50 per cent of women aged 25–29 employed in full-time jobs that amount to the top 40 per cent of jobs overall (Stanwick et al. 2013). While rates of participation in study for Degrees continue to climb, participation in other forms of education and training is declining (COAG 2012b). But in an economy that places a higher premium on certain forms of knowledge and skills, what will become of those for whom higher education is not the preferred pathway and for whom full-time work remains elusive? Increasing levels of education mean that those with poor education outcomes are likely to find entering the labour market more difficult. It is increasingly difficult for unqualified people to get a 'good' job (Stanwick et al. 2013). Wage penalties await many young people who start work in low-skill jobs, although this is arguably better than having no job at all (Karmel et al. 2013). For those who do go on to further study, the qualifications received at the end may not necessarily land them employment in their intended field of study.

Those in jobs face two additional challenges. Firstly, the safety net for those in work is being steadily eroded. In recent years, there have been persistent suggestions to lower penalty rates and minimum wages, following the publication of a series of issue papers by the Productivity Commission (2015). These recommendations were ostensibly to stimulate employment, but have a number of implications for young people.

In March 2015, penalty rates were removed in South Australia in retail (big employers of young people), indicating that this suggestion is gaining traction. The largest reduction in penalty rates 'occurs if a small business rosters a permanent employee after 6pm on weeknights and from 9am to 5pm on weekends, when penalties are scrapped or halved' (Hannan 2015). This recommendation is part of a larger chorus of calls by business peak bodies to also reduce weekend penalty rates. In 2014, for example, the Australian Chamber of Commerce and Industry (ACCI) led a campaign to lower Sunday penalty rates, arguing that it will create jobs for young people (Mayer 2014). This idea has also been floated by the Australian government at a national level. In 2015, Prime Minister Abbott suggested that if employees 'don't want to work on a weekend, fair enough, don't work on a weekend . . . But if you do want to work on a weekend – and lots of people, particularly young people, particularly students, would love to work on a weekend – you want the employers open to provide jobs' (Abbott, cited in Toscano et al. 2015). This policy suggestion has important implications for young people – particularly those working while studying. For students studying full-time, weekends play at least two important roles. Firstly, for those needing the money, it is a time when they can work beyond the study timetable. Secondly, like many other Australians, the weekend can also be a valuable time for rest and for catching up with family and friends. Making every working day the same in terms of pay level removes the weekend as a time for relaxation and maintaining other necessities of everyday life. Aside from being traditionally important times for a number of religious communities, weekends perform an important role in cultural and social ways, as well as for maintaining personal wellbeing. Knowing that weekends are 'sacred', young people can plan their lives accordingly. But as we saw in Chapter One, one of the effects of fluid working hours on young people is that it can impact negatively on their ability to plan. Having to work variable hours in areas of employment, such as hospitality, can interfere with other things that are important in life, such as family and other significant relationships. For those who 'choose' to work on weekends, a penalty rate provides an incentive for trading off this valuable time to maintain a living. But for many, the 'choice' to work on weekends is somewhat illusory; this is because for many, this income is needed to survive, particularly while studying.

Lowering the minimum wage has also been under consideration for some time now as the National Commission of Audit recommended lowering the minimum wage from AU$622.20 a week to around AU$488.90 a week, or 44 per cent of average weekly earnings (Australian Government National Commission of Audit 2014). Doing so could compel students to work more to maintain income levels. This could be counterproductive, as working too much can compromise student outcomes. Research has shown that a challenge for some university students is that working too much can compromise their study (Krause et al. 2005). The same applies to young people working while at school. As discussed in Chapter One, the 2009 House of Representatives' *Inquiry into Combining School and Work: Supporting Successful Youth Transitions* identified a risk that too much work can impact negatively on study in school (House of Representatives 2009).[2]

There are deeper implications for young people beyond potentially negatively affecting study. Student poverty has been an increasing problem over the last decade, and lowering wages could exacerbate this. This applies particularly to students who struggle to make ends meet. This is, in part, due to the rising costs of living. Research by the Canadian Educational Policy Institute in 2005 found that living costs for university students in Australia were the third highest in the world, behind New Zealand and the UK (Educational Policy Institute 2005, p. 18). Sixty per cent of students were living below the poverty line. Around half of undergraduate students lived on less than a third of the national minimum wage. It was reported that by 2012, costs of living, including accommodation, increased around twofold since that earlier study (Bita 2012). Those on youth allowance lived on far less than the minimum wage. Earning while learning is necessary for many students just to make ends meet.

Despite a persistent interest in lowering the minimum wage, the economic impact of changing the minimum wage to alter employment outcomes is debatable. While the Productivity Commission has explored 'whether or not there is an impact from the minimum wage on employment' (Massola 2015), there is consensus among influential economists that 'the weight of evidence now [shows] that increases in the minimum wage have had little or no negative effect on the employment of minimum-wage workers, even during times of weakness in the labor [sic] market' (Economic Policy Unit 2014). In the Australian context, 20 years of unbroken economic growth has taken place despite the fact that minimum wage rates in Australia are double that of the US (Matthews 2013).

In contrast to Australian proposals to cut (or even remove) the minimum wage and other safety nets, maintenance of a social safety net continues to be an important feature of European policy responses, by 'offering a good balance between rights to benefits and targeted activation measures based upon mutual obligation, in order to avoid young people, especially the most vulnerable, falling outside any social protection system' (European Commission 2010, p. 15). Protective mechanisms include proposals to introduce 'an open-ended "single contract" with a sufficiently long probation period and a gradual increase of protection rights, access to training, life-long learning and career guidance for all employees. Introducing minimum incomes specifically for young people and positively differentiated non-wage costs to make permanent contracts for youngsters more attractive' (European Commission 2010, p. 15).

But in a global context in which more people are studying higher education in increasingly competitive labour markets, there is a broader question of whether the promise of education as a means to a better, secure working life is still tenable. Alongside a shift in the nature of youth transitions discussed in this book is a wider shift from 'a work society to a knowledge society' (Beck 2000, p. 1) in which 'mental rather than manual production has become the mainstay of capitalism; the knowledge economy rather than the industrial economy is its cornerstone'. But whether a knowledge society is the logical product of a knowledge economy is itself a subject of debate (Kenway et al. 2006). We still see large numbers of young Australians seeking work in areas in which manual labour is required, which leads to the next perception.

Perception 4: young people should just go to where the work is

Increasing workforce mobility figures prominently on European agendas. Mobility is promoted through the identification of available jobs in Europe and the skills needed via a 'European Vacancy Monitor' (European Commission 2010, p. 11). The European Skills Passport, which builds on the Europass, is another mechanism through which young people record the competences acquired 'throughout their lives in a variety of learning settings, including e-skills and informal and non-formal learning. This should facilitate mobility by easing the recognition of skills across countries' (European Commission 2010, p. 10). Inherent in these approaches is the development of incentives to relocate, which has been mooted by the Australian government alongside the more punitive tone adopted in the contemporary neoliberal discourse of recent Australian policy that was critiqued in Chapter Three.

In 2014, the then Australian federal Employment Minister Eric Abetz suggested that young people not in study or training could take up picking fruit in Tasmania (Cox 2014). At that time, he was defending a controversial proposal to changes in the Newstart unemployment welfare allowance to compel Australians under the age of 30 to wait six months before receiving unemployment benefits. Compelling vulnerable young people to leave key support networks, such as family, places them at risk of marginalisation and isolation. Implicit in this type of approach was an expectation that young people have the capacity to leave valuable local support networks to pursue low-paying job opportunities in seasonal markets. Those in regional and remote communities already face particular challenges in finding work. Removing support may exacerbate these. This approach additionally strikes at real and complex tensions between addressing the challenges of marginalisation by those who never move beyond their suburb and the socio-economic disadvantage associated with their marginalisation and the idea that success in life is reducible to being economically 'fit for purpose'.

An additional challenge arises from the ethnoscape of migratory flows of labourers, who are intensifying competition for work. Further to our discussion in Chapter Two, the number of Working Holiday Makers from overseas in 2012–13 roughly equalled the number of young people who left school to seek work (Birrell & Healy 2013a). Working Holiday Makers from overseas (all aged 30 or less) are competing with young Australians who leave school and look for work, such as picking fruit in Tasmania. Birrell and Healy (2013b) link this to high levels of local youth unemployment. Given the government's consideration of increasing the import of foreign labour through 457 and other visas (Patty 2015), there is a marked absence of an overarching vision as to how this relates to forcing young Australians to find work without assistance. In this approach, young people faced a 'double-whammy' of being compelled to seek work without support while competing in a globalised job market.

Perception 5: getting young people into a job – any job – will improve their prospects

As noted in the Introduction to this book, recent national surveys of Australian youth by Mission Australia have consistently shown the high level of importance to young people of getting a job. They face a casualised, insecure workforce in which part-time work is the norm. The Australian Industry Group (AIG) has argued that people in casual work 'do not want to lose their flexibility or their casual loading' and that those with family responsibilities or study commitments prefer casual work (AIG 2015, p. 87). This may be true for some, but what of the vast number of others who are seeking more secure work and want to be able to plan their lives, secure a loan for a house and not be tethered to the ever-changing hours of a fluid job market?

Having a part-time job can be important to building self-esteem but the assumption that this will lead to secure work is problematic. As mentioned in Chapter One, data show that statistically people aged 15–19 who have part-time jobs are only slightly more likely to move into full-time work than those who are unemployed (Robinson et al. 2011), which leads us to the next perception.

Perception 6: Work for the Dole improves young people's chances of finding work

In 2014, it was announced that the Newstart Allowance would not be cancelled for over 100,000 dole recipients under the age of 30 as initially suggested (Karvelas 2014b). Instead, recipients would have the option of working for the dole if they worked for 25 hours per week for welfare. Evidence from the US and previous Work for the Dole programmes suggests that being in a mandatory programme may discourage young people from looking for work. Researchers have observed a 'chilling' effect, whereby young people in Work for the Dole programmes spend less time searching for other work. For those young people affected, a preoccupation with 'busy-work' in such programmes could result in them spending less time looking for a real job, as has been the case in Work for the Dole schemes in the US (Borland & Tseng 2003). Or to take Senator Abetz's example, let us say a young person gets a job in Tasmania picking fruit. Being on a limited salary, isolated and fully occupied may inhibit the capacity of young people to seek better paying jobs, attend interviews and escape a cycle of low-paying work far from home, and other employment and training opportunities, trapping them in seasonal currents of insecure work.

In addition, the Social Services Minister at that time, Kevin Andrews, expressed interest in a recommendation that '[c]onsideration should be given to incorporating income management as part of a package of support services available to job seekers who need to stabilise their circumstances and develop a pathway to work or study' (DSS 2014, p. 10).

As mentioned in Chapter Three, it has been recommended that the government should be able to determine how recipients spend their welfare benefits. This is presumably to stop young people from spending their dole on non-necessities, such as alcohol. Putting the intention aside, this sends a contradictory message from a conservative government that espouses personal autonomy and responsibility on the one hand, while apparently threatening to wield the regulatory hand of the seemingly reviled 'nanny state' on the other.

The policy proposals critiqued in Chapter Three, such as prolonging eligibility for welfare to the age of 30 and income management of welfare payments, position young people in an interstitial zone, in which they are simultaneously treated as both adults and young people. In the European context, Stein et al. (2003, p. 6) evoke 'the metaphor of "yo-yo" transitions to refer to the ups and downs, "either-ors" and "neither-nors" of young people living adult and young lives simultaneously' (see also Walther et al. 2001). Neoliberal efforts to defer eligibility for the social safety net to the age of 30 in Australia would exacerbate the 'yo-yo-isation of transitions' to adulthood.

In addition, responsibilising young people to navigate globalised labour markets alongside older citizens with life-experience, qualifications and other potential assistance, such as home ownership and spousal support, risks creating a generational divide, which has been observed elsewhere in the world as we saw in Chapter Two. Furthermore, many of the recently proposed 'earning or learning' measures in Australia have been more lax for older age groups. For example, it was proposed in 2014 that physically able job seekers aged under 30 would have to sign up for 25 hours of work for the dole for at least half of each year, whereas those aged between 30 and 50 would be expected to do 15 hours of work for the dole every six months (Barlow 2014). Is this evidence of 'age apartheid' said to be emerging in Britain (Howker & Malik 2010)?

Perception 7: working life becomes more stable and secure as one gets older

A folly of neoliberal policy arises from the misconception that young people who want and are able to work can do so. Put bluntly, this policy is doomed to failure if there are no jobs available. In May 2014, it was reported that a total of 146,100 job vacancies were available in Australia (ABS 2014), while a total of 740,000 Australians were unemployed (Martin 2014). The greatest growth was in casual and part-time work. However, as we have seen, those in part-time work who want more secure employment are not necessarily in a better position to gain full-time employment.

Australia is now in a policy context in which funding has been reduced to organisations seeking to support young people in transition, and which is seeking to transfer the burden of financial debt onto young people to undertake training and higher education. An important question arises as to what investment is being made into constructively supporting pathways to earning and learning, rather than penalising young people or burdening them with a study or training mortgage when they leave school. Another question is whether forced-labour through Work for the Dole or compelling young people to move to work is necessary in a strong economy that has just undergone unprecedented growth and has a debt-to-GDP ratio that is the envy of most other countries.

As suggested above, the promise of better jobs through post-school study and training is also contested. Neoliberal policies closely connect education and work (Cuervo et al. 2013). Assuming that learning will lead to earning, these policies target education and training as a basis for gaining employment. Brown et al. (2011, p. 5) suggest that this 'neoliberal opportunity bargain' is decreasingly tenable in a globalised job market. As we saw in Chapter Two, globalisation has ramped up competition for work in ways that are profoundly reshaping local job markets that challenge the conventional wisdom that getting a qualification will lead to secure work. Consequently, Cuervo et al. (2013, p. 11) observe that this link 'is not as strong as neoliberal policies in the last two decades have assumed'. In the US, the 'promise of education, jobs, and rewards' that underpins the mobility of middle-class youth is being compromised by the influx of professionals internationally from emerging economies such as India and China. Countries such as the UK and Australia are not immune to these consequences of globalisation. Brown et al. (2011, p. 5) describe an emergent 'global auction' in which competition for good quality jobs has intensified. They provide an unsettling example of the global Dutch auction in operation in the form of a German website advertising 'cleaning, clerical, and catering jobs . . . offered by employers with a maximum price for the job; those looking for employment then underbid each other, and the winner was the person willing to work for the lowest wages'. In a highly competitive global labour market, could this be the future of working life? If so, given the challenges discussed throughout this book, how adequately are our schools preparing young people for fluid worlds of work? It continues to be the case that those young people who complete Year 12 or equivalent fare better in life. But within this, and especially beyond this for those who disengage from school, the explicit development of adversity capital that positively improves young people's resilience is potentially valuable.

Regardless, the effectiveness of any effort to boost the skills of young people will depend on the jobs being available. Efforts to stimulate job opportunities represent an important policy trajectory; however, this alone cannot address the challenges outlined in the previous chapters. As the European Commission (2011) suggests, 'Growth enhancing measures are necessary to create new jobs'; however, these 'could not in themselves be sufficient to tackle the problem of youth unemployment' (p. 5). Nevertheless, adversity capital assumes particular significance here; in particular, its emphasis on developing the capacity of individuals to survive in precarious circumstances. But its value is delimited when fewer opportunities are available.

The promise by governments to provide pathways to earning and learning is problematic given the prevailing norm that higher education is a preferred pathway over vocational alternatives. But what is equally problematic of neoliberal responses is the way that they shift responsibility for addressing this 'problem' onto young people and their families. Also implied in neoliberal policy is that young people are suspected of being unwilling, incapable or unprepared to reflexively navigate and negotiate the fluid and flexible labour markets (Black & Walsh 2015). As we saw in Chapter Three, the contemporary individual is understood both to be the source or cause of risk and to be the agent responsible for risk minimisation. The impact of disengagement, therefore, has a wider significance. The stigmatisation of unemployment, for example, is associated with a characterisation of young people as failed citizens, or 'anti-citizens' (Rose 1999, p. 259). Sir Ken Henry has argued that 'unemployment is a powerful source of "capability deprivation". In essence, what this means is that young people who are not in the education system and who are denied work are deprived of the freedom to lead a life they would choose. They are being denied the capability to participate fully in the activities of their community' (Henry 2014b). In the absence of work, building resilience in young people to negotiate adversity is particularly salient in building this capability.

Perception 8: responding to the challenges of the contemporary workforce is a matter of individual choice

Efforts to develop entrepreneurial skills in young people to create their own work opportunities have become more prominent in the European policy discourse (European Commission 2010). Though valuable, they become problematic: firstly, in the context of a deficit of resources to support young people to generate their own work, and secondly, when they are promoted within a neoliberal view that shifts the burden of addressing unemployment onto the young. I have carefully and deliberately avoided using the voguish notion of entrepreneurialism in this discussion because it typically locates the young individual as the main determinant of her/his future and adopts a quasi-corporate language that assumes young people can 'innovate' their way out of precarity. While some may have the agency and social and financial capital to do so, the concept of entrepreneurialism has been captured by neoliberal ideology that has at its core, a valorisation of the individual over the social. Entrepreneurship features prominently in the language of international organisations, such as the UN, which identifies the importance of 'investing in education and fostering empowerment of youth will allow for their entrepreneurship to flourish' (UNRIC 2012a). Entrepreneurialism is often attached to a hope that it will lead to self-employment, but as Williamson (2014) has argued, 'Among the young, this may work for a very few. For most who try it, it is likely to be a temporary measure in predictable, under-capitalised and saturated sectors of the labour market – as young people wait for something more secure to turn up.' He further points to 'strong arguments that entrepreneurship is not for the young'. A third risk is that 'blaming enterprising young people who give something a go and then are deemed to "fail"'. A risk is that being marked as a failed 'anti-citizen' compounds what is already a desperate situation for some young people. They become the problem, the solution and a failure simultaneously.

This stigma of failure is not confined to entrepreneurs. Returning to our young British correspondent from Chapter Two: 'Various government policies over the past decades have structurally prohibited most of us from attaining the lifestyle and material security that our parents associated with success and peace of mind. Adding insult to injury, we have to deal with what feels like the entire country blaming us for our misfortune. You know the drill: we're uncultured, narcissistic, entitled babies who lack the soft skills necessary to take our place as functioning adults' (Robertson 2014). Perhaps she is right to some extent about the patronising and infantilising suggestion about lacking soft skills. It is not argued here that young people lack soft skills; the case I am making is for these skills to be more explicitly developed in, recognised and harnessed by young people.

A myth of neoliberalism perpetuates the idea that all young people can be treated as a homogenous group, in which individuals have equal capacity to navigate the challenges of the contemporary workforce. Writing in the UK context, Howker and Malik argue that broader politics has shifted towards attempting to meet the satisfaction of short-term goals and the false-empowerment of individuals (2010, p. 202). In part, they argue a focus on individual rights and self-expression has drawn the focus away from 'social inheritance', which 'has led us to assume that doing the best for ourselves will always be best for others, but this is demonstrably untrue' (Howker & Malik 2010, p. 202). This can also be said of Australia. As the trends in Part One of this book highlighted, young people from certain backgrounds and contexts (e.g. Indigenous, low SES, regional and remote) face persistent structural barriers and deeply embedded challenges. There is a tension between the neoliberal narrative of choice and the very real structural exclusions experienced by many young people, which render agentic notions of autonomy to be elusive if not illusory (Furlong & Cartmel 2007; Wyn & White 2000).

In light of the neoliberal discourse of policy described above, the need to develop soft skills in schools could be seen a basis for preparing young people for a responsibilised future post-school, thus entrenching the individualistic, reflexive aspects of neoliberalism. But as highlighted in Chapter Four, it forms part of a deeper form of resilience that draws on the wider social ecology in which young people live. While serving as a kind of adversity capital that enables young people to be more adaptive, flexible and resilient, these soft skills also reflect the need to prepare young people for more uncertain, fluid working lives in which the conventional notion of a career is outdated. These soft skills may also provide the basis for negotiating and even challenging dominant neoliberal modes of working and being.

There is a related danger here that fostering soft skills in schools may propagate a reflexive notion in which education and life, in general, are reduced to economic need, and one that is highly individualised. It may also be asked: is the development of soft skills to prepare young people to be responsive to global capital at the expense of other needs and capacities, such as the ability to plan or define themselves in relation to something other than the economy? Is it a means of preparing young people to be effectively subjugated to the needs of the economy?

Bottrell (2013) writes, '[s]ince the 1990s in Australia and the US, workfare has enshrined the neoliberal demonization of welfare "dependency", intensified surveillance through performance contracts and piled up conditions on recipients, including stricter eligibility criteria, reductions to benefit duration, participation in job readying or parenting programs, and an increasing range of "breach" criteria with accompanying penalties.'

She rightly points out that 'state rhetorical enthusiasm for resilient individuals and communities provides a smokescreen over its removal of barriers to market based accumulation, facilitation of accumulation by dispossession and policy failure in areas such as poverty reduction, educational equity and redress of damaging adverse conditions in marginalised communities' (Bottrell 2013). This is where adversity capital becomes important. The standard responses of contemporary neoliberal governments overlook the material realities of modern working life. Adversity capital is necessary to navigate these working conditions and interrogate government policy that works against the interests and contexts of young people. At best, it enables them to navigate a potentially hostile labour market. At worst, it provides them with the resilience to deal with marginalisation and potentially challenge the wider forces at work in creating the conditions of their exclusion. This is where the ability to critically analyse and engage the world as a core component of adversity capital is important. Young people need to be able to critically navigate, challenge and innovatively address global labour markets and power in general.

But again, it is important to recognise that young people should not be expected to 'manage risk' alone. Adversity capital assumes a level of individual agency, while recognising that young people and their families 'can't do it alone'. Social, political and economic support mechanisms remain as important as ever. The challenges facing young people in our time need targeted policy interventions, such as those proposed by the Gonski review and through community-based approaches supported by a wide range of actors, including government, business and the third sector, as explored in Chapter Six.

Through the concept of adversity capital, this book argues for a deeper form of resilience that recognises the pervasive conditions accompanying neoliberalism, while critically engaging the associated effects arising from this prevailing view. So while it may be argued that this notion of adversity capital is problematic because it responsibilises young people to navigate the choppy and uncertain seas of contemporary global labour markets, it additionally locates the challenges facing young people within the broader contexts in which they live. These contexts are characterised by structural problems and deep social, cultural and economic challenges that require collective responses. This is why schools will always be important – they continue to be a powerful means by which these challenges can be addressed.

Given that levels of employment have failed to match population growth, a major risk of this approach is that it overstates the importance of soft skills. As Mitchell (2015) suggests, 'the public narrative still focuses on the supply-side – the allegedly "lazy" and "unskilled" unemployed'. This is why adversity capital also encompasses the skills, competencies and predispositions to engage precarity and is not in itself 'a solution'. Systemic approaches to building employment and overcoming disadvantages continue to be important alongside this.

Perception 9: the market can solve some key problems in youth transitions

The Abbott government pursued another key tenet of neoliberalism when it (to date unsuccessfully) argued for the deregulation of higher education. Education Minister Pyne stated that he did not wish to see higher education go the way of car manufacturing as globally uncompetitive because of regulation (Walker 2014). This proposition implies that universities are somehow comparable to industry, and devalues their role as a public good and foundational basis of Australia's social and economic infrastructure.

Trainees were also affected by the proposal to introduce concessional trade support loans of up to AU$20,000 over a four-year apprenticeship. With the slashing of Tools for Your Trade in 2014, apprentices no longer received financial assistance for their tools. They instead would incur debt through the Trade Support Loans Programme. This measure would apparently save the government AU$914.6 million over four years, but for apprentices, loan repayments may take longer.

Deregulation was bundled with changes to student loans that would mean that many choosing to learn could start their post-school life in debt, having gambled on choosing a profession in an ever-changing job market in which a 'career' scarcely resembles what it did 20 years ago. Those who need to reskill in future, such as those in automotive manufacturing, will face dual challenges of unemployment without social security benefits and the added debt incurred by the need for additional training.

These kinds of neoliberal policies seek to shift debt from the government to the young and their families. They favour those who are already wealthy and can rely on support networks, such as family. They infantilise young people by stretching out the definition of youth to the age of 30. In so doing, these policies propose a perverse experiment in social engineering, in which the government may save money now, but at the risk of great social and economic cost in the future.

Perception 10: young people are optimistic about the future

The research findings vary with regard to this perception. According to the Melbourne Declaration, a purpose of schooling is to endow young people with 'a sense of optimism about their lives and the future' (MCEETYA 2008, p. 9). There is a powerful link between educational achievement and feelings of autonomy in young people. School completion increases the likelihood that young people will feel in control of their own lives (Robinson et al. 2010). Data from the World Values Survey (WVS) show that across almost all participating countries (including Australia), school completers are more likely to feel that they have control over their lives than their peers who do not complete school or its equivalent (World Values Survey Association 2009). Of young Australians surveyed in the WVS between 2005 and 2007, 56 per cent believed that they had a high degree of choice and control over their lives. A further 41 per cent felt that they had some degree of self-efficacy. Only 2 per cent stated that they had little or no choice and control. This kind of finding is consistent with that of a Mission Australia study, in which more than 64 per cent of 50,000 young respondents indicated that they felt either positive or very positive about the future (Mission Australia 2010). A sense of optimism and agency is visible in the testimonies of young people. One suggests, for example, 'At my school there are a lot of options open to me which is I think is a good thing, it makes me very ambitious . . . They help us access whatever we want to do, they really do their best to get us to where we want to be.' Another suggests, '[a]lthough [my parents] were influences, I always felt that I could choose. I chose not to go to [residential] college and I chose to travel, I chose to go to university but my parents really had no say in what I was studying, nor did anyone else. There's restrictions with money, that's probably the only thing where freedom is stunted, but I think that's student life.' In another example, it was found that '[e]arly on in my degree I discovered what I wanted to do and made positive steps to try and get to that. I've always tried to do work experience, most of that is on a volunteer basis because realistically you can't [expect to be paid] for a week or two when you're not really providing them any benefits, so I think that as a whole has put me in good stead for future prospects' (Robinson et al. 2010, p. 68).

These examples echo the wider WVS finding that 59 per cent of school completers felt that they had a lot of choice and control within their lives, while 39 per cent felt that they had some. For school non-completers, we see the reverse: only 39 per cent felt that they had a lot of choice and control, while 55 per cent felt that they had some. Three times as many non-completers felt that they had no choice and control within their lives as their counterparts who had completed school (Robinson et al. 2010, p. 70).

Two striking implications arise from this data. Firstly, young people from excluded groups are less likely to feel that they are autonomous agents within their own lives. This is reinforced by other research showing that young people from low socio-economic groups are less optimistic than their more affluent peers (Wyn et al. 2008). This is at odds with a pervasive view of young people as collectively 'confident, optimistic and trail blazing' (Wyn et al. 2008, p. 18).

Secondly, will this optimism be tempered by the sometimes-jarring realities of post-school study and employment outcomes outlined throughout this book? That is, as the promise of education as a pathway to secure and desirable work is challenged by the global economy, what effects (if any) will this have on 'generation next'?

The evidence indicates that young people see more to life than fulfilling economic need or being the products of 'slack'. Data from the 2011 World Values Survey, for example, indicated that three quarters of young adults prioritised the need to protect the environment over economic growth (Robinson et al. 2010) – although, concern amongst teenagers fell significantly according to the Mission Australia 2012 Youth Survey, which found a substantial number nominating 'the economy and financial matters' over the environment as a major issue of national importance (Mission Australia 2012). Some might abhor the idea that mobility is dictated exclusively by labour market need and seemingly relentless economic growth. The challenges of youth transitions should therefore be located in a richer world of values, contexts, expectations and possibilities for young people to participate in the economies and societies of the 21st century.

Recent global data also suggest a pervasive pessimism, one that permeates much of the world. High rates of global youth unemployment, the UN suggests, 'results in a lack of hope to young people and social instability' (UNRIC 2012a). A survey of 20 countries found that a majority believe that their prospects will be worse (42 per cent) rather than better (34 per cent) (Ipsos MORI 2014). This pessimism is particularly pronounced in Western Europe, including countries that are faring relatively well such as Sweden and Germany. Similarly, in Australia, the survey found that 42 per cent believed that the current generation would be worse off than their parents (versus 30 per cent who thought they would be better off).

That said, there are other signs of optimism amongst young people. Several years ago, in the wake of the GFC, I was involved in a small project investigating the attitudes and biographies of young Australians in transition, many of who were living in conditions of precarity and marginalisation from work and study. A recurring attitude was one of optimism. As I wrote at the time, 'Despite the often unsettling portrayal of young people in transition that emerges from the data, young people are resilient and optimistic about their futures . . . young people comprise a richly diverse range of individuals, defying easy categorisation. Young people are not a homogenous group. Making up nearly a quarter of Australia's population, they reflect a broad range of heritage cultures, socioeconomic backgrounds, political perspectives and other dispositions' (Walsh, in Robinson et al. 2010, p. vii). This optimism has also been observed elsewhere. A survey of around 2,000 British people aged 16 to 24 by The Work Foundation found that 63.4 per cent of young people believe that one day they will get their ideal job (Howell 2013). A challenge is to bolster that hope with the tools, resources and support needed to get young people into work. This includes not only developing adversity capital in a systematic way, but also building and expanding existing pathways to work through further study and training, as well as a safety net for those who fall along the way.

The bigger picture

The concerns raised above should be tempered by the positive achievements of education systems in Australia and throughout the world. While this book is focused on youth transitions to employment, it is worth briefly examining some of the wider trends, gains and challenges in improving education outcomes that enframe and significantly shape employment outcomes.

Despite both government rhetoric and the very real challenges outlined in this book, there have been some solid gains during the last decade, particularly in educational participation as one critical means of improving opportunities and life chances of young people (Robinson & Lamb 2012). School retention rates have reached the highest level ever recorded, though falling short of government targets. The evidence continues to affirm the benefits of completing Year 12 or equivalent. As previously noted, educational attainment improves the labour market and broader life prospects of young people. University-level attainment among 24- to 35-year-olds also increased from 24 per cent in 2001 to 35 per cent in 2011, tracking well for the Bradley target of 40 per cent (Robinson & Lamb 2012).

However, over this period, some national and state initiatives have only had modest returns in some areas. The gap between Indigenous Australians and non-Indigenous Australians, for example, remains wide despite some gains in year 12 completion by Indigenous Australians (DPMC 2015; Long & North 2009). Targets set at halving the gap in reading, writing and numeracy achievements for Indigenous students, as well in employment outcomes between Indigenous and non-Indigenous Australians by 2018, are not on track (DPMC 2015). There have been no overall gains in Indigenous reading and numeracy, and employment outcomes have declined since 2008 (DPMC 2015). Certain policy responses have failed to gain traction because of policy myopia. For example, programmes with an established link to Indigenous engagement, such as bilingual education, have lacked coherent, long-term support.

Too often, inconsistent policy has undermined the role of educational institutions in preparing young people, in general, for work. Over the last few decades, investment by successive governments in vocational education and training pathways and programmes within schools has, for example, varied dramatically and discouraged the development of a coherent and stable response to changes in the labour market. In Australia, the provision of multiple pathways to work needs development. Changes in student transitions over the past decade have added significantly to the complexities that young people face. Although governments and school systems have invested in a range of information and guidance resources, most young people are located in Australian schools where the dominant pathway is that of university study. Other pathways and measures of successful learning need to be developed. Sustained investment in support programmes and services, such as learning coaches and mentors, seems to have had a positive impact. Similar services and interventions are also provided through other agencies, including NGOs. It is important that these services be well designed, of high quality and targeted in an optimal manner that takes into consideration the contemporary realities of youth transitions.

In the longer term, it is important to note that the patterns of poor transition vary considerably across social groups and location. However, prior to the Gonski reforms, Australian Commonwealth funding policies over the past decade have not effectively directed resources towards these groups, locations and schools. Rather, resources have tended to go to groups, locations and schools with the lowest capacity for marginal improvements, rather than those areas that have the greatest needs. While it is argued that there has been a 'disappearance of inequality from government policy and the agenda of daily life' during the last few decades (Beck 1992, p. 92), there have been notable exceptions, such as the Gonski *Review of Funding for Schooling*, which stimulated widespread discussion over the best ways to address educational disadvantage in targeted ways (Gonski et al. 2011).

In so far as the contemporary labour force is characterised by precarity, policy responses are too often framed by a particular world view – that of neoliberalism. The fixation of this approach on austerity measures that responsibilise individuals and their communities is stifling innovative responses and the adaptation necessary to enable young people to thrive. At the systems level, economists have argued that unemployment rates could be lowered through the creation of large-scale job programmes; however, these would require government to move away from a border-line obsession with creating budget surpluses (Mitchell 2015). Where policy tends to 'lag behind the changing realities of young people's lives' (Wyn et al. 2010, p. 13), the need to address youth transitions becomes all the more urgent given how profoundly the last two economic slowdowns impacted upon young people.

At the individual level, the need to develop well-rounded, critical and creative thinkers becomes all the more important to enable young people to navigate uncertainty and change as well as critique it, challenge it and, where necessary, develop alternatives. This requires the development of adversity capital alongside deep content knowledge. Schleicher (2013) is perhaps half-right in asserting that the 'world economy doesn't pay you for what you know, but what you can do with what you know'. The contemporary labour force demands adaptability and the need for skills to navigate change. But deep content knowledge is also important and will differentiate prospective employees. In a competitive global labour market, pressures to specialise and acquire deep content knowledge often counterbalance the need for generic soft skills. Specialisation certifications and postgraduate qualifications, for example, continue to be required by employers. Ortlieb (2015) provides the examples of 'a teacher with a Certificate of Gifted Education, a midwife who has advanced training in neonatal health, or a computer programmer who can code in multiple languages'. Deep content knowledge, therefore, remains important alongside the development of adversity capital.

The types of responses outlined in this book have in some ways been recognised in various policies. For example, in its 2010 report, *Building Stronger Pathways for Young Aboriginal People*, the Ministerial Taskforce on Aboriginal Affairs recommended a number of measures to improve retention and attainment, including bringing the world of work through the school gate; developing partnerships between the private sector, philanthropic organisations and the Aboriginal community; offering enhanced career advice and managing Individual Pathway Plans from Year 7; targeting Aboriginal students using sport, art and culture; providing mentors and role models; and establishing Transition Coordinators to facilitate the process (Samms 2010). These kinds of approaches suggest that the arguments made in this book for a combination of adequately resourced systemic responses and a shift in thinking about how and where learning takes place are not foreign to education systems. But they do need to recognise and respond to the profound challenges facing young people's transitions into the contemporary global economy.

In a sense, there is a need to reclaim the idea of 'transition' in two ways. Firstly, education systems should not be treated as something that is rigid or fixed, but rather as an ecological system of institutions, practices, individuals and organisations that is evolving and can be changed. They are perpetually in a state of transition (however glacial). Secondly, youth transitions have changed so significantly in recent decades that conventional markers are less relevant. Where adulthood is typically characterised as a state in which individuals experience 'full employment and independent living' (Wyn & White 2000, p. 170), the transition to 'adulthood' is being pushed out later in life for many young people. At the same time, the kinds of policy outlined in Chapter Three suggest that young people are at the same time expected to grow up more quickly. Some will find themselves in uncertain seas perpetual fluidity and precarity. They are shaped by – and themselves shape – the intersecting scapes described in Chapter Two.

The notion of transition has consequently been contested for some time now, and with changes to traditional markers of transition moving to later in life, such as getting full-time work, buying a house and starting a family, its meaning has become porous if not irrelevant. There is an argument, on the other hand, to reclaim a notion of transition that emphasises how critical the move beyond the school gates is, along with developing adversity capital to navigate changing worlds of work during a critical stage of young people's personal, social and economic development. Young lives cannot indeed be relived.

Notes

Introduction

1 Full-time work is defined here as involving 35 hours or more work per week (Robinson & Lamb 2009, p. vi).
2 Part-time work includes less than 35 hours per week (Robinson & Lamb 2009, p. vi).
3 Those classified as 'unemployed' include those not employed in the week of the relevant labour force survey 'and who had actively looked for and were available for work in the previous four weeks' (Robinson & Lamb 2009, p. vi).

1 Young People, Precarity and a Workforce in Transition

1 Not in the labour force 'refers to those not in work and not seeking work' (Robinson & Lamb 2009, p. vi).
2 'School completers' includes 'young people who have attended school and completed Year 12' (Robinson & Lamb 2009, p. vi).
3 Early school leavers are defined here as 'young people who have left school without completing Year 12' (Robinson & Lamb 2009, p. vi).
4 7.8 per cent of 15- to 19-year-olds and 11.7 per cent of 20- to 24-year-olds compared to the OECD averages of 8.2 per cent and 18.4 per cent (OECD 2013a, cited in FYA 2014).
5 There has been substantial attrition from the study over time. The sample of young people from Cohort One stood at 2,000 in 1996, and by 2013 was at 284 (14.2 per cent retention; 85.8 per cent attrition). The sample from Cohort Two stood at 3,977 in 2005–06, but was at 626 as of 2013 (15.7 per cent retention; 84.3 per cent attrition).

2 The Big Four: Structural Marginalisation, Globalisation, Demographic Change and Technology

1 It is argued that the regional or remote status of Indigenous young people only explains part of the problem. Comparing Indigenous and non-Indigenous schools in the same remote locations, Hughes and Hughes (2010) found significant discrepancies in levels of attainment that are not explicitly linked to location. These discrepancies may be explained by inadequate staffing and facilities, shorter school hours, low community expectation, low attendance, and separate Indigenous curriculums with lower standards of learning (Hughes & Hughes 2010, p. vii).

2 High fertility is defined as 'a period total fertility level greater than 3.2 children per woman in 2005–2010' (United Nations, Department of Economic and Social Affairs, Population Division 2014, p. 24).

3 Within longer-term demographic changes, there are 'mini baby booms' from time to time, most recently since the turn of the millennium in Australia.

3 Neoliberal Policy and Precarity

1 Policy prescriptions by the European Commission, such as *Europe 2020*, are limited in influence. As the Commission states, youth unemployment is primarily the responsibility of the member states. The European Commission and EU can play a supportive role through reviewing national policies and performances and by providing financial support to national and transnational action (European Commission 2011).

2 Interestingly, participants in a Work for the Dole scheme are not counted as employed by the ABS. Such individuals are classified based on their behaviour outside of this scheme. This contrasts with participants of Community Development Employment Projects, who are classified as employed. The distinction is a product of different remuneration structures (i.e. welfare benefits, compared with award wages and conditions), which implies that a genuine employee–employer relationship exists for the latter, but not for the former group (ABS 2013a).

4 Adversity Capital

1 Pavlidis differentiates adversity capital from 'the concept of "resilience" in that it is not necessarily prevention focused' (2009, p. 11); however, adversity capital is used here as a basis for resilience that can serve as a form of prevention to negotiate the contemporary labour force.

5 Teachers in Transition: Current Challenges

1 'Year 12 or equivalent' is defined to have involved 'completion of a school certificate (such as the South Australian Certificate of Education or the Tasmanian Certificate of Education) or an equivalent qualification defined as VET certificate III or higher' (Robinson & Lamb 2009, p. vi).

2 Part of this dropout rate has been linked to the contractual arrangements in place (Walters 2012).

3 Following the commencement of a Liberal–National coalition government in 2013, a review of the Australian Curriculum reviewed its focus on the seven 'general capabilities' rather than specific subject knowledge (Crowe 2014). However, at the time of writing, no official determinations on this review had been implemented.

6 Beyond the School Gates: Are Our Education Institutions Obsolete?

1 Disclosure: the author previously worked for the Foundation for Young Australians.
2 It uses the term '21st century skills and competencies'.

Conclusion: Where to for Young People?

1 This chapter builds on a discussion by the author published in *The Canberra Times* entitled 'Casualisation of Youth Employment Is Mortgaging the Future' (Walsh 2014).
2 The risk mainly arises in relation to people who work more than 20 hours per week; otherwise, no negative connection has been found between part-time work and educational outcomes (Patton & Smith 2009; Vickers 2011).

Bibliography

AAP (Australian Associated Press) (2014). 'Minister "Appalled" by Child's McDonald's Shifts.' *WA Today*, 23 February 2014. Accessed 13 April 2015 at: http://www.watoday.com.au/wa-news/minister-appalled-by-childs-mcdonalds-shifts-20140223-33a0e.html

Abbott, T. (2010). *Our Action Contract: A Strong Plan for Australia*. Accessed 30 April 2015 at: http://shared.liberal.org.au/Share/LPA-Contract-A4.pdf

Abbott, T. (2012). *Tony Abbott Press Release – The Coalition's Jobs Pledge*, 28 November 2012. Accessed 18 May 2015 at: http://www.liberal.org.au/latest-news/2012/11/28/tony-abbott-press-release-coalitions-jobs-pledge

Abbott, T. (2013). *Leader of the Opposition's Address to the 56th Federal Council of the Liberal Party of Australia*. Accessed 8 May 2015 at: http://www.liberal.org.au/latest-news/2012/06/30/leader-oppositions-address-56th-federal-council-liberal-party-australia

ABC PM (2013). 'Young More Likely to Leave Murray-Darling Towns.' *ABC PM* [radio], 30 May 2013. Accessed 4 May 2015 at: http://www.abc.net.au/pm/content/2013/s3771228.htm

ABS (Australian Bureau of Statistics) (2001–09). *Education and Work*, Australia Catalogue No. 6227.0. Canberra: ABS.

ABS (Australian Bureau of Statistics) (2003). *4102.0 – Australian Social Trends, 2003*. Retrieved from http://www.abs.gov.au/AUSSTATS/abs@.nsf/2f762f958454 17aeca25706c00834efa/3d196e4d297f42c9ca2570eb0082f628!OpenDocument

ABS (Australian Bureau of Statistics) (2005). *Australian Demographic Statistics*. Canberra: Australian Bureau of Statistics.

ABS (Australian Bureau of Statistics) (2006). *4102.0 – Australian Social Trends, 2006*. Retrieved from http://www.abs.gov.au/AUSSTATS/abs@.nsf/7d12b0f6763c78cac a257061001cc588/a428496a0ccd9af8ca2571b00016e4d8!OpenDocument

ABS (Australian Bureau of Statistics) (2007a). *Patterns of Internet Access in Australia*. Canberra: Australian Bureau of Statistics.

ABS (Australian Bureau of Statistics) (2007b). *4840.0.55.001 – Mental Health of Young People, 2007*. Retrieved from http://www.abs.gov.au/ausstats/abs@.nsf/Latestproducts/4840.0.55.001Main%20Features12007?opendocument&tabname=Summary&prodno=4840.0.55.001&issue=2007&num=&view=

ABS (Australian Bureau of Statistics) (2008). *4102.0 – Australian Social Trends, 2008*. Retrieved from http://www.abs.gov.au/AUSSTATS/abs@.nsf/Lookup/4102. 0Chapter3002008

ABS (Australian Bureau of Statistics) (2010). *4102.0 – Australian Social Trends, Mar 2010*. Retrieved from http://www.abs.gov.au/AUSSTATS/abs@.nsf/Lookup/4102. 0Main+Features40Mar+2010

ABS (Australian Bureau of Statistics) (2011a). *6265.0 – Underemployed Workers, Australia, Sep 2011*. Accessed 22 April 2015 at: http://www.abs.gov.au/ausstats/abs@.nsf/Previousproducts/6265.0Main%20Features4Sep%202011?opendocument&tabname=Summary&prodno=6265.0&issue=Sep%202011&num=&view=

ABS (Australian Bureau of Statistics) (2011b). *2071.0 – Reflecting a Nation: Stories from the 2011 Census, 2012–2013.* Accessed 22 April 2015 at: http://www.abs.gov.au/ausstats/abs@.nsf/Lookup/2071.0main+features902012-2013

ABS (Australian Bureau of Statistics) (2012). *Article – 50 Years of Labour Force: Now and Then. Year Book Australia, 2012.* Cat. No. 1301.0. Canberra: Australian Government.

ABS (Australian Bureau of Statistics) (2013a). *6102.0.55.001 – Labour Statistics: Concepts, Sources and Methods, 2013.* Accessed 23 March 2015 at: http://www.abs.gov.au/ausstats/abs@.nsf/Latestproducts/6102.0.55.001Contents12013?opendocument&tabname=Summary&prodno=6102.0.55.001&issue=2013&num=&view=

ABS (Australian Bureau of Statistics) (2013b). *3222.0 – Population Projections, Australia, 2006 to 2101.* Accessed 17 April 2015 at: http://www.abs.gov.au/AUSSTATS/abs@.nsf/Lookup/3222.0Main+Features12006%20to%202101?OpenDocument

ABS (Australian Bureau of Statistics) (2013c). *6105.0, Australian Labour Market Statistics, July 2013.* Accessed 7 May 2015 at: http://www.abs.gov.au/ausstats/abs@.nsf/featurearticlesbytitle/EF44F37DA92FDDEECA2571A3001A4180?OpenDocument

ABS (Australian Bureau of Statistics) (2014). *6354.0 – Job Vacancies, Australia, May 2014.* Released 26 June 2014. Accessed 18 August 2014 at: http://www.abs.gov.au/ausstats/abs@.nsf/mf/6354.0

ACMA (Australian Communications and Media Authority) (2009). *Click and Connect: Young Australians' Use of Online Social Media 02: Quantitative Research Report.* Canberra: Australian Government.

ACMA (Australian Communications and Media Authority) (2013). *Like, Post, Share: Young Australians' Experience of Social Media Quantitative Research Report.* Canberra: Australian Government.

ACMA (Australian Communications and Media Authority) (2014). *Key Indicators of Aussie Teenagers Online, December 2013.* Accessed 11 April 2015 at: http://www.acma.gov.au/~/media/Research%20and%20Reporting/Research/Spreadsheet/Aussie%20teens/Figure1%20xlsx.xlsx

ACARA (Australian Curriculum, Assessment and Reporting Authority) (undated). *Work Studies Introduction.* Accessed 30 April 2015 at: http://www.australiancurriculum.edu.au/work-studies/introduction

ACARA (Australian Curriculum, Assessment and Reporting Authority) (2011). *National Assessment Program – ICT Literacy Years 6 and 10 Report 2011.* Accessed 16 March 2011 at: http://www.acara.edu.au/reporting/national_report_on_schooling_2011/student_achievement/nap_ict_literacy_1_1.html

ACARA (Australian Curriculum, Assessment and Reporting Authority) (2012). *The Shape of the Australian Curriculum.* Australian Curriculum and Assessment Authority, May 2012. Accessed 1 May 2015 at: http://www.acara.edu.au/verve/_resources/The_Shape_of_the_Australian_Curriculum_V3.pdf

ACARA (Australian Curriculum, Assessment and Reporting Authority) (2013a). *General Capabilities in the Australian Curriculum.* Accessed 4 February 2015 at: http://www.australiancurriculum.edu.au/GeneralCapabilities/Pdf/Overview

ACARA (Australian Curriculum, Assessment and Reporting Authority) (2013b). *Draft Australian Curriculum: Work Studies, Years 9–10, August 2013.* Accessed 27 April 2015 at: http://consultation.australiancurriculum.edu.au/Static/docs/

WorkStudies/Draft%20Australian%20Curriculum%20Work%20Studies%20
Years%209-10.pdf
ACARA (Australian Curriculum, Assessment and Reporting Authority) (2014a).
Australian Curriculum: Cross-curriculum Priorities. Accessed 29 July 2015 at:
http://www.acara.edu.au/curriculum/cross_curriculum_priorities.html
ACARA (Australian Curriculum, Assessment and Reporting Authority) (2014b).
Intercultural Understanding – General Capabilities. Accessed 29 July 2015 at:
http://www.australiancurriculum.edu.au/GeneralCapabilities/Pdf/Intercultural-
understanding
ACT Government (2011). *Engaging Canberrans. A Guide to Community Engagement*.
Canberra: ACT Government. Accessed 24 April 2015 at: http://www.timetotalk.
act.gov.au/storage/communityengagement_FINAL.pdf
ACTU (Australian Council of Trade Unions) (2012). *Lives on Hold. Unlocking the
Potential of Australia's Workforce. The Report of the Independent Inquiry into Insecure
Work in Australia*. Melbourne: Australian Council of Trade Unions.
ADEST, ACCI & BCA (Australia Department of Education, Science and Training,
Australian Chamber of Commerce and Industry & Business Council of Australia)
(2002). *Employability Skills for the Future*. Canberra: Department of Education,
Science and Training.
AEU (Australian Education Union) (2014). *More Teachers than Ever on Contract*, 5
August 2014. Accessed 10 April 2015 at: http://www.aeuvic.asn.au/604195.html
AIG (Australian Industry Group) (2015). *Ai Group Submission, Productivity Com-
mission Inquiry into the Workplace Relations Framework. A Workplace Relations
Framework for the 21st Century, March 2015*. Accessed 11 April 2015 at: http://
www.aigroup.com.au/portal/binary/com.epicentric.contentmanagement.servlet.
ContentDeliveryServlet/LIVE_CONTENT/Policy%2520and%2520Repre
sentation/Submissions/Workplace%2520Relations/2015/PC%2520Ai%2520
Group%2520workplace%2520release%2520Final.pdf
AIHW (Australian Institute of Health and Welfare) (2011). *Young Australians:
Their Health and Wellbeing 2011*. Cat. No. PHE 140. Canberra: AIHW. Accessed
25 May 2015 at: http://www.aihw.gov.au/WorkArea/DownloadAsset.aspx?id=
10737419259
AITSL (Australian Institute for Teaching and School Leadership) (2011a).
National Professional Standards for Teachers. February 2011. Melbourne: AITSL.
AITSL (Australian Institute for Teaching and School Leadership) (2011b).
Accreditation of Initial Teacher Education Programs in Australia. Melbourne: AITSL.
Accessed 30 April 2015 at: http://www.aitsl.edu.au/docs/default-source/default-
document-library/accreditation_of_initial_teacher_education_file
AITSL (Australian Institute for Teaching and School Leadership) (2011c).
National Professional Standards for Principals. February 2011. Melbourne: AITSL.
Aldenmyr, S. I., Wigg, U. J., & Olson, M. (2012). 'Worries and Possibilities in
Active Citizenship: Three Swedish Educational Contexts.' *Education, Citizenship
and Social Justice*, 7(3), 255–270.
Alexander, R. J. (ed.) (2010). *Children, Their World, Their Education: Final Report of
the Cambridge Primary Review*. London: Routledge.
Allen, N. L. (2014). 'As a Result of the Expansion of Enrollments, the Wage Levels
of Graduates Are Decreasing in Many Fields.' *The LSE's Daily Blog on American
Politics and Policy*, 21 April 2014. Accessed 16 February 2015 at: http://bit.ly/
1lvLXzS

Ananiadou, K. & Claro, M. (2008). '21st Century Skills and Competences for New Millennium Learners in OECD Countries.' *OECD Education Working Papers, No. 41.* Paris: OECD Publishing. Accessed 24 May 2015 at: http://www.oecd.org/officialdocuments/publicdisplaydocumentpdf/?cote=EDU/WKP(2009)20& doclanguage=en

Andres, L. & Wyn, J. (2010). *The Making of a Generation: The Children of the 1970s in Adulthood.* Toronto: University of Toronto Press.

Appadurai, A. (1996). *Modernity at Large: Cultural Dimensions of Globalization.* Minnesota: University of Minnesota Press.

Arvanitakis, J. & Sidoti, E. (2011). 'The Politics of Change – Where to for Young People and Politics.' In Walsh, L. & Black, R. (eds.), *In Their Own Hands: Can Young People Change Australia?* Camberwell: ACER Press, pp. 11–25.

Asia Education Foundation (2010). *The Current State of Chinese, Indonesian, Japanese and Korean Language Education in Australian Schools. Four Languages, Four Stories.* Carlton: Education Services Australia.

Asialink (2012). *Developing an Asia Capable Workforce a National Strategy.* Melbourne: Asialink, University of Melbourne.

Austrade (The Australian Trade Commission) (2014). *Why Australia? Benchmark Report 2014.* Canberra: Austrade.

The Australian (2014). 'Lifting, Not Leaning, Is the Way ahead for Our Nation.' *The Australian,* 31 May 2014. Accessed 11 April 2015 at: http://www.theaustralian.com.au/opinion/editorials/lifting-not-leaning-is-the-way-ahead-for-our-nation/story-e6frg71x-1226937788213

Australian Government (2010). *Australia to 2050: Future Challenges.* Canberra: Commonwealth of Australia.

Australian Government (2012). *Australia in the Asian Century,* White Paper, October 2012. Accessed 8 February 2015 at: http://www.asiaeducation.edu.au/verve/_resources/australia-in-the-asian-century-white-paper.pdf

Australian Government National Commission of Audit (2014). *Towards Responsible Government. The Report of the National Commission.* Canberra: Commonwealth of Australia.

The Australia Institute (2013). *Youth Survey.* Accessed 22 April 2015 at: http://www.tai.org.au/content/youth-survey-2013-election-issues-policies

Australian Workforce Productivity Agency (2014). *Labour Force Participation: Youth at Risk and Lower Skilled Mature-age People: A Data Profile, May 2014.* Canberra: Australian Government.

AYAC (Australian Youth Affairs Coalition) (2013). *Australia's Youth Matters. Young People Talk About What's Important to Them.* Sydney: Australian Youth Affairs Coalition.

Backstrom, L. (2011). *Anatomy of Facebook.* Accessed 1 April 2015 at: https://www.facebook.com/notes/facebook-data-team/anatomy-of-facebook/101503885159243859

Ball, S. (1994). *Education Reform: A Critical and Post-structural Approach.* Buckingham: Open University Press.

Ball, S. (2004). 'Education for Sale! The Commodification of Everything?' *King's Annual Education Lecture 2004.* University of London, 17 June 2004. Accessed 20 April 2015 at: http://nepc.colorado.edu/files/CERU-0410-253-OWI.pdf

Ball, S. (2010). 'New Class Inequalities in Education: Why Education Policy May be Looking in the Wrong Place! Education Policy, Civil Society and Social Class.' *International Journal of Sociology and Social Policy,* 30, 155–166.

Bansel, P. (2007). 'Subjects of Choice and Lifelong Learning.' *International Journal of Qualitative Studies in Education*, 20(3), 283–300.

Barlow, K. (2014). 'Unemployed to be Forced to Apply for 40 Jobs a Month as Part of $5 Billion Dole Overhaul.' *ABC News*, 29 July 2014. Accessed 18 August 2014 at: http://www.abc.net.au/news/2014-07-28/government-reveals-details-of-dole-overhaul/5627660

Bauman, Z. (2000). *Liquid Modernity*. Cambridge: Polity Press.

Bauman, Z. (2013). *The Individualized Society*. Cambridge: Polity Press.

Beck, U. (1992). *Risk Society: Towards a New Modernity*. Thousand Oaks, CA: Sage Publications.

Beck, U. (2000). *The Brave New World of Work*. Cambridge: Polity.

Beck, U. & Beck-Gernsheim, E. (2002). *Individualization*. London: Sage.

Beech, H. (2013). 'I Am Australian. So Am I.' *Time Magazine*, 19 August 2013. Accessed 23 March 2015 at: http://content.time.com/time/magazine/article/0,9171,2149091,00.html

Benderly, B. L. (2015). 'Workforce "Smoke and Mirrors" Down Under.' *Science*, 3 February 2015. Accessed 4 May 2015 at: http://sciencecareers.sciencemag.org/career_magazine/previous_issues/articles/2015_02_03/caredit.a1500031

Bentley, T. & Cazaly, C. (2015). *The Shared Work of Learning: Lifting Educational Achievement Through Collaboration*. Mitchell Institute Research Report No. 03/2015. Mitchell Institute for Health and Education Policy and the Centre for Strategic Education, Melbourne. Accessed 25 May 2015 at: http://www.mitchellinstitute.org.au

Berlant, L. (2011). *Cruel Optimism*. Durham and London: Duke University Press.

Bernardini, J. (2014). 'The Infantilization of the Postmodern Adult and the Figure of Kidult.' *Postmodern Openings*, 5(2), 39–55.

Bessant, J. (2009). 'Jobless Young Need Opportunities Not Punishment.' *The Age*, 8 May 2009. Accessed 6 August 2010 at: http://www.theage.com.au/opinion/jobless-young-need-opportunities-not-punishment-20090507-awk5.html

Birrell, B. & Healy, E. (2013a). 'Scarce Jobs: Migrants or Locals at the End of the Job Queue?' *The Conversation*, 28 August 2013. Accessed 20 May 2015 at: https://theconversation.com/scarce-jobs-migrants-or-locals-at-the-end-of-the-job-queue-17496

Birrell, B. & Healy, E. (2013b). *Scarce Jobs: Migrants or Locals at the End of the Job Queue?* Clayton: Centre for Population and Urban Research.

Bita, N. (2012). 'Inflation Rate Not a Patch on Cost of Living.' *The Australian*, 2 August 2012. Accessed 20 March 2015 at: http://www.theaustralian.com.au/business/economics/inflation-rate-not-a-patch-on-cost-of-living/story-e6frg926-1226440717571

Black, R. (2008). *Beyond the Classroom: Building New School Networks*. Melbourne: ACER Press.

Black, R. (2009). *Boardroom to Classroom: The Role of the Corporate and Philanthropic Sectors in School Education*. Melbourne: Department of Education and Early Childhood Development.

Black, R. (2012). *Educating the Reflexive Citizen: Making a Difference or Entrenching Difference?* PhD Thesis, Melbourne Graduate School of Education, The University of Melbourne. Accessed 25 May 2015 at: http://repository.unimelb.edu.au/10187/17319

Black, R. & Walsh, L. (2009). *Corporate Australia and Schools: Forming Business Class Alliances and Networks*. Melbourne: Centre for Strategic Education.

Black, R. & Walsh, L. (2015). 'Educating the Risky Citizen: Young People, Vulnerability and Schooling.' In Te Riele, K. & Gorur, R. (eds.), *Interrogating Conceptions of 'Vulnerable Youth' in Theory, Policy and Practice*. Rotterdam, The Netherlands: Sense Publishers, pp. 181–194.

Blackmore, J. (2010). 'Policy, Practice and Purpose in the Field of Education: A Critical Review.' *Critical Studies in Education*, 51, 101–111.

Borland, J. & Tseng, Y. (2003). *Does 'Work for the Dole' Work?*, June 2003. Melbourne: University of Melbourne. Accessed 18 August 2014 at: http://www.melbourneinstitute.com/downloads/labour/6_wfd_FinReport.pdf

Bottrell, D. (2013). 'Responsibilised Resilience? Reworking Neoliberal Social Policy Texts.' *M/C Journal of Media and Culture*, 16(5) October. Accessed 25 May 2015 at: http://journal.media-culture.org.au/index.php/mcjournal/article/viewArticle/708

Bourdieu, P. (1977). 'Cultural Reproduction and Social Reproduction.' In Karabel, J. & Halsey, A. (eds.), *Power and Ideology in Education*. New York: Oxford University Press, pp. 487–511.

Bourdieu, P. & Wacquant, L. (1992). *An Invitation to Reflexive Sociology*. Chicago: University of Chicago Press.

boyd, D. (2014). *It's Complicated*. New Haven: Yale University Press.

Boyd, D., Grossman, P., Lankford, H., Loeb, S., & Wyckoff, J. (2005). 'How Changes in Entry Requirements Alter the Teacher Workforce and Affect Student Achievement.' *NBER Working Paper No. 11844*. Accessed 22 May 2015 at: http://www.nber.org/papers/w11844

Boyd, D., Grossman, P., Lankford, H., Loeb, S., & Wyckoff, J. (2006). 'How Changes in Entry Requirements Alter the Teacher Workforce and Affect Student Achievement.' *Education Finance and Policy*, 1(2), 176–216.

Bradley, D., Noonan, P., Nugent, H., & Scales, B. (2008). *Review of Australian Higher Education: Final Report*. Canberra: Department of Education, Employment and Workplace Relations.

Breman, J. (2013). 'A Bogus Concept?' *New Left Review*, 84, 130–138.

Brotherhood of St Laurence (2014). *Australian Youth Unemployment 2014: Snapshot*. Fitzroy: Brotherhood of St Laurence.

Brown, P., Lauder, H., & Ashton, D. (2011). *The Global Auction: The Broken Promises of Education, Jobs, and Incomes*. New York: Oxford University Press.

Browne, R. (2014.) 'Budget will Save Vulnerable from Bleaker Future, Joe Hockey Tells Welfare Sector.' *The Sydney Morning Herald*, 22 May 2014. Accessed 18 August 2014 at: http://www.smh.com.au/federal-politics/political-news/budget-will-save-vulnerable-from-bleaker-future-joe-hockey-tells-welfare-sector-20140522-38puf.html#ixzz3Ai34xcMi

Bryce, J. & Withers, G. (2003). *Engaging Secondary School Students in Lifelong Learning*. Camberwell: Australian Council for Educational Research.

Caldwell, B. (2012). *Graduate Entry Teacher Education: A Case for Two Year Programs*, 31 January 2012. Brighton: Educational Transformations Pty Ltd. Accessed 20 April 2015 at: http://www.pc.gov.au/inquiries/completed/education-workforce-schools/submissions/subdr081-attachment.pdf

Campbell, I. (2013). 'An Historical Perspective on Insecure Work in Australia.' *Queensland Journal of Labour History*, 16, 6–24.

Cappelli, P. (2012). *Why Good People Can't Get Jobs: The Skills Gap and What Companies Can Do About It*. Philadelphia: Wharton Digital Press.

Casinader, N. & Walsh, L. (2014). 'Teacher Transculturalism and Cultural Difference: Addressing Racism in Australian Schools.' Paper presented at the *Australian and New Zealand Comparative and International Education Society*, 26 November 2014, Queensland University of Technology, Brisbane Australia.

Casner-Lotto, J. & Barrington, L. (2006). *Are They Really Ready to Work? Employers' Perspectives on the Basic Knowledge and Applied Skills of New Entrants to the 21st Century US Workforce.* New York: The Conference Board.

Cassidy, J. (2014). 'Piketty's Inequality Story in Six Charts.' *The New Yorker*, 26 March 2014. Accessed 21 April 2015 at: http://www.newyorker.com/online/blogs/johncassidy/2014/03/piketty-looks-at-inequality-in-six-charts.html

CBI (Confederation of British Industry) (2012). *Learning to Grow: What Employers Need from Education and Skills: Education and Skill Survey 2012.* London: CBI.

CCIQ (Chamber of Commerce and Industry Queensland) (2011). *The Right People at the Right Time: Developing a Skilled Workforce That Meets the Needs of Queensland's Economy.* Queensland: Chamber of Commerce & Industry Queensland.

Chalmers, J. (2013). 'Occupational Standing over the Life Course: What Is the Role of Part Time Work?' In Evans, E. & Baxter, L. (eds.), *Negotiating the Life Course: Stability and Change in Life Pathways.* Dordrecht: Springer, pp. 191–214.

Chalmers, J. & Hill, T. (2007). 'Marginalising Women in the Labour Market: "Wage Scarring" Effects of Part-time Work.' *Australian Bulletin of Labour*, 33(2), 180–201.

Chauvel, L. (2010). 'The Long-term Destabilization of Youth, Scarring Effects, and the Future of the Welfare Regime in Post-trente Glorieuses France.' *French Politics, Culture & Society*, 28(3), 74–96.

Chomsky, N. (2011). 'The "Great Moderation" and the International Assault on Labor.' *In These Times*, 2 May 2011. Accessed 29 April 2015 at: http://inthesitimes.com/article/7264/the_great_moderation_and_the_international_assault_on_labor

Cisco Systems Inc. (2010). *The Learning Society.* Accessed 23 May 2012 at: http://www.cisco.com/web/about/citizenship/socio-conomic/docs/LearningSociety_WhitePaper.pdf

COAG (Council of Australian Governments) (2008). *National Partnership Agreement on Improving Teacher Quality.* Canberra: Council of Australian Governments.

COAG (Council of Australian Governments) (2009). *Council of Australian Governments Meeting, Hobart, 30 April 2009, Communiqué.* Accessed 13 April 2015 at: https://www.coag.gov.au/sites/default/files/2009-04-30.pdf

COAG (Council of Australian Governments) (2012a). *Reform Agenda.* Canberra: Commonwealth of Australia. Accessed 22 January 2014 at: http://www.coag.gov.au/schools_and_education

COAG (COAG Reform Council) (2012b). *Overview – National Agreement for Skills and Workforce Development: Performance Report for 2011.* Accessed 27 March 2012 at: http://www.coagreformcouncil.gov.au/reports/docs/skills/swd2011/Skills_and_Workforce_Development_2011_overview.pdf

Cole, P. (2011). *Professional Learning That Works: A Guide for Teachers and School Leaders.* Australia: PTR Consulting. Accessed 20 April 2015 at: http://www.ptrconsulting.com.au/sites/default/files/Professional_Learning_that_Works_A_guide_for_teachers_and_school_leaders.pdf

Cole-Adams, K. (1993). 'Soft Sell Goes to School.' *Time Australia*, No. 46, 15 November 2013, pp. 52–55.

Colebatch, T. (2009). 'Quarter of a Million Teenagers in No Man's Land.' *The Age*, 10 April 2009, p. 1.

Côté, J. E. (2013). 'Towards a New Political Economy of Youth.' *Journal of Youth Studies*, 17(4), 527–543.

Cox, L. (2014). 'Young and Without Work? Take up Fruit Picking, says Liberal Senator Eric Abetz.' *The Age*, 16 May 2014. Accessed 18 August 2014 at: http://www.smh.com.au/federal-politics/political-news/young-and-without-work-take-up-fruit-picking-says-liberal-senator-eric-abetz-20140526-38xmb.html

Crowe, D. (2014). 'Christopher Pyne Tackles Leftist "Bias" in Classrooms.' *The Australian*, 10 January 2014 at: http://www.theaustralian.com.au/national-affairs/policy/christopher-pyne-tackles-leftist-bias-in-classrooms/story-fn59nlz9-1226798590821#

Cuervo, H., Crofts, J., & Wyn, J. (2013). *Generational Insights into New Labour Market Landscapes for Youth*. Research Report, 42 Youth Research Centre, Melbourne Graduate School of Education, December 2013. Parkville: The University of Melbourne.

Darling-Hammond, L. (2000). 'Teacher Quality and Student Achievement: A Review of State Policy Evidence.' *Education Policy Research Archives*, 8(1), 1–44. Accessed 20 May 2015 at: http://epaa.asu.edu/ojs/article/view/392/515

Darling-Hammond, L. (2010). 'Teacher Education and the American Future.' *Journal of Teacher Education*, 61(1–2), 35–47.

Darling-Hammond, L., Holtzman, D., Gatlin, S. J., & Heilig, J. V. (2005). 'Does Teacher Preparation Matter? Evidence About Teacher Certification, Teach for America and Teacher Effectiveness.' *Education Policy Analysis Archives*, 13(42), 1–51.

Davies, M., Lamb, S., & Doecke, E. (2011). *Strategic Review of Effective Re-engagement Models for Disengaged Learners*. Melbourne: Victorian Department of Education and Early Childhood Development.

DEECD (Department of Education and Early Childhood Development) (2013). *Towards Victoria as a Learning Community*. Melbourne: Department of Education and Early Childhood Development.

DEEWR (Department of Education, Employment and Workplace Relations) (2011). *Realising Potential: Businesses Helping Schools to Develop Australia's Future: Business-School Connections Roundtable*. Canberra: Department of Education, Employment and Workplace Relations.

DEEWR (Department of Education, Employment and Workplace Relations) (2013). *DEEWR Annual Report 2012–13*. Canberra: Department of Education, Employment and Workplace Relations.

Dempster, N., Lovett, S., & Flückiger, B. (2011). *Literature Review: Strategies to Develop School Leadership: A Select Literature Review*. Melbourne: AITSL.

Department of Employment (2014a). *Job Commitment Bonus for Young Australians*, 14 May 2014. Accessed 12 April 2015 at: https://employment.gov.au/job-commitment-bonus-young-australians-0

Department of Employment (2014b). *Labour Market Assistance Outcomes. Job Services Australia*. Canberra: Government of Australia.

DET (Australian Government Department of Education and Training) (2015a). *Teacher Education Ministerial Advisory Group: Action Now: Classroom Ready Teachers. February 2015. Australian Government Response*. Canberra: Australian Government.

DET (Australian Government Department of Education and Training) (2015b). 'Teacher Education Ministerial Advisory Group.' *Students First*. Accessed 24 February 2015 at: http://www.studentsfirst.gov.au/teacher-education-ministerial-advisory-group

Dewey, C. (2013). 'Map: More than Half of Humanity Lives Within this Circle.' *Washington Post*, 7 May 2013. Accessed 8 February 2015 at: http://www.washingtonpost.com/blogs/worldviews/wp/2013/05/07/map-more-than-half-of-humanity-lives-within-this-circle/

Dinham, S. (2011). *Pilot Study to Test the Exposure Draft of the National Professional Standard for Principals: Summary of Key Issues and Recommendations Arising from Draft Final Reports*, July 2011. Melbourne: AITSL.

Dockery, A. M. (2010). *Education and Happiness in the School-to-Work Transition.* South Australia: The National Centre for Vocational Educational Research (NCVER).

Dodd, T. & Tadros, E. (2014). 'The Degrees of Unemployment: Universities' Jobless.' *Australian Financial Review*, 18 August 2014. Accessed 18 February 2015 at: http://www.afr.com/p/national/education/the_degrees_of_unemployment_universities_e3nDZ8x89ziuXsEdNMOz9J

Doecke, B., Parr, G., North, C., Gale, T., Long, M., Mitchell, J., Rennie, J., & Williams, J. (2008). *National Mapping of Teacher Professional Learning Project.* Canberra: Department of Education, Employment and Workplace Relations.

Dooley, J. J. & Scott, A. J. (2013). 'Online Social Networking Behaviours, Cyber Bullying, Mental Health and Behavioural Functioning in Australian Students.' In Hanewald, R. (ed.), *From Cyber Bullying to Cyber Safety: Issues and Approaches in Educational Contexts*. Hauppauge, NY: Nova Science Publishers, pp. 117–130.

DPMC (Department of Prime Minister and Cabinet) (2015). *Closing the Gap: Prime Minister's Report 2015*. Canberra: Commonwealth of Australia.

DSS (Department of Social Services) (2014). *A New System for Better Employment and Social Outcomes – Interim Report of the Reference Group on Welfare Reform to the Minister for Social Services.* Canberra: Commonwealth of Australia.

Dumont, H., Istance, D., & Benavides, F. (eds.) (2010). *The Nature of Learning: Using Research to Inspire Practice.* Paris: OECD.

Economic Policy Unit (2014). *Over 600 Economists Sign Letter in Support of $10.10 Minimum Wage. Economist Statement on the Federal Minimum Wage*, 14 January 2014. Accessed 23 March 2015 at: http://www.epi.org/minimum-wage-statement/

The Economist (2013a). 'A Great Migration.' *The Economist*, 1 June 2013. Accessed 10 August 2014 at: http://www.economist.com/news/finance-and-economics/21578702-spain-needs-its-young-people-create-new-businesses-great-migration

The Economist (2013b). 'Generation Jobless.' *The Economist*, 27 April 2013. Accessed 25 March 2015 at: http://www.economist.com/news/international/21576657-around-world-almost-300m-15-24-year-olds-are-not-working-what-has-caused

The Economist (2013c). 'Generation Jobless: The Number of Young People Out of Work Globally is Nearly as Big as the Population of the United States.' *The Economist*, 27 April 2013. Accessed 9 September 2015 at: http://www.economist.com/news/leaders/21576663-number-young-people-out-work-globally-nearly-big-population-united

The Economist (2013d). 'Why is Youth Unemployment so High?' *The Economist*, 8 May 2013. Accessed 8 September 2015 at: http://www.economist.com/blogs/economist-explains/2013/05/economist-explains-why-youth-unemployment-so-high

The Economist (2014). 'The Onrushing Wave.' *The Economist*, 8 January 2014. Accessed 11 April 2015 at: http://www.economist.com/news/briefing/21594264-previous-technological-innovation-has-always-delivered-more-long-run-employment-not-less

Educational Policy Institute (2005). *Global Higher Education Rankings: Affordability and Accessibility in Comparative Perspective.* Canada: Educational Policy Institute.

Eggleston, J. (2012). *Ecology of the School.* Oxon and New York: Routledge.

European Commission (2010). *Youth on the Move. An Initiative to Unleash the Potential of Young People to Achieve Smart, Sustainable and Inclusive Growth in the European Union.* Communication from the Commission to the European Parliament, the Council, the Economic and Social Committee and the Committee of the Regions, COM (2010), 477 Final, 15 September 2010. Brussels: European Commission. Accessed 26 March 2015 at: http://eur-lex.europa.eu/legal-content/EN/TXT/PDF/?uri=CELEX:52010DC0477&from=EN

European Commission (2011). *Youth Opportunities Initiative.* Communication from the Commission to the European Parliament, the Council, the Economic and Social Committee and the Committee of the Regions, COM (2011), 933 Final, 20 December 2011. Brussels: European Commission.

European Commission (2014). *EU Measures to Tackle Youth Unemployment.* Brussels: European Union.

Eurostat (2015). *EU Labour Force Survey – Methodology.* Accessed 22 April 2015 at: http://ec.europa.eu/eurostat/documents/1978984/6037342/EU-LFS-explanatory-notes-from-2014-onwards.pdf/3dc95eb7-3b86-49f6-ba26-3707abbe4b97

Eurostat (2015, January 15). *Underemployment and Potential Additional Labour Force Statistics.* Retrieved 11 February 2015, from http://ec.europa.eu/eurostat/statistics-explained/index.php/Underemployment_and_potential_additional_labour_force_statistics

Eurostat (2015, January 30). *Unemployment Statistics.* Retrieved 11 February 2015, from http://ec.europa.eu/eurostat/statistics-explained/index.php/Unemployment_statistics

Eurostat (2015, February 2). *Employment Statistics.* Retrieved 11 February 2015, from http://ec.europa.eu/eurostat/statistics-explained/index.php/Employment_statistics

Farrugia, D. (2009). 'Responsibility, Intersubjectivity, and Recognition: The Case of Australian Young People Experiencing Homelessness.' In Lockie, S. et al. (eds.), *The Future of Sociology,* The Australian National University, Canberra, 1–4 December 2009. Canberra, Australia: TASA. Accessed 30 April 2015 at: https://www.tasa.org.au/wp-content/uploads/2015/03/Farrugia-David.pdf

Fejes, A. (2010). 'Discourses on Employability: Constituting the Responsible Citizen.' *Studies in Continuing Education,* 32(2), 89–102.

Ferguson, M., Hitt, L., & Tambe, P. (2013). *The Talent Equation: Big Data Lessons for Navigating the Skills Gap and Building a Competitive Workforce.* New York: McGraw-Hill.

Fielding, M. & Rudduck, J. (2002). 'The Transformative Potential of Student Voice: Confronting the Power Issues.' Paper presented at the *Annual Conference of the British Educational Research Association,* University of Exeter, England, 12–14 September 2002.

Finnish National Board of Education (2011). *Building an Ecosystem for Innovations in Education: The Case of Finland.* Accessed 17 April 2015 at: http://www.slideboom.com/presentations/459374/Kumpulainen-presentation?pk=42b3-bb9f-ee58-1e98-5b1e-498e-5a16-aeda

Foley, D. (2013). 'Indigenous Australia and the Education System.' In Connell, R., Welch, A., Vickers, M., Foley, D., Bagnell, N., Hayes, D., Proctor, H., Sriprakash,

A., & Campbell, C. (eds.), *Education, Change and Society*. South Melbourne: Oxford University Press, pp. 131–159.

Foster, K. R. & Spencer, D. (2011). 'At Risk of What? Possibilities over Probabilities in the Study of Young Lives.' *Journal of Youth Studies*, 14(1), 125–143.

Foster, S., Delaney, B., Bateman, A., & Dyson, C. (2007). *Higher-level Vocational Education and Training Qualifications: Their Importance in Today's Training Market*. Adelaide: NCVER.

France, A., Sutton, L., & Waring, A. (2010). 'Youth, Citizenship and Risk in UK Social Policy.' In Leaman, J. & Wörsching, M. (eds.), *Youth in Contemporary Europe*. New York and Oxon: Routledge, pp. 165–178.

Fullan, M. (2000). 'The Three Stories of Education Reform.' *Phi Delta Kappan*, 81(8), 581–584.

Fullan, M. (2005). *Leadership Sustainability: System Thinkers in Action*. Thousand Oaks: Corwin Press.

Furlong, A. (2007). 'The Zone of Precarity and Discourses of Vulnerability: NEET in the UK.' *The Journal of Social Sciences and Humanities* (Jinbun Gakuho), 381, 101–121.

Furlong, A. & Cartmel, F. (2007). *Young People and Social Change: New Perspectives* (Second ed.). Maidenhead: Open University Press.

Furlong, A. & Kelly, P. (2005). 'The Brazilianisation of Youth Transitions in Australia and the UK?' *Australian Journal of Social Issues*, 40(2), 207–225.

FYA (The Foundation for Young Australians) (2014). *Unlimited Potential*. Melbourne: The Foundation for Young Australians. Accessed 9 March 2015 at: www.fya.org

Garmezy, N. & Rutter, M. (1983). *Stress, Coping, and Development in Children*. New York: McGraw-Hill.

Garrett, P. (2013). '$6.1 Million to Kick-Start Careers.' *Media Release*, 23 May 2013. Accessed 24 April 2015 at: https://www.nesa.com.au/media/52007/130523_garrett_mr_$6.1%20million%20to%20kick-start%20careers.pdf

Gemici, S., Bednarz, A., Karmel, T., & Lim, P. (2014). *The Factors Affecting the Educational and Occupational Aspirations of Young Australians*. Longitudinal Surveys of Australian Youth Research Report No. 66. Adelaide: National Centre for Vocational Education Research.

Genda, Y. (2005). *A Nagging Sense of Job Insecurity: The New Reality Facing Japanese Youth*. Tokyo: International House of Japan.

Go8 (Group of Eight Australia) (2012). *Go8 Policy Note 6 – National Trends in Year 12 Course Completions*. Accessed 11 April 2015 at: https://go8.edu.au/sites/default/files/docs/go8policynote6_year12completions.pdf

Gonski, D., Boston, K., Greiner, K., Lawrence, C., Scales, B., & Tannock, P. (2011). *Review of Funding for Schooling. Final Report*, December 2011. Canberra: Department of Education, Employment and Workplace Relations.

Graduate Careers Australia (2014). *Postgraduate Destinations 2013. A Report on the Work and Study Outcomes of Recent Higher Education Postgraduates*. Melbourne: Graduate Careers Australia Ltd.

Green, L., Brady, D., Olafsson, K., Hartley, J., & Lumby, C. (2011). 'Parties' Risks and Safety for Australian Children on the Internet: Full Findings from the AU Kids Online Survey of 9–16 Year Olds and Their Parents.' *Cultural Science*, 4(1), 1–73.

Grice, A. (2013). 'Tories Fear Return of Nasty Party in Attacks on Welfare "Scroungers".' *The Independent*, 3 January 2013. Accessed 4 May 2015 at: http://www.independent.co.uk/news/uk/politics/tories-fear-return-of-nasty-party-in-attacks-on-welfare-scroungers-8442950.html

Guthrie, B. & Bryant, G. (2014). *Postgraduate Destinations 2013. A Report on the Work and Study Outcomes of Recent Higher Education Postgraduates*. Melbourne: Graduate Careers Australia.

Halsey, K., Murfield, J., Harland, J. L., & Lord, P. (2006). *The Voice of Young People: An Engine for Improvement? Scoping the Evidence*. Slough: National Foundation for Educational Research.

Hannan, E. (2015). 'SA Penalty Rate Deal No Champagne Moment for Employers.' *The Australian Financial Review*, 28 March 2015. Accessed 30 March 2015 at: http://www.afr.com/news/policy/industrial-relations/sa-penalty-rate-deal-no-champagne-moment-for-employers-20150327-1m7d4i

Hannon, V., Patton, A., & Temperley, J. (2011). *Developing an Innovation Ecosystem for Education*. Cisco White Paper, December 2011. Retrieved 2 June 2014 from: http://www.cisco.com/web/strategy/docs/education/ecosystem_for_edu.pdf

Harvey, D. (2005). *A Brief History of Neoliberalism*. Oxford: Oxford University Press.

Hattie, J. (2009). *Visible Learning: A Synthesis of Over 800 Meta-analyses Relating to Achievement*. London: Routledge.

Heilig, J. V. & Jez, S. J. (2010). *Teach for America: A Review of the Evidence*. East Lansing, MI: The Great Lakes Center for Education Research & Practice. Accessed 21 April 2015 at: http://www.greatlakescenter.org/docs/Policy_Briefs/Heilig_TeachForAmerica.pdf

Henry, K. (2014a). *Wise Words*. Melbourne: Brotherhood of St Laurence. Accessed 2 February 2015 at: http://www.bsl.org.au/media-centre/media-releases/media-release/we-can-t-afford-to-have-260000-youth-unemployed-former-treasury-head-ken-henry/

Henry, K. (2014b). 'Why Rising Youth Unemployment Demands Our Urgent Attention.' *The Conversation*, 29 April 2014. Accessed 2 February 2015 at: http://theconversation.com/why-rising-youth-unemployment-demands-our-urgent-attention-25990

Hillman, K. & McMillan, J. (2005). *Life Satisfaction of Young Australians: Relationships between Further Education, Training and Employment and General and Career Satisfaction*. Victoria: Australian Council for Educational Research.

Hopkins, D. (2008). 'Realising the Potential of System Leadership.' In Pont, B., Nusche, D., & Hopkins, D. (eds.), *Improving School Leadership Volume 2: Case Studies on System Leadership*. Accessed 20 May 2015 at: http://www.oecd.org/education/school/44375122.pdf

HOR (House of Representatives Standing Committee on Education and Training) (2009). *Adolescent Overload? Report of the Inquiry into Combining School and Work: Supporting Successful Youth Transitions*. House of Representatives Standing Committee on Education and Training, October 2009. Canberra: The Parliament of the Commonwealth of Australia.

House of Commons (2009). *House of Commons Children, Schools and Families Committee National Curriculum Fourth Report of Session 2008–09, Volume II. Oral and Written Evidence*. London: The Stationery Office Limited.

House of Representatives (2009). 'Study and Work: The Results Are in.' *About the House*, December, 17–18.

Howell, J. (2013). 'Young People More Optimistic about Futures.' *graduate-jobs. com*, 17 October 2013. Accessed 30 January 2015 at: http://www.graduate-jobs. com/news/12459/Young_people_more_optimistic_about_futures

Howker, E. & Malik, S. (2010). *Jilted Generation: How Britain has Bankrupted Its Youth.* London: Icon Books.

Hudson, P. & Hudson, S. (2008). 'Changing Preservice Teachers' Attitudes for Teaching in Rural Schools.' *Australian Journal of Teacher Education*, 33(4), 67–77. Accessed 24 May 2015 at: http://dx.doi.org/10.14221/ajte.2008v33n4.6

Hughes, H. & Hughes, M. (2010). *Indigenous Education.* St Leonards, NSW: Centre for Independent Studies, Policy Monograph 110.

Hugo, G. (2012a). 'The Cornerstone of Democracy: Why (and How) the Census Counts.' *The Conversation*, 21 June 2012. Accessed 23 April 2015 at: http:// theconversation.com/the-cornerstone-of-democracy-why-and-how-the-census-counts-7607

Hugo, G. (2012b). 'Challenge 3: Balancing Population Growth and Resources.' *The Conversation*, 12 June 2012. Accessed 23 April 2015 at: http://theconversation.com/challenge-3-balancing-population-growth-and-resources-7489

Human Rights Commission (2009). *Social Justice Report 2009.* Aboriginal and Torres Strait Islander Social Justice Commissioner, Sydney: Australian Human Rights Commission.

Huntley, R. (2006). *The World According to Y: Inside the New Adult Generation.* NSW, Australia: Allen & Unwin.

Hurst, D. (2014). 'Tony Abbott Praises US Idea of Schools in Partnership with Major Companies.' *The Guardian*, 12 June 2014. Accessed 24 April 2015 at: http://www.theguardian.com/world/2014/jun/12/tony-abbott-praises-schools-partnership-companies

IB (International Baccalaureate) (2015). *MYP Projects.* Accessed 9 March 2015 at: http://www.ibo.org/en/programmes/middle-years-programme/curriculum/myp-projects/

ILO (International Labour Organisation) (1982). *Resolution Concerning Statistics of the Economically Active Population, Employment, Unemployment and Underemployment, adopted by the Thirteenth International Conference of Labour Statisticians.* Geneva: International Labour Office. Accessed 25 May 2015 at: http://www.ilo. org/public/english/bureau/stat/download/res/ecacpop.pdf

ILO (International Labour Organisation) (2010). *Global Employment Trends for Youth.* Geneva: International Labour Office.

ILO (International Labour Organisation) (2012). *Global Employment Trends.* Geneva: International Labour Office.

ILO (International Labour Organisation) (2013). *Global Employment Trends for Youth 2013: A Generation at Risk.* Geneva: International Labour Office.

ILO (International Labour Organisation) (2015). *World Employment and Social Outlook Trends 2015.* Geneva: International Labour Office. Accessed 22 May 2015 at: http://www.ilo.org/wcmsp5/groups/public/---dgreports/---dcomm/---publ/documents/publication/wcms_337070.pdf

IMF (International Monetary Fund) (2013). *Global Housing Watch.* Accessed 16 September 2014 at: http://www.imf.org/external/research/housing/index.htm

The Independent (2014). 'Jobless must Sign on Every Day: Government to Dock Money from Long-term Unemployed If They Do Not Comply.' *The Independent*, 28 April 2014. Accessed 30 January 2015 at: http://www.independent.co.uk/

news/uk/politics/jobless-mustsign-on-every-day-government-to-dock-money-from-longterm-unemployed-if-they-do-not-comply-9294586.html

Inman, P. (2015). 'Almost 700,000 People in UK Have Zero-Hours Contract as Main Job.' *The Guardian*, 25 February 2015. Accessed 25 February 2015 at: http://www.theguardian.com/uk-news/2015/feb/25/zero-hours-contract-rise-staff-figures

Ipsos MORI (2014). *Ipsos MORI Global Trends Survey*, 14 April 2014. Accessed 30 January 2014 at: https://www.ipsos-mori.com/researchpublications/research archive/3369/People-in-western-countries-pessimistic-about-future-for-young-people.aspx#gallery[m]/0/

Istance, D. (2011). *Innovative Learning Environments: An International OECD Project*. Centre for Strategic Education Seminar Series, December 2011. East Melbourne: Centre for Strategic Education.

IYF (International Youth Foundation) (2013). *Getting Youth in the Door: Defining Soft Skills Requirements for Entry-level Service Sector Jobs*. Accessed 1 May 2015 at: http://library.iyfnet.org/library/getting-youth-door-defining-soft-skills-requirements-entry-level-service-sector-jobs

Jay, M. (2010). 'Liquidity Crisis: Zygmunt Bauman and the Incredible Lightness of Modernity.' *Theory, Culture & Society*, 27(6), 95–106.

Jensen, B. & Reichl, J. (2012). *Implementing a Performance and Development Framework*. Melbourne: Grattan Institute.

Jensen, B., Sandoval-Hernández, A., Knoll, S., & Gonzalez, E. (2012). *The Experience of New Teachers: Results from TALIS 2008*. Paris: OECD Publishing. Accessed 24 November 2014 at: http://www.oecd.org/edu/school/49846877.pdf

Johnson, M. (2012). 'Spanish Youth Urged to Seek Work Abroad.' *The Financial Times*, 2 May 2012. Accessed 27 April 2015 at: http://www.ft.com/cms/s/0/f2018cf0-9467-11e1-8e90-00144feab49a.html

Kahn, L., Abdo, M., Hewes, S., McNeil, B., & Norman, W. (2011). *The Way to Work: Young People Speak Out on Transitions to Employment*. London: The Youth of Today & The Young Foundation.

Kahn, L., McNeil, B., Patrick, R., Sellick, V., Thompson, K., & Walsh, L. (2012). *Developing Skills for Life and Work: Accelerating Social and Emotional Learning across South Australia*. London: Young Foundation.

Kalleberg, A. (2009). 'Precarious Work, Insecure Workers: Employment Relations in Transition.' *American Sociological Review*, 74(1), 1–22.

Karmel, T., Lu, T., & Oliver, D. (2013). *Starting Out in Low-skill Jobs*. Adelaide: NCVER.

Karvelas, P. (2014a). 'No Dole Before 25: Youth will have to Earn or Learn.' *The Australian*, 3 May 2014. Accessed 13 April 2015 at: http://www.theaustralian.com.au/national-affairs/budget-2014/no-dole-before-25-youth-will-have-to-earn-or-learn/story-fnmbxr2t-1226903967790

Karvelas, P. (2014b). 'Reprieve for Some before the Loss of Dole Payments.' *The Australian*, 28 May 2014. Accessed 19 May 2015 at: http://www.theaustralian.com.au/national-affairs/industrial-relations/reprieve-for-some-before-the-loss-of-dole-payments/story-fn59noo3-1226933815660

Keating, J. (2009). *A New Federalism in Australian Education: A Proposal for a National Reform Agenda*. Melbourne: The Foundation for Young Australians.

Kelly, J. F. & Mares, P. (2013). *Productive Cities: Opportunity in a Changing Economy*. Melbourne: The Grattan Institute.

Kelly, P. (2000). 'Youth as an Artefact of Expertise: Problematizing the Practice of Youth Studies in an Age of Uncertainty.' *Journal of Youth Studies*, 3(3), 301–315.

Kelly, P. (2001). 'Youth at Risk: Processes of Individualisation and Responsibilisation in the Risk Society.' *Discourse: Studies in the Cultural Politics of Education*, 22(1), 23–33.

Kelly, P. (2006). 'The Entrepreneurial Self and "Youth at Risk": Exploring the Horizons of Identity in the 21st Century.' *Journal of Youth Studies*, 9, 17–32.

Kelly, P. (2011a). *A Social Science of Risk: The Trap of Empiricism, the Problem of Ambivalence?* Geelong: Deakin University.

Kelly, P. (2011b). 'An Untimely Future for Youth Studies?' *Youth Studies Australia*, 30(3), 47–53.

Kenway, J., Bullen, E., Fahey, J., & Robb, S. (2006). *Haunting the Knowledge Economy*. London and New York: Routledge.

Kharas, H. (2010). 'The Emerging Middle Class in Developing Countries.' *OECD Development Centre Working Paper No. 285*. Paris: OECD.

King, A. (2012). 'Gen Y's Have Tickets on Themselves.' *Australian Financial Review*, 12 September 2012. Accessed 20 July 2015 at: http://www.afr.com/news/policy/industrial-relations/gen-ys-have-tickets-on-themselves-20120911-j1s99

Kirby, K. (2011). 'Learning to Live in the Asian Century.' *The Conversation*, 13 October 2011. Accessed 29 April 2015 at: https://theconversation.com/learning-to-live-in-the-asian-century-3586

Knight, J. (1994). *Internationalisation: Elements and Checkpoints*. Ottawa: Canadian Bureau for International Education.

Kozol, J. (1993). 'The Sharks Move In.' *New Internationalist*, 248(October), 8–10.

Krause, K. Hartley, R., James, R., & McInnis, C. (2005). *The First Year Experience in Australian Universities: Findings from a Decade of National Studies*. Centre for the Study of Higher Education University of Melbourne. Final Report January 2005. Canberra: Australian Government Department of Education, Science and Training.

Krockenberger, M. (2015). *Population Growth in Australia*. Canberra: The Australia Institute. Accessed 26 March 2015 at: http://www.tai.org.au/content/population-growth-australia

Laczko-Kerr, I. & Berliner, D. (2002). 'The Effectiveness of Teach for America and Other Under-certified Teachers on Student Academic Achievement: A Case of Harmful Public Policy.' *Education Policy Analysis Archives*, 10(37), 1–53. Accessed 20 May 2015 at: http://epaa.asu.edu/ojs/article/download/316/442

Lamb, S. & Mason, K. (2008). *How Young People Are Faring 2008*. Melbourne: The Foundation for Young Australians.

Lamb, S., Robinson, L., & Walstab, A. (2010). *How Young People Are Faring 2010*. Melbourne: The Foundation for Young Australians.

Lareau, A. & Weininger, E. (2004). 'Cultural Capital in Educational Research: A Critical Assessment.' In Swartz, D. & Zolberg, V. (eds.), *After Bourdieu Influence, Critique, Elaboration*. Dordrecht: Kluwer Academic, pp. 105–144.

Levin, B. (2008). *How to Change 5000 Schools*. Cambridge, MA: Harvard Educational Press.

Lewis, D. (with Esther Han) (2012). 'An Age of Hostility Looms.' *Sydney Morning Herald*. Accessed 23 September 2012 at: http://m.smh.com.au/national/an-age-of-hostility-looms-20120922-26doh.html

Lewis, M. (2014). *Flash Boys: Cracking the Money Code*. London: Allen Lane.

Long, M. & North, S. (2009). *How Young Indigenous People Are Faring: Key Indicators 1996–2006.* Canberra: Dusseldorp Skills Forum. Accessed 4 August 2009 at: http://www.dsf.org.au/get/index.php?id=208andn=How+Young+Indigenous+People+are+Faringandext=pdf andp=%2Fmedia%2Ffiles%2Fresource%2F208.pdf

Lonsdale, M. & Ingvarson, L. (2003). *Initiatives to Address Teacher Shortage. ACER Policy Brief,* Issue 5, 3 November 2003. Camberwell: Australian Council for Educational Research.

Luke, A. (2010). 'Will the Australian National Curriculum up the Intellectual Ante in Classrooms?' *Curriculum Perspectives,* 30(3), 59–64.

Lupton, D. (2006). 'Sociology and Risk.' In Mythen, G. & Walklate, S. (eds.), *Beyond the Risk Society: Critical Reflections on Risk and Human Security.* Berkshire: Open University Press, pp. 11–24.

MacDonald, R. (2009). 'Precarious Work: Risk, Choice and Poverty Traps.' In Furlong, A. (ed.), *Handbook of Youth Handbook of Youth and Young Adulthood: New Perspectives and Agendas.* London: Routledge, pp. 167–175.

Mann, A. (2012). *It's Who You Meet: Why Employer Contacts at School Make a Difference to the Employment Prospects of Young Adults.* London: Education and Employers Taskforce.

Mansouri, F. & Jenkins, L. (2010). 'Schools as Sites of Race Relations and Intercultural Tension.' *Australian Journal of Teacher Education,* 35(7), 93–108. Accessed 25 May 2015 at: http://ro.ecu.edu.au/cgi/viewcontent.cgi?article=1478&context=ajte

Mansouri, F., Jenkins, L., Morgan, L., & Taouk, M. (2009). *The Impact of Racism upon the Health and Wellbeing of Young Australians.* Melbourne: The Foundation for Young Australians.

Marks, G. & Ainley, J. (1999). 'School Achievement and Labour Market Outcomes.' *Discussion Paper No. 408.* Paper presented to the *Centre for Economic Policy Research, ANU Conference on Labour Market Trends and Family Policies: Implications for Children,* 14–15 July 1999. Accessed 20 April 2015 at: https://digitalcollections.anu.edu.au/bitstream/1885/40226/2/DP408.pdf

Marshall, G., Cole, P., & Zbar, V. (2012). *Teacher Performance and Development in Australia: A Mapping and Analysis of Current Practice.* Melbourne: AITSL.

Martin, O. (2014). 'Lousy Days Loom for Small Businesses Bombarded by Job-Seekers.' *The Sydney Morning Herald,* 29 July 2014. Accessed 18 August 2014 at: http://www.smh.com.au/federal-politics/political-opinion/lousy-days-loom-for-small-businesses-bombarded-by-jobseekers-20140728-3cpxb.html#ixzz3AinFYA3n

Martin, P. (2009). 'Women Make Jobs Gains While Men Lose Out.' *The Age,* 10 July 2009. Accessed 25 May 2015 at: http://www.theage.com.au/national/women-make-jobs-gains-while-men-lose-out-20090709-dep7.html

Maslen, G. (2009). '24/7 Teens.' *About the House,* 36, 20–25.

Massola, J. (2015). 'Penalty Rates, Minimum Wage: All Bets Are Off.' *Sydney Morning Herald,* 22 January 2015. Accessed 22 March 2015 at: http://www.smh.com.au/federal-politics/political-news/penalty-rates-minimum-wage-all-bets-are-off-20150122-12vxa2.html

Matthews, D. (2013). 'The U.S. has a $7.25 Minimum Wage. Australia's Is $16.88.' *The Washington Post,* 19 August 2013. Accessed 23 March 2015 at: http://www.washingtonpost.com/blogs/wonkblog/wp/2013/08/19/the-u-s-has-a-7-25-minimum-wage-australias-is-16-88/

Mavromaras, K., Mahuteau, S., Sloane, P. & Wei, Z. (2012). *The Persistence of Overskilling and Its Effect on Wages.* Adelaide: NCVER.

Mayer, D. & Lloyd, M. (2011). *Professional Learning: An Introduction to the Research Literature October 2011*. Melbourne: AITSL.

Mayer, S. (2014). 'Business Push on Sunday Penalties.' *The Australian*, 23 June 2014. Accessed 20 March 2015 at: http://www.theaustralian.com.au/national-affairs/industrial-relations/business-push-on-sunday-penalties/story-fn59noo3-1226940798835

McDougall, B. (2013). 'Generation Consigned to the Scrapheap.' *The Australian*, 29 April 2013. Accessed 25 May 2015 at: http://www.theaustralian.com.au/news/generation-consigned-to-the-scrapheap/story-e6frg6n6-1226631159132

McDougall, B. (2014). 'No School Jobs Available for Thousands of Trained Teachers throughout NSW Schools.' *The Daily Telegraph*, 8 July 2014. Accessed 13 March 2014 at: http://www.dailytelegraph.com.au/news/nsw/no-school-jobs-available-for-thousands-of-trained-teachers-throughout-nsw-schools/story-fni0cx12-1226980912361

MCEETYA (Ministerial Council on Education, Employment, Training and Youth Affairs) (2008). *Melbourne Declaration on Educational Goals for Young Australians*. Canberra: Australian Government.

McGregor, J. (2013). 'Businesses Must Rise Up to Meet the Asian Century.' *The Age*, 25 July 2013. Accessed 29 April 2015 at: http://www.theage.com.au/comment/businesses-must-rise-up-to-meet-the-asian-century-20130724-2qjj3.html

McKenzie, P., Weldon, P., Rowley, G., Murphy, M., & McMillan, J. (2014). *Staff in Australia's Schools 2013: Main Report on the Survey*, April 2014. Camberwell: Australian Council for Educational Research.

McLintock, P. (2014). 'Budget 2014: Young Unemployed to Work for the Dole, University Students to Pay More.' *ABC News*, 14 May 2014. Accessed 13 April 2015 at: http://www.abc.net.au/news/2014-05-13/young-unemployed-work-dole-university-students-pay-more-budget/5450878

Mission Australia (2010). *National Survey of Young Australians 2010: Key and Emerging Issues*. Sydney: Mission Australia.

Mission Australia (2011). *National Survey of Young Australians 2011*. Sydney: Mission Australia.

Mission Australia (2012). *Mission Australia Youth Survey – 2012*. Sydney: Mission Australia.

Mission Australia (2013). 'Employer Survey Paints a Tough Picture for Young Job Seekers.' *Media Release*, 1 March 2013. Accessed 25 May 2015 at: http://bsllibrary.org.au/employment-training/employer-survey-paints-a-tough-picture-for-young-job-seekers-mission-australia-30016/

Mitchell, W. (2015). 'Punishment Dished Out to Unemployed Is On Par with Our Treatment of Refugees.' *The Guardian*, 25 February 2015. Accessed 25 February 2015 at: http://www.theguardian.com/commentisfree/2015/feb/24/punishment-dished-out-to-unemployed-is-on-par-with-our-treatment-of-refugees

Modestino, A. S. (2010). *Mismatch in the Labor Market: Measuring the Supply of and Demand for Skilled Labor in New England*. New England Public Policy Center Research Report 10 – 2 November 2010. Boston: Federal Reserve Bank of Boston.

Morton, A. (2009). 'First Climate Refugees Start Move to New Island Home.' *The Age*, 29 July 2009. Accessed 25 May 2015 at: http://www.theage.com.au/national/first-climate-refugees-start-move-to-new-island-home-20090728-e06x

Mourshed, M., Farrell, D., & Barton, D. (2012). *Education to Employment: Designing a System That Works*. Washington, DC: McKinsey Center for Government.

Muir, K., Mullan, K., Powell, A., Flaxman, S., Thompson, D., & Griffiths, M. (2009). *State of Australia's Young People: A Report on the Social, Economic, Health and Family Lives of Young People.* Sydney: Social Policy Research Centre, University of New South Wales.

National Foundation for Australian Women (NFAW) (2013). *Election 2013.* Accessed 18 August 2014 at: http://www.nfaw.org/nfaw-election-2013/

news.com.au (2011). 'Anger Boils over in Global GFC Protests.' *news.com.au*, 16 October 2011. Accessed 25 May 2015 at: http://www.news.com.au/breaking-news/anger-boils-over-in-global-gfc-protests/story-e6frfku0-1226167634623

news.com.au (2013). 'Facebook Fatigue Sets in with Thousands Abandoning the Social Network.' *news.com.au*, 28 April 2013. Accessed 1 April 2015 at: http://www.news.com.au/technology/facebook-fatigue-sets-in-with-thousands-abandoning-the-social-network/story-e6frfro0-1226630663227

news.com.au (2014). 'Welfare Expert Patrick McClure in Push to Restrict Dole Spending for Young Jobseekers.' *news.com.au*, 30 June 2014. Accessed 25 May 2015 at: http://www.news.com.au/national/welfare-expert-patrick-mcclure-in-push-to-restrict-dole-spending-for-young-jobseekers/story-fncynjr2-12269 71487479

Niemi, H. (2011). 'Educating Student Teachers to Become High Quality Professionals – A Finnish Case.' *CEPS Journal.* Center for Educational Policy Studies 1(1), 43–66.

Niemi, H. & Jakku-Sihvonen, R. (2006). 'In the Front of the Bologna Process: Thirty Years of Research-based Teacher Education in Finland.' In Jakku-Sihvonen, R. & Niemi, H. (eds.), *Posodobitev pedagoških študijskih programovv mednarodnem kontekstu: Modernization of study programmes in teachers' education in an international context.* Ljubljana: Univerza v Ljubljani, Pedagoška fakulteta 2006, 50–69.

Niemi, H. & Jakku-Sihvonen, R. (2009). *Teacher Education Curriculum of Secondary School Teachers.* Helsinki: University of Helsinki. Accessed 1 May 2015 at: http://www.revistaeducacion.mec.es/re350/re350_08ing.pdf

OECD (Organisation for Economic Co-operation and Development) (2008). *Improving School Leadership. Volume 1: Policy and Practice.* Paris: OECD.

OECD (Organisation for Economic Co-operation and Development) (2009). *Jobs for Youth Australia.* Paris: OECD.

OECD (Organisation for Economic Co-operation and Development) (2010). *Off to a Good Start? Jobs for Youth.* Paris: OECD. Accessed 1 May 2015 at: http://www.oecd.org/els/emp/46717876.pdf

OECD (Organisation for Economic Co-operation and Development) (2012a). *AUSTRALIA – Country Note – Education at a Glance 2012: OECD Indicators.* Paris: OECD. Accessed 23 March 2015 at: http://dx.doi.org/10.1787/eag-2012-en

OECD (Organisation for Economic Co-operation and Development) (2012b). *CERI – Innovative Learning Environments (ILE).* Paris: OECD. Accessed 1 May 2015 at: http://www.oecd.org/edu/ceri/The%20ILE%20project.pdf

OECD (Organisation for Economic Co-operation and Development) (2013a). *Education at a Glance 2013: OECD Indicators, Table C5.2d.* Paris: OECD.

OECD (Organisation for Economic Co-operation and Development) (2013b). *OECD Stat Extracts.* Accessed 20 February 2013 at: http://stats.oecd.org/Index.aspx?DatasetCode=INVPT_I

OECD (Organisation for Economic Co-operation and Development) (2015). *Education Policy Outlook 2015: Making Reforms Happen.* Paris: OECD. Accessed 17 April 2015 at: http://dx.doi.org/10.1787/9789264225442-en

Ortlieb, E. (2015). 'Just Graduating from University Is No Longer Enough to Get a Job.' *The Conversation*, 12 February 2015. Accessed 16 February 2015 at: http://theconversation.com/just-graduating-from-university-is-no-longer-enough-to-get-a-job-36906

Ozga, J. (2000). *Policy Research in Educational Settings: Contested Terrain*. Buckingham: Open University Press.

Partnership for 21st Century Skills (2009). *P21 Framework Definitions*. Washington, DC: P21. Accessed 25 May 2015 at: http://www.p21.org/storage/documents/P21_Framework_Definitions.pdf

Patton, W. & Smith, E. (2009). 'Part-Time Work of High School Students and Impact on Educational Outcomes.' *Australian Journal of Guidance and Counselling*, 19(2), 216–224.

Patty, A. (2015). 'Overseas Workers Will Be Allowed to Work for a Year without Applying for 457 Visas.' *The Sydney Morning Herald*, 7 January 2015. Accessed 12 April 2015 at: http://www.smh.com.au/nsw/overseas-workers-will-be-allowed-to-work-for-a-year-without-applying-for-457-visas-20150107-12jf3r.html

Pavlidis, A. (2009). 'The Diverse Logics of Risk: Young People's Negotiations of the Risk Society.' In Lockie, S., Bissell, D., Greig, A., Hynes, M., Marsh, D., Saha, L., Sikora, J., & Woodman, D. (eds.), *The Future of Sociology*, The Australian National University, Canberra, 1–4 December 2009. Canberra, Australia: TASA.

Pegg, G., McPhan, G., Mowbray, B., & Lynch, T. (2010). *Validation of the Australian Professional Standards for Teachers: Executive Summary*. Melbourne: AISTL.

PhillipsKPA Pty Ltd. (2010). *Unfolding Opportunities: A Baseline Study of School Business Relationships in Australia*. Richmond: Department of Education, Employment and Workplace Relations. Accessed 20 April 2015 at: https://education.gov.au/partnerships-between-schools-businesses-andcommunities-reports-and-research

Pocock, B., Skinner, N., & Pisaniello, S. (2010). *How Much Should We Work: Working Hours, Working Holidays and Working Life: The Participation Challenge. The Australian Work and Life Index 2010*. South Australia: The Centre for Work + Life, University of South Australia.

Pope, J. (2006). *Indicators of Community Strength: A Framework and Evidence*. Melbourne: Department for Victorian Communities.

Price, D. (2010). *Learning Futures: Engaging Students*. London: Paul Hamlyn Foundation.

Priest, N., Ferdinand, A., Perry, R., Paradies, Y., & Kelaher, M. (2014). *Mental Health Impacts of Racism and Attitudes to Diversity in Victorian Schools: A Summary of Survey Findings*. Melbourne: VicHealth.

Pro Bono (2014). 'Jobless Generation on Cards for Australia.' *Pro Bono*, 24 February 2014. Accessed 13 April 2015 at: http://www.probonoaustralia.com.au/news/2014/02/jobless-generation-cards-australia#

Productivity Commission (2002). *Independent Review of the Job Network*. Inquiry Report No. 21, 3 June 2002. Canberra: Government of Australia.

Productivity Commission (2009). *Overcoming Indigenous Disadvantage: Key Indicators 2009*. Canberra: Australian Government.

Productivity Commission (2012). *Schools Workforce*. Research Report, May. Accessed 30 April 2015 at: http://www.pc.gov.au/projects/study/education-workforce/schools/report

Productivity Commission (2014). *Overcoming Indigenous Disadvantage: Key Indicators 2014*. Canberra: The Australian Government.

Productivity Commission (2015). *Workplace Relations Framework: The Inquiry in Context.* Canberra: The Australian Government. Accessed 20 March 2015 at: http://www.pc.gov.au/inquiries/current/workplace-relations/issues/workplace-relations-issues-combined.pdf

Quiggin, J. (1999). 'Globalisation, Neoliberalism and Inequality in Australia.' *The Economic and Labour Relations Review*, 10(2), 240–259.

Quinlan, M. (2012). 'The "Pre-invention" of Precarious Employment: The Changing World of Work in Context.' *Economic and Labour Relations Review*, 23(4), 3–24.

Rawolle, S. & Lingard, B. (2008). 'The Sociology of Pierre Bourdieu and Researching Education Policy.' *Journal of Education Policy*, 23, 729–741.

Rigsby, L. (1994). 'The Americanization of Resilience: Deconstructing Research Practice.' In Wang, M. & Gordon, E. (eds.), *Educational Resilience in Inner-City America: Challenges and Prospects.* New York: Routledge, pp. 85–94.

Roberts, A. & Wignall, L. (2010). *Briefing on Foundation Skills for the National VET Equity Advisory Council (NVEAC).* Melbourne: TVET. Accessed 18 August 2014 at: http://www.nveac.natese.gov.au/__data/assets/pdf_file/0008/56348/Briefing_on_Foundation_Skills_-_Roberts_and_Wignall.pdf

Roberts, Y. (2009). *Grit: The Skills for Success and How They Are Grown.* London: The Young Foundation.

Robertson, E. (2014). 'Generation Y Didn't Go Crazy in a Vacuum. How Can We Enjoy Life When Our Future Is So Uncertain?' *The Guardian*, 17 October 2014. Accessed 30 January 2014 at: http://www.theguardian.com/commentisfree/2014/oct/17/generation-y-didnt-go-crazy-in-a-vacuum-how-can-we-enjoy-life-when-our-future-is-so-uncertain

Robinson, L. & Lamb, S. (2009). *How Young People Are Faring 2009.* Melbourne: The Foundation for Young Australians.

Robinson, L., & Lamb, S. (2012). *How Young People Are Faring 2012.* Melbourne: The Foundation for Young Australians.

Robinson, L., Lamb, S., & Walstab, A. (2010). *How Young People Are Faring 2010.* Melbourne: The Foundation for Young Australians.

Robinson, L., Long, M., & Lamb, S. (2011). *How Young People Are Faring 2011.* Melbourne: The Foundation for Young Australians.

Rodgers, G. (1989). 'Precarious Work in Western Europe: The State of the Debate.' In Rodgers, G. & Rodgers, J. (eds.), *Precarious Jobs in Labour Market Regulation: The Economic and Labour Relations Review the Growth of Atypical Employment in Western Europe.* Geneva: International Institute for Labour Studies, pp. 1–16.

Rose, N. (1998). *Inventing Our Selves: Psychology, Power, and Personhood.* New York: Cambridge University Press.

Rose, N. (1999). *Powers of Freedom: Reframing Political Thought.* Cambridge, UK: Cambridge University Press.

Rose, N. (2014). *From Risk to Resilience: Responsible Citizens for Uncertain Times.* Public Lecture, 28 August 2014, Ian Potter Auditorium, Kenneth Myer Building, Royal Parade, Parkville, Australia.

Rothman, S. & Hillman, K. (2008). *Career Advice in Australian Secondary School: Use and Usefulness.* LSAY Research Report 53. Camberwell: Australian Council for Educational Research.

Samms, J. (2010). *Building Stronger Pathways for Young Aboriginal People.* Canberra: Ministerial Taskforce on Aboriginal Affairs, Department of Planning & Community Development.

Savelsberg, H. J. (2010). 'Setting Responsible Pathways: The Politics of Responsibilisation.' *Journal of Education Policy*, 25(5), 657–675.

Schleicher, A. (ed.) (2012). *Preparing Teachers and Developing School Leaders for the 21st Century: Lessons from around the World*. Paris: OECD Publishing. Accessed 19 May 2015 at: http://www.oecd.org/site/eduistp2012/49850576.pdf

Schleicher, A. (2013). *OECD Dialogue*. Presentation on 3 July 2013, Bastow Institute of Educational Leadership, North Melbourne, Australia.

Seccombe, M. (2013). 'What Happens When Half the World Stops Making Babies.' *The Global Mail*, 12 March 2013. Accessed 9 February 2015 at: http://www.theglobalmail.org/feature/what-happens-when-half-the-world-stops-making-babies/573/

Sikora, J. & Saha, L. J. (2011). *Lost Talent? The Occupational Ambitions and Attainments of Young Australians*. South Australia: National Centre for Vocational Education Research.

SiMERR (The National Centre of Science, ICT, and Mathematics Education for Rural and Regional Australia) (2012a). *AITSL Pilot Projects, July–November, 2011 REVISED DRAFT Summary Report* (February 2012). NSW, Australia: SiMERR National Research Centre, University of New England.

SiMERR (The National Centre of Science, ICT, and Mathematics Education for Rural and Regional Australia) (2012b). *AITSL Pilot Projects, Draft Final Report – Appendix C, Executive Summaries*. NSW, Australia: SiMERR National Research Centre, University of New England. Accessed 30 April 2015 at: http://simerr.une.edu.au/pages/projects/aitsl_reports/AITSL%20Pilot%20Projects%20Appendix%20C%20-%20Executive%20Summaries-final.pdf

Skoczylas, T. & Mrozowicki, A. (2012). 'The Precariat: The New Dangerous Class.' (Book Review). *Labor History*, 53(4), 588–589.

Stacey, D. (2013). 'The Real Problem with Gen Y.' *The Age*, 1 July 2013. Accessed 29 April 2015 at: http://www.dailylife.com.au/news-and-views/dl-opinion/the-real-problem-with-gen-y-20130628-2p0z8.html

Standing, G. (2011). *The Precariat: The New Dangerous Class*. London: Bloomsbury.

Standing, G. (2012). 'The Precariat: From Denizens to Citizens?' *Polity*, 44(4), 588–608.

Stanwick, J., Lu, T., Karmel, T., & Wibrow, B. (2013). *How Young People Are Faring 2013*. Melbourne: The Foundation for Young Australians.

Stein, T. G., Stauber, B., & Walther, A. (2003). *Misleading Trajectories? An Evaluation of the Unintended Effects of Labour Market Integration Policies for Young Adults in Europe*. Tübingen: Institut fuer regionale Innovation und Sozialforschung. Accessed 19 May 2015 at: http://cordis.europa.eu/documents/documentlibrary/70601461EN6.pdf

Sum, A. & McLaughlin, J. (2011). *Changes in the Weekly and Annual Earnings of Young Adults from 1979–2010: Progress and Setbacks amidst Widening Inequality*. CDF Policy Brief No. 3. Accessed 20 April 2015 at: http://www.childrensdefense.org/zzz-child-research-data-publications/changes-in-the-weekly-and.pdf

SVA (Social Ventures Australia Consulting) (2013). *Partnership Brokers Program: Baseline Social Return on Investment Analysis Summary Report*, February 2013. Accessed 31 March 2015 at: http://partnershipbrokers.org/w/wp-content/uploads/2013/07/Partnership-Brokers-SROI-Summary-Report.pdf

Svendsen, G. & Svendsen, G. (2004). 'On the Wealth of Nations: Bourdieuconomics and Social Capital.' In Swartz, D. & Zolberg, V. (eds.), *After Bourdieu Influence, Critique, Elaboration*. Dordrecht: Kluwer Academic, pp. 239–263.

Tatham, P. & McIlveen, P. (2009). 'Improving the Career Literacy of Australian Students.' In *TAFE Directors Australia and the Career Industry Council of Australia Round Table: Improving the Career Literacy of Australian Students*, 10 August 2009, Melbourne, Australia.

Tennant, L., Tayler, C., Farrell, A., & Patterson, C. (2005). 'Social Capital and Sense of Community: What Do They Mean for Young Children's Success at School?' *Proceedings Australian Association for Research in Education International Research Conference*, Sydney, Australia.

Thomas, S. (2008). 'Leading for Quality: Questions About Quality and Leadership in Australia.' *Journal of Education Policy*, 23, 323–334.

Thomas, T. (2009). 'The Age and Qualifications of Special Education Staff in Australia.' *Australasian Journal of Special Education*, 33(2), 109–116.

Thomson, P. (2009). *School Leadership – Heads on the Block?* Oxon and New York: Routledge.

Timperley, H. (2011). *A Background Paper to Inform the Development of a National Professional Development Framework for Teachers and School Leaders*. Melbourne: AITSL.

Timperley, H., Wilson, A., Barrar, H., & Fung, I. (2007). *Teacher Professional Learning and Development: Best Evidence Synthesis Iteration*. Wellington, New Zealand: New Zealand Ministry of Education. Accessed 21 April 2015 at: http://www.oecd.org/edu/school/48727127.pdf

Todhunter, J. (2009). 'The Effect of Permanent Income on Completed Schooling in Australia.' Paper presented at the *HILDA Survey Research Conference*, Melbourne, 16–17 July 2009.

Toscano, N., Bagshaw, E., & Massol, J. (2015). 'Unions Vow to Mobilise as Abbott Plans to Make Industrial Relations a Major Election Issue.' *Sydney Morning Herald*, 23 January 2015. Accessed 22 March 2015 at: http://www.smh.com.au/federal-politics/political-news/unions-vow-to-mobilise-as-abbott-plans-to-make-industrial-relations-a-major-election-issue-20150123-12x1zo.html

Treanor, P. (2005). *Neoliberalism: Origins, Theory, Definition*. Online. Accessed 8 May 2015 at: http://web. inter.nl.net/users/Paul.Treanor/neoliberalism.html

UN (United Nations) (2012a). *World Youth Report*. New York: International Labour Organization and United Nations, Department of Economic and Social Affairs. Accessed 30 January 2015 at: http://www.unworldyouthreport.org/index.php?option=com_k2&view=item&id=62:growing-gaps-in-decent-work-for-young-people-in-the-aftermath-of-the-global&Itemid=122

UN (United Nations) (2012b). *World Youth Report. Report Summary*. New York: International Labour Organization and United Nations, Department of Economic and Social Affairs. Accessed 30 January 2015 at: http://www.un.org/esa/socdev/unyin/documents/wyr11/summaryreport.pdf

UN (United Nations) (2014). *Definition of Youth*. Accessed 21 November 2014 at: http://www.un.org/esa/socdev/documents/youth/fact-sheets/youth-definition.pdf

UN (United Nations) (2015). *Millennium Development Goal Indicators: Metadata*. Accessed 5 February 2015 at: http://mdgs.un.org/unsd/mdg/Metadata.aspx

UNESCO (United Nations Educational, Scientific and Cultural Organization) (2006). *Synergies between Formal and Non-formal Education: An Overview of Good Practices*, March 2006. Paris: UNESCO.

Ungar, M. (2008). 'Resilience across Cultures.' *British Journal of Social Work*, 38, 218–235. Accessed 21 April 2015 at: doi:10.1093/bjsw/bcl343

Ungar, M. (2013). 'Introduction to the Volume.' In Ungar M. (ed.), *The Social Ecology of Resilience: A Handbook of Theory and Practice*. New York and London: Springer, pp. 1–12.

United Nations, Department of Economic and Social Affairs, Population Division (2014). *World Fertility Report 2013: Fertility at the Extremes*. New York: United Nations.

Universities Australia (2014). *Key Facts & Data*, 7 July 2014. Accessed 16 February 2015 at: https://www.universitiesaustralia.edu.au/australias-universities/key-facts-and-data#.VOEhcb9D_Kl

UNRIC (United Nations Regional Information Centre for Western Europe) (2012a). *Youth: The Hardest Hit by the Global Financial Crisis*. Accessed 29 January 2015 at: http://www.unric.org/en/youth-unemployment/27414-youth-the-hardest-hit-by-the-global-financial-crisis

UNRIC (United Nations Regional Information Centre for Western Europe) (2012b). *Youth Unemployment*. Accessed 29 January 2015 at: http://www.unric.org/en/youth-unemployment/

Vickers, M. (2011). 'Juggling School and Work and Making the Most of Both.' In Price, R., McDonald, P., Bailey, J., & Pini, B. (eds.), *Young People and Work*. Surrey: Ashgate, pp. 105–120.

Walker, J. (2014). '"One Chance" for University Reform, says Christopher Pyne.' *The Australian*, 27 August 2015. Accessed 25 May 2015 at: http://www.theaustralian.com.au/national-affairs/education/one-chance-for-university-reform-says-christopher-pyne/story-fn59nlz9-1227038023822

Walsh, L. (2010). 'Six Challenges to the Social Inclusion of Young People in Times of Economic Uncertainty.' *Developing Practice: The Child, Youth and Family Work Journal*, 26(Spring), 21–29.

Walsh, L. (2013). 'Incentives Not Enough to Tackle Youth Unemployment.' *The Drum*, 28 August 2013. Accessed 30 March 2015 at: http://www.abc.net.au/news/2013-08-28/walsh-incentives-not-enough-to-tackle-youth-unemployment/4919112

Walsh, L. (2014). 'Casualisation of Youth Employment Is Mortgaging the Future.' *The Canberra Times*, 28 May 2014. Accessed 4 May 2015 at: http://www.canberratimes.com.au/comment/casualisation-of-youth-employment-is-mortgaging-the-future-20140529-zrqoh.html#ixzz3A2xKPnJK

Walsh, L. & Black, R. (2009). 'Students in the Lead: Increasing Participation by Young People in a Distributed Leadership Framework.' *CSE Seminar Series*, Paper 188, September. Melbourne: Centre for Strategic Education.

Walsh, L. & Black, R. (2011). *In Their Own Hands: Can Young People Change Australia?* Camberwell: ACER Press.

Walsh, L., Black, R., Arthurson, D., & Hooper, G. (2009). *Response by The Foundation for Young Australians to The Learning Society, Global Education, Cisco*. Unpublished Commissioned Review, 15 August 2009. Melbourne: Education Foundation.

Walsh, L., Lemon, B., Black, R., Mangan, C., & Collin, P. (2011). *The Role of Technology in Engaging Disengaged Youth: Final Report. Report for the Australian Flexible Learning Framework*. Canberra: Commonwealth of Australia.

Walters, I. (2012). 'In the Trenches, the Teach for Australia Program Is Working.' *The Age*, 16 January 2012. Accessed 25 May 2015 at: http://www.theage.com.

au/opinion/society-and-culture/in-the-trenches-the-teach-for-australia-program-is-working-20120115-1q1bf.html#ixzz20SOv71pb

Walther, A., Stauber, B., Biggart, A., Bois-Reymond, M. D., Furlong, A., López Blasco, A., Mørch, S., & Pias, J. M. (2001). *Misleading Trajectories – Integration Policies for Young Adults in Europe?* Hechingen/Tübingen: Institute for Regional Innovation and Social Research.

Ware, G. (2015). 'Only One in Ten Education Reforms Analysed for Their Impact: OECD.' *The Conversation*, 20 January 2015. Accessed 30 January 2015 at: https://theconversation.com/only-one-in-ten-education-reforms-analysed-for-their-impact-oecd-36461

White, H. (2012). 'White-Papering the Cracks: A Blueprint for the Asian Century?' *The Monthly*. Accessed 9 February 2015 at: http://www.themonthly.com.au/issue/2012/december/1354762584/hugh-white/white-papering-cracks

White, R. & Wyn, J. (2008). *Youth and Society.* South Melbourne: Oxford University Press.

White, S. & Forgasz, R. (in press). 'The Practicum: The Place of Experience?' In Loughran, J. & Hamilton, M. (eds.), *International Handbook of Teacher Education.* Dordrecht: Springer Press.

Williams, T. (2014). 'UniSA Education Professor Stephen Dobson says Oral Exams More Critical Than Written Tests for "21st Century Skills".' *The Advertiser*, 14 May 2014. Accessed 30 January 2015 at: http://www.adelaidenow.com.au/news/south-australia/unisa-education-professor-stephen-dobson-says-oral-exams-more-critical-than-written-tests-for-21st-century-skills/story-fni6uo1m-1226916322776?nk=5fd3765d2b356e6bfd49d641de07f90d

Williamson, H. (2014). 'More Places Available at University, but Future Precarious for Many School Leavers.' *The Conversation*, 14 August 2014. Accessed 30 January 2015 at: https://theconversation.com/more-places-available-at-university-but-future-precarious-for-many-school-leavers-30440

Willox, I. (2012). 'Insecure Work Claim a Union Beat-up.' *The Australian Financial Review*, 4 December 2012. Accessed 18 August 2014 at: http://www.afr.com/p/insecure_work_claim_union_beat_up_BBih9jxHDIO4LIPz4pjZnJ

Wilson, M. (2013). *Precarious Work: The Need for a New Policy Framework.* Sydney: The Whitlam Institute.

Woodman, D. (2012a). 'Life out of Synch: How New Patterns of Further Education and the Rise of Precarious Employment Are Reshaping Young People's Relationships.' *Sociology*, 46(6), December, 1074–1090.

Woodman, D. (2012b). 'Biting the Hand That Feeds You.' *The Age*, 16 January 2012. Accessed 20 February 2015 at: http://www.theage.com.au/federal-politics/political-opinion/biting-the-hand-that-feeds-you-20120115-1q1be.html

Woodman, D. & Wyn, J. (2011). 'Youth Research in a Changing World.' In Beadle, S., Holdsworth, R., & Wyn, J. (eds.), *For We Are Young and . . . ? Young People in a Time of Uncertainty.* Melbourne: Melbourne University Press, pp. 5–28.

World Bank (2014). *Internet Users (per 100 People).* Accessed 11 April 2015 at: http://data.worldbank.org/indicator/IT.NET.USER.P2/countries?order=wbapi_data_value_2013+wbapi_data_value+wbapi_data_value-last&sort=asc

World Values Survey Association (www.worldvaluessurvey.org). (2009). *World Values Survey 2005.* Official Data File v. 20090901, 2009. Accessed 20 February 2015 at: http://www.wvsevsdb.com/wvs/WVSData.jsp

Wyn, J. (2009). *Touching the Future: Building Skills for Life and Work*. Melbourne: Australian Council for Educational Research.

Wyn, J. & Cuervo, H. (2014). 'Pain Now, Rewards Later? Young Lives Cannot be Relived.' *The Conversation*, 16 June 2014. Accessed 18 August 2014 at: https://theconversation.com/pain-now-rewards-later-young-lives-cannot-be-relived-27376

Wyn, J., Cuervo, H., Smith, G., & Woodman, D. (2010). *Young People Negotiating Risk and Opportunity: Post-school Transitions 2005–2009*. Parkville: Youth Research Centre.

Wyn, J., Lantz, S., & Harris, A. (2011). 'Beyond the "Transitions" Metaphor: Family Relations and Young People in Late Modernity.' *Journal of Sociology*, 48(1), 3–22.

Wyn, J., Smith, G., Stokes, H., Tyler, D., & Woodman, D. (2008). *Generations and Social Change: Negotiating Adulthood in the 21st Century*. Parkville: Youth Research Centre.

Wyn, J. & White, R. (2000). 'Negotiating Social Change: The Paradox of Youth.' *Youth & Society*, 32(2), 165–183.

Zhao, Y. (2009). *Catching Up or Leading the Way: American Education in the Age of Globalization*. Alexandria, VA: Association for Supervision & Curriculum Development.

Index

Printed and bound by CPI Group (UK) Ltd, Croydon, CR0 4YY